# CONTINUING PROFESSIONAL DEVELOPMENT

Continuing Professional Development (CPD) is the means by which professions across the world ensure that their knowledge and skills remain up-to-date and relevant to changing needs and environments. CPD significantly contributes to the quality and reputation of professions and therefore to the quality of national and international social life and economic wellbeing.

Starting with a discussion on what CPD encompasses, the author analyses how professional bodies govern CPD, what support they provide to individual professionals and how they measure or evaluate what individuals do under the provenance of CPD. *Continuing Professional Development* explains why, up to now, CPD has been a relatively neglected subject in spite of it being carried out by millions. It argues whether a variety of perspectives or visions of CPD has held back wider public appreciation of it, and if greater co-ordination by professional bodies, or the introduction of new players to the field, will change this in the future.

Providing the first comprehensive study of the subject, this innovative book will be required reading for CPD professionals and researchers and will be useful supplementary reading for all those involved with human resources development and management/leadership development.

**Andrew L. Friedman** is Professor of Management and Economics at Bristol University and Managing Director of PARN. He has written 26 books and many articles which have appeared in adjudicated journals. Many of these publications cover CPD and most other aspects of professional body activities.

CPD is now a key element of ongoing trust in the professions – and it is here to stay. This book is an invaluable reference tool in relation to the history of CPD and ways in which it might evolve in the future.

*Helen Brand, Chief Executive,*
*The Association of Chartered Certified Accountants (ACCA)*

CPD performs a pivotal role in ensuring that professionals maintain and develop their skills and knowledge throughout their careers and so maintain public confidence in the services that they provide. This book provides an invaluable analysis of the origins of, and rationale behind, the development of CPD together with an insightful look at the ways in which it may develop in the future.

*Desmond Hudson, Chief Executive, The Law Society*

# CONTINUING PROFESSIONAL DEVELOPMENT

## Lifelong learning of millions

*Andrew L. Friedman*

Routledge
Taylor & Francis Group

LONDON AND NEW YORK

First published 2012
by Routledge
2 Park Square, Milton Park, Abingdon, Oxon OX14 4RN

Simultaneously published in the USA and Canada
by Routledge
711 Third Avenue, New York, NY 10017

Routledge is an imprint of the Taylor & Francis Group, an informa
business

*British Library Cataloguing in Publication Data*
A catalogue record for this book is available from the British Library

*Library of Congress Cataloging in Publication Data*
Friedman, Andrew L.
Continuing professional development: lifelong learning of millions /
Andy Friedman.
p. cm.
Includes bibliographical references and index.
1. Career development. 2. Professions. 3. Employees–Training of. I. Title.
HF5549.5.C35F75 2011
658.3'124–dc22
2011006149

ISBN: 978-0-415-67791-2 (hbk)
ISBN: 978-0-415-67925-1 (pbk)
ISBN: 978-0-203-80616-6 (ebk)

Typeset in Bembo by Prepress Projects Ltd, Perth, UK

For Carla

# CONTENTS

*List of figures and tables*                                                    *xi*
*List of exhibits*                                                              *xiii*
*List of abbreviations*                                                          *xv*
*Preface*                                                                      *xvii*
*Acknowledgements*                                                            *xviii*

**Introduction**                                                                  1

**PART I**                                                                        7

**1   What is CPD? Complex and varied!**                                          9
   *1.1   Introduction  9*
   *1.2   How CPD is formally defined  9*
   *1.3   A process definition: the CPD cycle  14*
   *1.4   Professional Development Value (PDV)  17*
   *1.5   'Valid' CPD activities  19*
   *1.6   Actual activities regarded as CPD  26*

**2   CPD: Who? Who from? For whom?**                                            29
   *2.1   Introducing players and stakeholders in and around a field  29*
   *2.2   The CPD field  30*
   *2.3   Players in the CPD field  32*
   *2.4   Individual professionals  34*
   *2.5   Professional bodies  39*
   *2.6   CPD specialists and CPD aficionados  40*
   *2.7   Employers of professionals  43*
   *2.8   IT intermediaries for recording, supporting and delivering CPD  45*

2.9   *(Potential) suppliers of CPD activities: higher and further education institutions  46*

2.10  *Government  49*

2.11  *Broadcast media and public commentators  51*

2.12  *The players/stakeholders and governance of CPD  51*

2.13  *Appendix  54*

**3  Visions of CPD**                                                                 **57**

3.1   *Introduction  57*

3.2   *Prehistory of CPD: what professionals just did (Vision 1)  58*

3.3   *Prehistory of CPD: the trajectory of member services from professional associations (Vision 2)  63*

3.4   *Prehistory of CPD: maintenance of professional standards (Vision 3)  64*

3.5   *Prehistory of CPD: yet another of a stream of trappings to legitimate professionalism (unjustifiably) (Vision 4)  65*

3.6   *Why did CPD emerge?  67*

3.7   *Why did CPD emerge in the late 1970s and 1980s?  68*

3.8   *Prehistory of CPD: educationalist ideas and ideals for lifelong learning (Vision 5)  71*

3.9   *Picture of CPD in its early years  77*

**PART II**                                                                          **79**

**4  CPD governance: compliance policies**                                           **81**

4.1   *Introduction  81*

4.2   *Types of compliance policies  81*

4.3   *History of policies  91*

4.4   *Professional associations and regulatory bodies  96*

4.5   *International comparisons  98*

**5  CPD governance: programme support**                                             **100**

5.1   *Introduction  100*

5.2   *A model of support for and governance of the CPD process by professional bodies  101*

5.3   *Forms of support  101*

5.4   *Accreditation and support for choosing activities to undertake  106*

5.5   *Mentoring and coaching  107*

5.6   *Competency frameworks  110*

5.7   *Evaluation tools supporting self-assessment  111*

5.8   *Support personnel and the spread of techniques for supporting CPD  112*

6   **CPD governance: regulatory procedures**                    **114**
    6.1   *Introduction  114*
    6.2   *Evidence of Vision 4: CPD as a sham  114*
    6.3   *Monitoring  115*
    6.4   *Sanctions  118*
    6.5   *Evidence from Vision 3: CPD as a form of public protection
          through active regulation: a form of quality assurance  120*
    6.6   *CPD as a disciplinary tool, as 'punishment' or remedial
          activity  125*

7   **CPD measurement and the paradox of CPD: effective
    achievement of Professional Development Value?**            **130**
    7.1   *Introduction  130*
    7.2   *Inputs versus outputs  133*
    7.3   *Measuring Professional Development Value (PDV)  147*
    7.4   *A model of CPD measurement and PDV  147*
    7.5   *Applying the model to particular professional bodies  153*
    7.6   *Research into the effectiveness of CPD  156*
    7.7   *Conclusions  157*

**PART III**                                                     **161**

8   **Complexity, paradox and mystery: potential of CPD yet to
    be realized**                                               **163**
    8.1   *Introduction  163*
    8.2   *Complexity: multiple aims  163*
    8.3   *Complexity: multiple visions associated with alternative and
          overlapping concepts  165*
    8.4   *Vision 6: CPD as training for professional employees  170*
    8.5   *Confusion among players and stakeholders  173*
    8.6   *Paradox and complexity contributing to mystery  176*

9   **Dynamics: CPD today and tomorrow**                        **178**
    9.1   *Introduction  178*
    9.2   *Growth in the CPD field: more today and most likely more
          tomorrow  179*
    9.3   *More compulsion and clearer sanctions for non-compliance  181*
    9.4   *Regulatory bodies and the third pillar of professional standards
          regulation  182*
    9.5   *IT-based support for CPD recording and assessment, online delivery
          and social networking  182*
    9.6   *Outputs measures: more directly measuring Professional
          Development Value  184*

9.7 *Progress on measuring the immeasurable: evidence for positive outcomes from CPD for clients and other stakeholders 185*

9.8 *Professionalization of CPD contributing to raising professionalism in general 188*

**10 CPD field beyond tomorrow: affecting players and passive stakeholders**     **191**

10.1 *Introduction 191*

10.2 *Coalescence of positive visions of CPD based around professional bodies 192*

10.3 *Significance for professional bodies 194*

10.4 *Significance for professionals 197*

10.5 *Significance for CPD specialists 197*

10.6 *CPD and mass media 198*

10.7 *Significance for suppliers of CPD: Vision 7 – CPD as a lucrative market based on a valuable commodity to be purchased and sold 198*

10.8 *CPD and higher education institutions 199*

10.9 *CPD and employers (and recruitment agencies) 203*

10.10 *CPD, Professional Development Value, clients and the general public 204*

10.11 *CPD and government 206*

10.12 *Shifting situation of the players and stakeholders 207*

**11 Visions and fulfilment: will the *real* CPD please stand?**     **209**

11.1 *Introduction 209*

11.2 *Realizing the visions: a virtuous circle 210*

11.3 *Withering of the CPD field? Missing/breaking links 212*

11.4 *Alternative futures 218*

11.5 *Centring the CPD field within a wider vision of lifelong learning 225*

11.6 *Conclusions 226*

*Notes*     *231*

*Bibliography*     *247*

*Author index*     *261*

*Organization index*     *263*

*Word and concept index*     *265*

# FIGURES AND TABLES

## Figures

2.1 Ways of classifying knowledge 31
2.2 People in and around a field 31
2.3 Map of players/stakeholders' power to influence the CPD field 52
2.4 Map of players/stakeholders potential power to influence 53
4.1 The virtuous 'circle' of compulsory CPD 86
4.2 The game of opening and closing loopholes in the law or any other form of compulsory regulation 89
4.3 Percentage of professional bodies with a CPD policy 92
4.4 S-shaped curve showing growth of penetration of CPD policies among UK professional bodies 93
5.1 The CPD wheel and arch 103
7.1 Model of CPD measurement evaluation 148
7.2 Suggested PDV pattern for CIMA 154
7.3 Suggested PDV pattern for Institute of Auditors in Germany 155
10.1 Map of players and stakeholders in the CPD field showing shifts in positions on an optimistic view of its future 207

## Tables

1.1 Relating reflection to practice and CPD 17
1.2 Average hours spent on CPD activities in previous 12 months 27
3.1 Early view of CPD policies and programmes 78
4.1 CPD policy by size of membership: UK professional bodies in 2006 and 2009 83

4.2 Professional bodies' CPD compliance policies in the UK
and Ireland                                                            95
4.3 Professional bodies' CPD compliance policies in four countries      99
7.1 Measurement of CPD participation by professional bodies:
Australia, Canada, UK, Ireland                                        135
7.2 Professional bodies' basis for inputs measures of CPD
participation                                                         136
7.3 Methods of gathering evidence of CPD participation                 136
7.4 Advantages and disadvantages of inputs and outputs
approaches to CPD measurement                                         143
7.5 Criteria for judging each dimension of the PDV model              150
7.6 Self-assessed effectiveness of CPE by accountants in the USA      157

# EXHIBITS

1.1 Definitions of CPD   10

1.2 Example of a CPD cycle (RPSGB)   15

1.3 The CIMA professional development cycle   16

1.4 Views on CPD activities from professional bodies   20

1.5 Examples of CPD from the UK Health Professions Council   21

1.6 HIMAA professional credentialling scheme CPD points   24

1.7 *British Dental Journal* and 'verifiable' CPD   25

2.1 Hypothetical set of reasons individual professionals do their CPD in ascending order of morality or ethics   37

2.2 Motivations for doing CPD   38

2.3 AoR approval scheme for CPD events   42

2.4 CPD support scheme for employed financial professionals at UK Bus   44

2.5 KPMG on training and development of staff   45

2.6 Towards McDonald's university?   46

2.7 Linking departments at higher education institutions and professional bodies   47

3.1 Milton Friedman on physicians   66

3.2 Three steps to CPD in educationalist terms   75

4.1 Automotive technician accreditation – ATA Kitemark   87

4.2 Compulsory CPD follows regulatory changes: case of accounting in the UK   97

5.1 Benefits of CPD according to the Chartered Institute of Personnel and Development   102

5.2  Professional development at the Chartered Institute of
      Marketing                                                           105
5.3  Mentoring at the Institution of Engineering and
      Technology (IET)                                                    108
5.4  Royal Institution of Chartered Surveyors (RICS)
      competency framework                                                110
5.5  Planning tool for CIPD members                                      112
6.1  UK GDC view of CPD                                                   122
6.2  UK Health Professions Council view of requirement for
      registrants                                                         123
6.3  CPD definition from RIBA                                             124
6.4  Architects Registration Board (ARB) – guidance on CPD               125
6.5  CPD and quality assurance among health professionals
      in Canada                                                           128
7.1  Example of an effectiveness scale to guide self-assessment
      of CPD                                                              138
7.2  Peer review groups for CPD at the Royal College of
      Psychiatrists                                                       139
8.1  Drucker on professionalism and management                           171
8.2  Excellent companies according to Peters and Waterman                172
8.3  Learning organizations according to Peter Senge                     174
10.1  Training gateway                                                    202
10.2  Engineers Ireland's accreditation of CPD scheme for employers      205

# ABBREVIATIONS

| | |
|---|---|
| ACCA | Association of Chartered Certified Accountants |
| AoR | Association of Reflexologists |
| APC | Assessment of Professional Competence |
| APEL | Accreditation of Prior Experiential Learning |
| ARB | Architects Registration Board |
| ATA | Automotive Technician Accreditation |
| BIS | Department for Business, Innovation and Skills |
| CIC | Construction Industry Council |
| CIM | Chartered Institute of Marketing |
| CIMA | Chartered Institute of Management Accountants |
| CIPD | Chartered Institute of Personnel and Development |
| CIPFA | Chartered Institute of Public Finance and Accountancy |
| CME | Continuing Medical Education |
| CMPD | Continuing Medical Professional Development |
| CPD | continuing personal/professional development |
| CPE | Continuing Professional Education |
| CRA | Centre for Recording Achievement |
| DES | Department of Education and Science |
| DfEE | Department for Education and Employment |
| DfES | Department for Education and Skills |
| DIUS | Department for Universities, Innovation and Skills |
| ECTS | European Credit Transfer System |
| EUSCCCIP | European Project for the use of Standards of Competence in CPD for Construction Industry Practitioners |
| FEC | further education college |
| FEE | Fédération des Experts Comptables Européens |
| GDC | General Dental Council |
| GP | general (medical) practitioner |
| GTCE | General Teaching Council for England |

| | |
|---|---|
| HEFCE | Higher Education Funding Council for England |
| HEI | higher education institution |
| HIMAA | Health Information Management Association of Australia |
| HPC | Health Professions Council |
| HR | human resources |
| HRD | human resources development |
| IBS | International Benchmarking Survey |
| ICAEW | Institute of Chartered Accountants in England and Wales |
| ICAS | Institute of Chartered Accountants of Scotland |
| IEE | Institution of Electrical Engineers |
| IES | International Education Standard |
| IET | Institution of Engineering and Technology |
| IfA | Institute for Archaeologists |
| IFAC | International Federation of Accountants |
| IMI | Institute of the Motor Industry |
| IoP | Institute of Physics |
| IOSH | Institution of Occupational Safety and Health |
| ITI | Institute of Translation and Interpreting |
| MSSSB | Marketing and Sales Standards Setting Body |
| OECD | Organisation for Economic Co-operation and Development |
| OFT | Office of Fair Trading |
| ONS | Office for National Statistics |
| OU | Open University |
| PARN | Professional Associations Research Network |
| PCC | Professional Conduct Committee |
| PDV | Professional Development Value |
| PICKUP | Professional, Industrial and Commercial Updating Programme |
| QAA | Quality Assurance Agency for Higher Education |
| RCP | Royal College of Physicians |
| RCPsych | Royal College of Psychiatrists |
| RCVS | Royal College of Veterinary Surgeons |
| RDR | Retail Distribution Review |
| RIBA | Royal Institute of British Architects |
| RICS | Royal Institution of Chartered Surveyors |
| RPB | recognized professional body |
| RPSGB | Royal Pharmaceutical Society of Great Britain |
| RSB | registered supervisory body |
| SCOPME | Standing Committee on Postgraduate Medical and Dental Education |
| SMART | specific, measurable, achievable, realistic and time-bound |
| SOCAM | The Society of Accountants in Malawi |
| SWOT | strengths, weaknesses, opportunities and threats |
| UKIPG | UK Inter-Professional Group |
| UNSCEAR | United Nations Scientific Committee on the Effects of Atomic Radiation |
| VLL | Vocational Lifelong Learning |

# PREFACE

I began working on continuing professional development (CPD) in 1998 by carrying out the first of several projects funded by the then Department for Education and Employment. I was at the time in the Economics Department at Bristol University and on the way to establishing the Department of Management there. These projects were commissioned by Graham Cheetham, an early champion for CPD, and were crucial for the establishment and early success of PARN (Professional Associations Research Network) at the University.

PARN is a not-for-profit mission-led company. It operates as a research enriched network and a membership organization for professional bodies in the UK and around the world. Along with my colleagues at PARN we have worked to identify interesting and good practice among professional bodies and to support what we call the professionalization of professional bodies. To my knowledge we are the only organization in the world dedicated to this. In 2005 PARN was relocated to its own premises in Bristol and is independent of any one university.

So far six books and numerous articles and reports have been produced on CPD by PARN. Although we have been investigating a wide range of subjects concerning professional bodies during the past decade – their governance, strategic and operational development, professional qualifications, ethics and other professional standards, as well as how they support access to the professions and equality and diversity within the professions – CPD remains a central part of our work. This book builds upon this work.

# ACKNOWLEDGEMENTS

This book has had a long gestation period. During the five years of writing and rewriting I have had support from many. The following were involved in the research and writing of previous books and reports on CPD produced by PARN: Natasha Afitska, Judith Croston, Isla Cruickshank, Kelly Davis, Catherine Durkin, Sarah Ellingham, Katherine Farquharson, Sam Friedman, Pinder Gill, Amy Hannington, Helen Harper, Hazel Harvey, Sarah-Louise Hopkins, Nicola Hurran, Lowri Jackson, Will Jessop, Brett Lambe, Chris Lynas, Jane Mason, Mary Phillips, Gemma Robertson, Emily Senior, Mark Summers, Rose Timlett, Elena Voltsinguer, Jeff Watkins, David Watts, Christina Williams and Susannah Woodhead.

I would like particularly to thank William Hanson, who provided substantial research assistance during the past two years. In addition, Sara Llewellyn read the entire manuscript and provided extremely useful comments.

# INTRODUCTION

At the breakfast table yesterday Jane's son George reminded her that today is a teacher training day. His whole school is closed. 'Bloody inconvenient', Jane thinks, 'I could use a day off – let off steam or even have somebody lecture me about how to be a good mother, AND be paid for it.'

'George! Put that down. Sarah! Pulling Georgie's hair will not make him do what I say any faster. Can you *pleeease* just keep an eye on him like a big sister while I answer the door?'

Jane returns and is horrified to find seven-year-old Sarah stuffing something into George's wide open mouth and proudly announcing 'Mummy's medicine will make you a good boy.' After extracting as many of the tablets as she can, Jane rushes into her tiny study to check the list of side effects of her birth control pills. 'Should I call an ambulance? Ring my doctor? Or maybe just stop, calm down with a cup of tea and think this through?' Jane suddenly realizes the list she is staring at from the piece of paper in the box of pills refers to adults, not five-year-old boys. She begins frantically searching the internet for other sites that could tell her if George is in danger. None have exactly what she needs to know. More worrying is the bewildering array purporting to give medical advice. 'Just how reliable are these sites?'

Soon Jane is confronting Dr Smith with George and Sarah in tow. The birth control pills Jane takes are new. Dr Smith reassures her, 'George will be ok.'

'How do you know? Has anyone considered this situation?'

'I read about these pills before I prescribed them for you.' Dr Smith recalls the seminar on side effects of these pills that she attended sponsored by the drug company. 'George will be fine.'

Jane is reassured but while driving home she begins to worry again. 'If the pills are new, have they had a chance to find out if they have a long-term effect on children? Would Dr Smith know if they had?' Jane spends more time on the internet, but finds nothing about effects if taken by toddlers.

In the afternoon Jane goes to her health club. They have a crèche for Sarah and George. She asks one of the trainers to recommend stress-busting exercises, reminding the trainer that she has had serious shoulder pains as well as the headache from the morning's trauma. The trainer is not particularly helpful, but suggests Jane makes an appointment with the physiotherapist connected to the club. Fortunately the physio is available at short notice. 'At last some good news today!' Jane answers some detailed questions about her current condition. The physio checks health club records and recommends certain exercises. Sorted, Jane goes for it in the gym.

The scene at the health club canteen late that afternoon is raucous. Sarah is hungry and unhappy and pestering George, who is retaliating by throwing plastic spoons at her. There seems to be nothing on the menu that Sarah wants to eat, and George, bless him, seems to be allergic to almost everything. After a long chat with Philip, the catering manager, about what George can and cannot eat, he suggests a special off-the-menu meal. Jane is impressed.

Unfortunately on the way home Jane hears a funny noise as she accelerates. Better safe than sorry, she pulls into the Toyota dealership. The mechanic shakes his head slowly and tut-tuts. 'Oil too low. This will cost you.'

'Damn! I put in oil last month. I thought the indicator must have been broken.'

'She's leaking. See that patch under there.'

'What is this going to cost?'

'Depends on the engine damage. Leave it with us.'

Jane shouts, 'I can't do that!' gesturing towards her children. 'Damn car repairs! I wish I really knew what they should be charging. Do they really know what they're doing? Maybe I'll try somewhere else in the morning.'

Many attitudes and concerns are expressed here in what might be only a slightly more hectic day in an ordinary life. Jane had to deal with five different professionals, paraprofessionals or potential professionals that day.

The doctor is clearly a professional, arguably the archetypal professional in the public mind. As far back as 1964, a trend towards professionalization of almost all occupations, was noted (Wilensky 1964). Physiotherapists are recognized health professionals by law in many countries; for example in the UK they are covered by the Health Professions Act and they, along with a range of other health-related occupations, are also covered by similar acts in the states of the USA and Australia and in the provinces of Canada. These occupations, which have been called professions supplementary to medicine or allied health professionals may also be considered by some to be paraprofessionals (people trained to assist a doctor, lawyer, teacher or other professional, but not licensed to practise in that profession). School teachers have long fought for professional status, though they teeter between professionalism and trade unionism.[1] Certainly parents and the general public expect teachers to behave in a professional manner. Catering managers are covered by the professional body, the Institute of Hospitality, in the UK. Managers and public services specialists may be thought of as the new 'frontier' of occupations that have been professionalizing since the mid-twentieth century. Car mechanics are a particularly interesting case. Traditionally they would be thought of as skilled workers rather than professionals. However, there are clear signs that they too are on the track of a 'professionalization' project in the UK supported by the Institute of the Motor Industry (IMI). People in Jane's position would certainly benefit from motor mechanics behaving in a professional manner.

Other days Jane may have to see a lawyer or accountant, various other types of managers or health specialists. In all these situations she wants, often needs, some service or advice from these people. She will think that others ought to know more than she does about these things. She will feel vulnerable in these situations. How can she be sure she is getting an effective, reliable, up-to-date service if she is not herself an expert in any of these subjects? These people are available to her, each with a recognizable label or job title that credits them to be experts and she expects they will use their expertise to sort out her issues in a trustworthy manner. At least she hopes they will, but may have less confidence owing to the knocks the public image of some types of professionals have taken in recent years.

The internet can help. Jane can check up on what experts tell her. This may give her confidence in their advice, or it can encourage her to question what she is told. She can find advice without consulting an expert directly. She could dispense with experts altogether in certain circumstances. But the internet can be confusing: too much information, often none of it exactly what is needed, and always doubts about authenticity and reliability. Who is behind the site? Are they trying to sell me something? What are their qualifications? What about sites that give conflicting advice?

Just because someone has a certificate to show they are a professional – a school teacher, a doctor, physiotherapist, catering manager or car mechanic – does not automatically mean that they are competent and trustworthy. They may have been up-to-date the day they qualified, but who is to say that 10, 20, even 40 years later that individual is still up-to-date and has the expected range of competencies? Just as important, can Jane trust them to use their expertise in her interests and not rip her off or treat her problem carelessly? Will they know the long-term consequences of their advice or actions? Will they consider the consequences of their actions and advice beyond solving her immediate problem? Will they tell Jane what they really think and discuss different options with her in the light of both short- and long-term consequences?

What if Dr Smith had not just happened to attend that course? Would it not be difficult to compel all doctors to take such a course, which may not even deal with the consequences of little boys taking the drug?

And the car repair man? Perhaps there is a tendency for engines of Jane's model of Toyota to develop serious problems when the oil level is very low. Should the mechanic warn Jane to deal with it urgently? What if the opposite were true, that the engine problem is not serious and will disappear as soon as the oil is topped up? Should Jane expect the mechanic to know these things? Should Jane expect the mechanic to tell her that the expensive repairs are not really necessary, or that the repairs he is suggesting will not solve the problem in the long run? Should she regard the repair man as a professional? Is there some sort of badge or certificate to inform the public that he can be regarded as a professional? Can any occupation become a profession? Even if they are called professional, can they be truly what in the past would have been expected of professionals; trustworthy, ethical, up-to-date and competent?

Jane's attitude to teachers having a day for their own education is interesting. After a moment's reflection it would be clear to Jane that all the specialists she encountered on that day could not have the expertise required to deal with her needs based only on whatever they learned when they first trained or qualified. Would she have been so annoyed with her doctor to learn that the very day Jane wanted specifically to see her, Dr Smith was off learning about side effects of birth control pills? Perhaps not. It is important for all professionals to maintain their competence and continue their learning. It is perhaps less obvious that whatever teachers do in this regard will directly benefit Sarah and George. Most teachers do not provide a direct service to clients for money. As an employee, just as the catering manager at the health club, these occupations do not command such high expectations of personal professional service. Complaints about inadequate service would be addressed to their employers rather than a professional body.[2] Much of what teachers may learn if they were to trying to keep up-to-date may have more to do with esoteric theory of education or for managers, aspects of team building. But the training of these employees is presumed to take place within the closed social space of company policy, away from the gaze of the general public.

It seems to be the accepted public view, as evidenced by the media, that the way to control professionals is through complaints and disciplinary procedures. If a professional is incompetent or misbehaves, they should be punished. They should be struck off. This way the bad apples are removed and the lesson is clear to potential bad apples – misbehave and you are out. However, this approach leaves the feeling that few are caught. High-profile cases make people wonder: how long can bad professionals get away with misbehaviour or incompetence? How many bad apples are out there and never caught? It is fundamental to the nature of services professionals provide that they will know more than clients or patients. How are they to be caught if clients or patients do not know if they are receiving up-to-date and competent services? Punishment is not much of a deterrent if there is little chance of being caught. Another way is needed.

In the past, at least before the last quarter of the twentieth century, it had been sufficient to accept the trustworthiness of professionals based on evidence of initial qualifications (unless we had information to the contrary). Nowadays this is not enough. Increasingly procedures that could encourage the needed reassurance are being undertaken. Professionals themselves, through professional bodies, are pursuing what is known as Continuing Professional Development, or CPD (called Continuing Professional Education or CPE in the USA[3]). CPD can include formal or structured educational activities – courses or other organized activities – but it can also include informal or unstructured activities; reading, discussions at social gatherings. As yet there are no generally accepted standards on how much of this should be done, what the content should be or how it should be measured or assessed.

Nevertheless, a great deal of CPD is being undertaken. Millions of professionals at all ages in adult life are following CPD programmes. CPD occupies them every year, often every month, for many even every day.[4] Yet this is hardly ever reported in the mass media. It is a major component of expenditure on education and training in developed countries, and yet just how much is spent on CPD is unknown and it is hardly ever mentioned in government education policies or plans.[5] It is a new market in high-level education and training, and yet only in the last few years have universities woken up to the new opportunities it represents to alleviate their seemingly perpetual financial straits. Research into CPD has not been supported by research councils, at least at anything like the level given to education of undergraduates or those on postgraduate courses. Academics rarely undertake research into it in spite of the vast array of economic, management, social studies or education journals where the subject could appear. Often when articles on CPD do appear, they tend to be in specialized journals, limited to particular narrowly defined professions, or most likely they are part of a 'grey literature' comprising limited distribution reports, which soon become even harder to access as they are archived or lost.

What is CPD? How widespread is it? How does it operate? These seem to be straightforward questions, largely of description. The answers are not straightforward. CPD is not a simple concept and it is not clear how it relates to more common terms such as professional qualifications and standards, lifelong learning, company training, organization learning or the learning society. In the following chapters evidence to answer these questions will be provided, but the lack of attention CPD has received up to now limits how comprehensive this evidence can be.

There are other questions we will attempt to answer; deeper *Why, What* and *How* questions. These are more difficult. They cannot be answered merely by reporting surveys or official statements. Why has CPD arisen recently and what is really new about it? Why is it spreading? How is it changing? How important is CPD for those who do it, those who supply it, and those who organize or 'accredit' it? These are questions of interpretation and judgement. So what if millions are doing CPD! What does this imply for their material situation, for their status and reputation? In addition, CPD is viewed differently by different groups of people because it is a complex and developing concept. There are different 'visions' of CPD. How are they changing? Do they influence the overall direction and significance of CPD?

More significantly what does CPD imply for the whole population of professional services users whose lives are affected by the work of those millions of

CPD practitioners? Are users more likely to receive better services from professionals because they have kept up their CPD? How would we assess an answer to this question? Even more broadly, what does the coming of CPD imply for society and the economy as a whole? What does it imply for how people interact and for their economic prospects? Arguably it is critically important for the quality of our society: for the trust that many believe is the essential oil that allows social as well as economic relations to flourish. If so, it will be a major contributor to the quality of life as well as the competitive position of countries. Is this potential for CPD's influence being realized? Is it likely to be realized in the foreseeable future?

Finally, there is the *CPD mystery*. Why has this subject been ignored in spite of the extent of its practice and the widespread and potentially deep significance of its effects? Is it not really effective, or only potentially of significance? Is it mere window dressing or worse, yet another gimmick used by professionals to dupe the public into thinking they are competent? Or are there other reasons for it being ignored?

# Part I

In Part I we attempt to answer questions posed at the end of the Introduction. We focus on what is CPD and provide a general framework for understanding the complexity of this question.

We first examine the 'what' of CPD in common sense or surface terms. How is it formally defined, what is the process of doing CPD, what counts as CPD and what activities are undertaken as CPD?

Second, we introduce the concept of the CPD field and examine its key players or stakeholders. We believe this will help us to explore and understand the deeper meaning of CPD, or rather the different meanings underlying CPD according to different types of players and stakeholders.

Third, we examine the prehistory of CPD and its emergence. This is done through a series of different visions that encourage the explanation of the emergence of CPD to focus on different things. We argue that all these visions are helpful for understanding not only what CPD is, but also its significance for professionals, professionalism and ultimately for society as a whole. Or rather what its potential significance is, because we argue that this significance is not widely recognized. For that potential to be realized, it must be more widely recognized and understood.

# 1

# WHAT IS CPD? COMPLEX AND VARIED!

*Define complexity! Differing definitions? Many parts? Many ways of identifying the phenomenon?*

## 1.1 Introduction

Understanding what CPD is, is itself complex. We begin by examining definitions; there are many. Different definitions produce different views of what CPD is meant to achieve. This is one reason for the CPD mystery: why it is not well understood or appreciated by the general public, in spite of how widespread and potentially important it is. To deal with this variety we introduce the concept of Professional Development Value (PDV).

There are other ways of understanding what CPD is, beyond formal definitions; by exploring the types of learning activities involved, as well as the *processes* of carrying out and administering CPD. Definitions, activities and processes can be linked by considering what *counts* as CPD; what are regarded as *valid* CPD activities.[1]

## 1.2 How CPD is formally defined

The definitions in Exhibit 1.1 are recognizable as describing a common phenomenon; but only just. Is CPD a commitment, a requirement, a process? Is it educational, learning or training activities, or a combination of approaches, ideas and techniques? What is it for? To understand the aims of CPD, consider a particular definition.

The most commonly used definition by professional bodies in the UK was put forward by the Construction Industry Council (CIC) in 1986:

> The systematic maintenance, improvement and broadening of knowledge and skills, and the development of personal qualities necessary for the execution of professional and technical duties throughout the individual's working life.

Out of 102 professional bodies surveyed, 55 published a definition of CPD and 22 of these used the CIC definition (Friedman, Davis *et al.* 2000: 41). The majority were from construction and building and from the engineering sector (15 of them). However, other professional bodies using this definition were spread widely; three from health, two from finance, one education and one ecological.

---

## EXHIBIT 1.1  DEFINITIONS OF CPD

The systematic maintenance, improvement and broadening of knowledge & skills, and the development of personal qualities necessary for the execution of professional and technical duties throughout the member's working life.

(Royal College of Veterinary Surgeons; RCVS 2006)

CPD (Continuing Personal/Professional Development) is defined as the holistic commitment to structured skills enhancement and personal or professional competence.

(Strategic Forum for Construction 2002)

CPD (Continuing Professional Development) is the requirement that the members of a profession or organization undertake training to maintain their competence, knowledge, skills and integrity on a regular, structured basis after they qualify.

(Royal Institute of British Architects; RIBA 2008)

CPD is the process by which pharmacists and pharmacy technicians keep up-to-date through learning. It includes everything you learn that enables you to do a better job. We all learn from experience at work as well as from formal education activities. CPD includes both learning from work and learning from continuing education.

(Royal Pharmaceutical Society of Great Britain; RPSGB 2008)

CPD is an abbreviation for Continuing Professional Development. It refers to the postgraduate educational activities physicians are expected to undertake in order to ensure that they remain up-to-date in their field and continue to develop and enhance the knowledge and skills required to be successful in their working lives.

(Royal College of Physicians; RCP 2008)

CPD is a combination of approaches, ideas and techniques that will help you manage your own learning and growth. The focus of CPD is firmly on results – the benefits that professional development can bring you in the real world. Perhaps the most important message is that one size doesn't fit all. Wherever you are in your career now, and whatever you want to achieve, your CPD should be exactly that: yours.

(Chartered Institute of Personnel and Development; CIPD 2008)

Continuing Professional Development (CPD) helps you create a structured career path, as well as safeguard your professional status. CPD is about your skills, knowledge and expertise, and reflecting on what you've gained or achieved.

(Institution of Occupational Safety and Health; IOSH 2010)

Continuing Professional Development (CPD) is a process by which individuals take control of their own learning and development by engaging in an on-going process of reflection and action. This process is empowering and exciting and can stimulate people to achieve their aspirations and move towards their dreams.

(Megginson and Whitaker 2007: 3)

The Health Professions Council (HPC) has defined Continuing Professional Development as: 'A range of learning activities through which health professionals maintain and develop throughout their career to ensure that they retain their capacity to practise safely, effectively and legally within their evolving scope of practice.

(Health Professions Council; HPC 2009)

The University of Kent defines 'Training and Professional Development' as: 'A range of short and long training programs, some of which have an option for accreditation, which foster the development of employment related knowledge, skills and understanding.

(University of Kent 2009)

## 1.2.1 CPD is systematic and formal

Perhaps the most significant word in the most common definition is *systematic*. There are parallels with some of the definitions in Exhibit 1.1 (holistic – Strategic Forum for Construction; structured – RIBA), though others use weaker terms (combination of approaches – CIPD; range of learning activities – HPC). We interpret systematic or structured as having two aspects:

- organized in a way that is capable of being made *public in a comparable manner* or in relation to a standard,[2] and
- *strategic* or capable of being understood in a *purposive and comprehensive manner.*

One way of interpreting CPD is as *systemizing or formalizing* what most (or at least those we would consider to be 'good') professionals would recognize as things that they 'just do'. They would regard learning and developing as part and parcel of what they understand to be ordinary professional practice and participation in ordinary professional community life. However, CPD is different. It is the *formal wrapping* of some, often most, of those things good professionals just do. Or at least CPD is something standardized enough to be identified by a policy and programme. Beyond what a good professional 'just does' post-qualification, CPD is what that professional is *seen* to do. The wrapping only includes those things that are 'counted' as CPD, though in some professions some, or even all, CPD activities are self-certified and self-assessed.[3]

Arguably this wrapping changes the nature of what it is that professionals just do. At least it is likely to change how professionals regard what they do, their consciousness of it. CPD leads certain facets of professional practice and community life to shift from informal activities, tacitly generating knowledge, into conscious generation of knowledge. Learning and development that occurs only unconsciously or dimly consciously during actual professional practice comes to be reflected upon as actual learning and development.[4]

Conversations around a dinner table at a social function organized by a professional body; reading about a leader in the professional news magazine; attending a branch meeting of the association: these are informal activities that can be transformed into formally counted CPD activities. They can be measured against other activities (including formal training), in terms of their contribution to professional development through a CPD programme. Thinking with some amusement of the curious tip about how to operate a new bit of software mentioned over cheese and biscuits, or musing on how that professional leader went about mentoring a recent graduate with a physical disability, may not in the past have been regarded as professional development. CPD allows formalization or structuring of casual, informal and off-work thoughts and actions.

Even more connected to what professionals 'just do' is the learning and practice development that occurs during work or practice itself. Learning-by-doing can be thought of as several different learning and practice development activities: learning by reflecting on what is about to be done, on what is being done and on what has recently been done are all part of professional practice; or should be. For many, a distinguishing feature of professionals is reflective practice. The terms reflecting on practice and reflecting in practice are well known in many professional communities based on the influential work of Schön (1983, 1984).

Sometimes professionals are very aware of reflecting, learning and developing their expertise and professionalism during the hurly burly of practice.

Sometimes professional practice is anything but a hurly burly. Much of professional practice involves reading notes and instructions or filling out forms. However, there are times when one's senses are operating more intensely. This occurs during interactions with clients, employers and individuals in agencies with which professionals must negotiate to deliver services (such as the need for architects to deal with planning authorities or for doctors who are general practitioners to deal with hospital authorities).[5] These situations, which may be regarded as the situated activities of professional practice, generate learning and practice changes that are arguably the most important aspects of professional development. Individual professionals will be more aware of the learning and practice development aspects of these situations, more alive to lessons to be learned, in early years, or when dealing with something new to them; a new technique or delivering a new service or advice on a new situation.

Under a formal CPD programme these situations, which may stimulate some to learning and practice development unconsciously, can be made more conscious and possibly more likely to influence practice if they are incorporated into CPD, and legitimated as such through formal reflection on practice implications and incorporation into a planning framework. Informal chat, interesting reading and exciting client interactions *can* have implications for knowledge, behaviour and practice even if they are not part of a CPD scheme, but they are more likely to have such implications if a context is provided for them to be reflected upon. CPD therefore does not merely formalize what professionals would do anyway in the sense of adding a layer of bureaucracy to these things. It not only allows informal activity to be standardized and thereby legitimated and made more transparent and accountable. Formalization itself can have positive outcomes for professional development. It can draw the attention of practitioners into a system of planning and reflection on their development as members of a profession.[6] It can also bring the learning professionals do to the attention of the public.

### 1.2.2  CPD as including development of personal qualities

Including development of personal qualities as well as professional development particularly distinguishes the aims of CPD from merely keeping up-to-date. To some, personal development is part of professional development, even if it involves learning things that do not seem to be directly relevant to current practice. Members of the public may find this odd, and even resent it (note Jane's attitude to her children's teachers' day off for training in the Introduction). However, personal development can be an essential support for trustworthiness of professionals: encouraging self-confidence, awareness of ethical pitfalls and openness to new ways of doing things.[7] These relatively intangible aspects of CPD can be just as important to clients/patients, even if they are only aware of them by their absence, when barely conscious expectations are unfulfilled.

### *1.2.3 A range of different facets to a single definition*

CPD contains three different facets according to the CIC definition (as well as others):

- maintenance of knowledge, skills and competencies;
- improvement and broadening of knowledge, skills and competencies;
- development of personal (and professional) qualities such as integrity, as well as flexibility and openness to new technologies and services.

These are not mutually exclusive and different definitions take up various combinations of them. Such differences in interpretation of CPD have consequences for which activities are regarded as legitimate CPD.[8] This makes it difficult for those outside a particular profession to understand what those professionals mean by CPD. This fragmentation is one of the reasons why employers, the government and the general public have been slow to recognize CPD or understand its importance.

### *1.2.4 CPD as being of benefit to others*

Although the CIC definition does not explicitly identify particular beneficiaries of CPD, some definitions do mention: clients/patients, the profession as a whole, the professional association, employers, and/or the general public/society as a whole, in addition to practitioners themselves (Friedman, Davis *et al.* 2000). That all do not make this explicit is another reason for lack of public awareness of CPD. If CPD is merely support for career aspirations of professionals, it is of less interest to the general public. Some professions give this impression.[9]

### 1.3  A process definition: the CPD cycle

The definitions listed in Exhibit 1.1 tend to focus on what CPD is for. Another approach is to describe what someone undertaking CPD does. Thought of this way, CPD is more than a collection of activities, though some do think of it this way, or at least give this impression.[10] The systematic aspect of CPD can be appreciated by seeing it as a process.

From the outset, certain professional bodies, particularly those in the construction and engineering sectors, adopted a process model known as the CPD cycle. With interesting variations this model has since been adopted by many professional bodies in the UK and around the world.[11] We have adapted it to help structure our discussions of support and measurement of CPD in Part II. Exhibit 1.2 demonstrates a basic CPD cycle model adapted from the Royal Pharmaceutical Society of Great Britain (RPSGB 2009).

CPD is not directed towards a single goal which is then achieved: end of story. It is a continual striving for, achieving and renewing of learning and

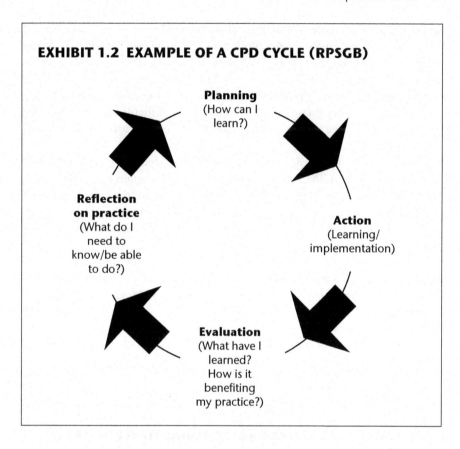

**EXHIBIT 1.2  EXAMPLE OF A CPD CYCLE (RPSGB)**

**Planning**
(How can I
learn?)

**Reflection
on practice**
(What do I
need to
know/be able
to do?)

**Action**
(Learning/
implementation)

**Evaluation**
(What have I
learned?
How is it
benefiting
my practice?)

development goals. The CPD cycle usefully illustrates this continuing aspect. This model allows us to map different aims of CPD by concentrating on different phases of the cycle. The UK CIC described their approach as:

> essentially a fairly simple, cyclical model that focused on the use of outputs and more particularly standards as the hub around which CPD should focus. So we had a 4-phase cyclical model which suggested that people should review where they were now, identify where they wanted to be, plan how they could get there, carry out that process of development and then review where they got to and so the process continues. At the hub of that are standards which allow people to set targets against which they could measure their development.

> (Friedman and Woodhead 2008: 135)

Some professional bodies have more complicated models. Some divide the planning phase into identification of gaps in current competencies compared with needed competencies, and development of procedures to fill those gaps. The Chartered Institute of Management Accountants (CIMA) divide planning further into three phases, or steps, calling them Define, Assess and Design before the common phases of Act, Reflect and Evaluate (see Exhibit 1.3). Many think of CPD as limited to post-qualification learning activities, or even post-graduate degrees. The CPD cycle shows CPD to be more, or at least potentially more, according to many professional bodies. Learning activities are only one of the four (or more) phases around the cycle. In particular professionals are expected to plan their own activities, rather than merely accept what is presented to them.

Notice that the term *reflection* is used in two different ways in the RPSGB CPD cycle and the CIMA cycle. For the former, the subject of reflection is practice and its purpose is to clarify development needs; for the latter the subject is development activities and the purpose how to apply them to practice and to future development activities. These are two of four possible combinations (see Table 1.1).

One can reflect on learning in order to develop knowledge and understanding and also to develop practice, to change one's behaviour in practice. One can also reflect on practice in order to develop knowledge and understanding and to develop practice.[12]

Reflection and reflective practice are terms often used in academic literature with reference to professionals. These issues are explored in more detail in Sections 3.2, 5.7 and 7.4.

---

## EXHIBIT 1.3 THE CIMA PROFESSIONAL DEVELOPMENT CYCLE

Step 1: Define what is expected of you in your current role, and consider what you might like to do in the future. Draw up brief descriptions of these roles and expectations.

Step 2: Assess your development needs and outcomes. Compare what is expected of you in your current, or a future role, against your current capabilities.

Step 3: Design your professional development programme around activities you believe are relevant to your role. Document these activities.

Step 4: Act. Undertake the development activities planned in Step 3.

Step 5: Reflect on your development activities, consider how well they went, what you learnt, how you can apply your learning and changes you would make next time.

Step 6: Evaluate your actual development against your development needs and outcomes. Any outstanding development can be carried over into the next cycle.

(CIMA 2008, with permission)

**TABLE 1.1**  Relating reflection to practice and CPD

|  |  | Subject of reflection | |
|---|---|---|---|
|  |  | CPD activity | Practice |
| Purpose of reflection | Gain understanding | Learn by reflecting on CPD | Learn by reflecting on practice |
|  | Improve practice | Improve practice by reflecting on CPD | Improve practice by reflecting on practice |

Professionals are encouraged, or even required, to take control of their own development. They need to evaluate learning activities, not merely in terms of what they have learned, measured perhaps by what grades they get, but rather in terms of professional practice. CPD programmes expect them to answer the question: how can what was learned improve services or reduce risks to clients or employers in practice?[13] In addition, professionals need to reflect on the implications of their learning activities for the CPD they will do next and for longer-term goals. The cycle must be repeated continually. The CPD cycle supports active responsibility for one's long-term development: one way of distinguishing what it is to be a professional.

The cycle may also be thought of as a spiral in several ways. One is in terms of more independent evaluation methods. According to the European Project for the Use of Standards of Competence in CPD for Construction Industry Practitioners (EUSCCCIP):

> it was on a kind of spiral basis, if you can imagine the model itself being a circle, if you can imagine that then moving up to a spiral in terms of people policing it . . . one could do it simply by policing oneself at one extreme, moving up to formal structured independent assessment of achievement at the opposite extreme.
>
> (cited in Friedman and Woodhead 2008: 135)

Targets for achievement through CPD rise with successive journeys around the cycle. In particular they should rise in terms of achieving whatever are defined as the goals of CPD. To express this concept for the complex and varied approaches to CPD we introduce the term Professional Development Value.

## 1.4 Professional Development Value (PDV)

How can we judge the extent to which aims are being achieved? How can we communicate those judgements in ways which are acceptable and accepted in general discourse? If the aim is clear, consistent and measurable, this is fairly easy. Let us say the aim is to maximize profits in general and to achieve a 10 per cent profitability rate in the coming year. Assuming we can find an acceptable procedure for measuring profits achieved,[14] this gives us a way of judging success and finding acceptance for those judgements. If profits achieved were only 5 per cent of the value of assets, then we would judge that company as not having reached its objective. If in the following year 8 per cent profitability is achieved, the company would be clearly moving closer to its aim. In addition, this number allows us to discuss the performance of this company compared with others. This company can be viewed as twice as successful as one that achieved a 4 per cent profitability.

How might we decide if a profession's policies and programmes are successful at achieving the aims of CPD? How could we compare professions in terms of their relative success at achieving the aims of CPD? We are a long way from a single number that may be regarded by a professional body as an accurate summary of how well that profession is doing in this respect, and even less close to a widely accepted common way of summarizing this information for different professions in order to compare them. We may never be able to summarize this in a simple and consistent manner with a single number, at least until a common definition of CPD is adopted. However, we can begin to develop a language by which we can describe the achievement of CPD aims that will encourage conversations about the idea of success. This is critical among those who come to see CPD as so important as proposed in the Introduction. Arguably the dearth of such conversations has hampered more widespread appreciation of the importance of CPD.

We propose to begin to develop a language for developing narratives about the achievement of the aims of CPD, while allowing for different aims to be articulated in different professions, by introducing the concept of Professional Development Value (PDV). We introduce the term here and elaborate on it more fully in Chapter 7, when we examine ways professional bodies attempt to measure the extent to which individual professionals carry out CPD as defined locally.

We define PDV most broadly as the impact CPD has on an individual's professionalism (Friedman and Woodhead 2008). The way this may be assessed or measured will vary according to the way the aims and purposes of CPD are defined, the way CPD is expected to contribute to an individual's professionalism in different professions. A narrower definition of PDV as applied to a particular profession is the contribution of any CPD activity or procedure to the specific aims and objectives of CPD as defined by that particular professional body. What exactly contributes to PDV, and by how much, will depend particularly on the balance in the CPD definition between maintenance and enhancement of competency on one hand, and personal and professional development on the other.

The intention behind defining PDV is to translate various definitions into common scales of achievement applicable no matter how the aims of CPD are defined. PDV concerns how well whatever is done accords with or contributes to those aims.

Here we elaborate PDV in terms of a range of positive effects that CPD may have which may be formally recognized as aims of CPD by professional bodies. These may be grouped into three broad categories:

1 personal support and enhancement of personal characteristics and professional careers;
2 forms of knowledge or competence; and
3 practice and client/patient or employer outcomes.

First, there are claims that CPD can support professional confidence, assertiveness and even empowerment. Similarly it can contribute to a sense of personal growth, improved morale, job satisfaction and camaraderie. In addition, it can support autonomy at work and career progression. It can encourage internalization of motivation for improvement and in particular to encourage self-directedness in the pursuit of whatever may be the stated aims of CPD.[15] In this sense CPD may not only raise the quality of individual practitioner practise, but also contribute to practitioner understanding of the importance of maintaining and enhancing their competence. This aspect of PDV complicates its assessment. Assessments of PDV would have to be made over a long time to take into account the contribution of CPD to motivational aspects of professionalism. This may be measured in the long run by individuals carrying out more or more intensive CPD than specified by CPD policies.

Second, CPD is claimed to lead to maintenance and development of knowledge and competence. This can be expressed in terms of particular techniques and procedures to learn about; skills and competence in applying those techniques and procedures; and, importantly, self-directedness in terms of understanding what techniques to apply when, and which techniques to refrain from applying, why and when.

Third are practice outcomes and more specifically practice outcomes that lead to positive benefits to clients/patients or employers. A critical aspect of this is understanding when to refrain from applying certain techniques, not merely because they are unlikely to be successful, but also because it is ethically wrong to apply those techniques knowing or suspecting negative consequences for a client or patient in the long run, or negative consequences for others: ethical competence as well as technical competence (see Friedman 2007). As we will see in Chapter 6, this is important for the credibility of CPD, particularly for clients and employers, but also for regulatory bodies.

## 1.5 'Valid' CPD activities

At one extreme some professional bodies accept as valid everything and anything their members choose to report (Exhibit 1.4). This is based on the idea that professionals ought to know *themselves* what they need to do to keep up

---

## EXHIBIT 1.4  VIEWS ON CPD ACTIVITIES FROM PROFESSIONAL BODIES

We accept anything that is relevant to their job, their particular circumstances. It can be online, reading, it can be seminar attendance, discussion with peers about technical points. It's very broad based.

(Friedman and Williams 2008: 36)

We want them [the members] to understand that CPD is a generic term for anything you can learn from, provided that it relates to [our subject] or running their business . . . so we are trying to get them around the idea that so many things can count, from the very little, going up to the advanced degree and everything in between.

(Friedman and Williams 2008: 36)

We believe that CPD takes many forms and that we should not set down exactly how health professionals should learn. Consequently, we do not approve education programmes which registrants must take after they have registered with us. Education providers can offer programmes for the purpose of CPD, but there is no requirement for them to be approved or monitored by us.

(HPC 2009 – This view is taken from the Allied Health Professions project, *Demonstrating competence through CPD* 2002)

---

and develop as professionals.[16] This approach relieves professional bodies of the need to judge the value of activities, at least in deciding what is acceptable.

There is a trade-off between accepting that most professionals will have unique knowledge of their development needs from their understanding of their practice situation, and the view that their choices may be governed by less than desirable motivation or less than complete understanding of their own needs.[17]

One step removed from this total acceptance of whatever individual practitioners consider to be valid (or whatever they can show has been of value to them) are long lists of valid activities. This can lead to what outsiders consider to be odd choices. The list in Exhibit 1.5 may surprise some. Note that it includes:

* reading journals/articles, but not reading books;
* updating knowledge through the internet or TV;
* attending branch meetings and voluntary work.

The first two of these are difficult to assess or audit. The third may not be regarded by members of the public or clients/patients as contributing to competence, at least not directly.

## EXHIBIT 1.5 EXAMPLES OF CPD FROM THE UK HEALTH PROFESSIONS COUNCIL

### Appendix 1: examples of types of CPD activity

This list should give you an idea of the kinds of activity that might make up your continuing professional development.

*Work-based learning*
- learning by doing
- case studies
- reflective practice
- clinical audit
- coaching from others
- discussions with colleagues
- peer review
- involvement in the wider work of the employer (for example, being a representative on a committee)
- workshadowing
- secondments
- job rotation
- journal club
- in-service training
- supervising staff or students
- visiting other departments and reporting back
- expanding your role
- analysing significant events
- filling in self-assessment questionnaires
- project work or project management
- evidence of learning activities undertaken as part of your
- progression on the Knowledge and Skills Framework

*Professional activity*
- involvement in a professional body
- membership of a specialist interest group
- lecturing or teaching
- mentoring
- being an examiner
- being a tutor
- branch meetings
- organizing journal clubs or other specialist groups
- maintaining or developing specialist skills (for example, musical skills)
- being an expert witness

- membership of other professional bodies or groups
- giving presentations at conferences
- organizing accredited courses
- supervising research
- being a national assessor
- being promoted

*Formal/educational*
- courses
- further education
- research
- attending conferences
- writing articles or papers
- going to seminars
- distance learning
- courses accredited by professional body
- planning or running a course

*Self-directed learning*
- reading journals/articles
- reviewing books or articles
- updating knowledge through the internet or TV
- keeping a file of your progress

*Other*
- public service
- voluntary work
- courses

(HPC 2008: 5–7, with permission)

CPD activities may be defined much more tightly, for example, as only structured (in this case meaning accredited and examined) courses.[18]

What different professional bodies count as CPD reflects differences in the aims of CPD. If the aims are primarily individual development as a professional, or even personally, the range of what counts as CPD would be much wider, and up to the practitioner to initiate and discriminate. If the purpose is proof of competence, then 'legitimate' activities will tend to be more restricted and specified by the professional body or an employer. This is only a tendency and there are plenty of exceptions. Also what counts will, for some professional bodies, depend on how easy it is to monitor activities.

Consider the list in Exhibit 1.6 from the Health Information Management Association of Australia (HIMAA). Here we have a list of activities with allowed points for each. Notice how long the list is. Notice also how arbitrary the allocation of points is. Higher points are given for reading the house journal, *HIM Journal*, compared with another relevant journal. No points are given for any other reading. Notice also double points are awarded for those living 150 km (straight line distance) from certain activities involving physical presence. Why double? Why 150 km? Why straight line distance? These decisions seem sensible. Defining by straight line distance means not having to change the rules due to road or rail changes; 150 km as what can conveniently be achieved by car round trip in a day; double because it would then take two days if coming by car. But what if someone flies to the location? What if they go by car and spend the extra day visiting relatives or carrying out normal work in their company's office in the location of the CPD event? Some people may find a 305 km round trip journey little more onerous than a 295 km journey. The problem is not that these rules are unreasonable, rather the more detailed they are, the more arbitrary they appear to be.

It is worth pointing out that the HIMAA is not a regulatory body and membership is voluntary. This is likely to be why their points allocation is affected by the level of convenience or resources required. Otherwise it would be harder to attract members in rural/remote locations (though there are other ways to deal with this, such as by price reduction on activities and by travel grants).

More generally, once a professional body moves towards excluding some of the things an individual professional might consider to be part of their professional development, or giving different weights to activities or allowing for any aspect of the personal situation of the individual professional, the criterion can seem arbitrary. This is because there is, as yet, no generally accepted basis for such variations.

Limiting what counts for CPD is interpreted here as an attempt to evaluate PDV in advance, to judge what will be useful or valuable for achieving the aims of CPD, based on the *type of activity, not on the actual activity undertaken by a particular individual*. This may be a reasonable approach for formal activities that are accredited by a trusted organization, but can be very problematic for most informal activities. Reading an article about the difficulties a practitioner had in dealing with certain ethical dilemmas, even if that practitioner was from a different profession to one's own, may have a greater effect on how a professional behaves compared with a formal course in professional ethics. Rules which limit or assign different points to these activities will always seem arbitrary because they cannot be connected to PDV in a transparent and commonly accepted manner.[19]

Many professional bodies define their CPD requirements in terms of a number of hours to be achieved per year, with a portion of those hours subject to a more stringent criterion (see Exhibit 1.7).

## EXHIBIT 1.6  HIMAA PROFESSIONAL CREDENTIALLING SCHEME: CPD POINTS

*Qualifications Gained During Qualification Period Points*
Postgraduate degree in a relevant discipline 120
Undergraduate degree in a relevant discipline 100
Graduate Diploma in a relevant discipline 90
Graduate Certificate in a relevant discipline 80
Diploma in a relevant discipline 70
Other relevant, post-secondary qualifications/training 50 per instance

*Professional Development*
Attendance at a HIMAA Seminar (2–4 hours) 15*
Attendance at a HIMAA Seminar (5+ hours) 20*
Presentation of a paper/topic at a HIMAA Seminar 10 per paper/topic*
Attendance at a relevant seminar, other than HIMAA 10*
Presentation of a paper/topic at a relevant seminar, other than HIMAA 5 per paper/topic*
Attendance at an HIMAA National Conference/Symposium (including associated workshops)
30 (full conference/symposium and workshops); or 5 per half day
Presentation of a paper/topic at a HIMAA National Conference (including associated workshops) 15 per paper/topic
Attendance at a relevant National Conference, other than HIMAA 15
Presentation of a paper at a relevant National Conference, other than HIMAA 10 per paper
Attendance at a relevant international conference 30
Presentation of a paper at a relevant international conference 15 per paper
Reading *HIM Journal* 5 per edition
Published article in *HIM Journal* (peer reviewed) 15 per article
Published article in *HIM Journal* (not peer reviewed) 10 per article
Reading a relevant journal, other than *HIM Journal* 3 per edition
Published article in a relevant journal, other than *HIM Journal* (peer reviewed) 5 per article
Published article in a relevant journal, other than *HIM Journal* (not peer reviewed) 3 per article

*Service to HIMAA*
Service on the HIMAA National Board 20 per year
Service on the HIMAA National Executive 15 per year
Service on the HIMAA State Branch Executive 15 per year*

Service on other HIMAA committees (Editorial Board, Education Committee, National Conference Committee etc.) 15 per year
Membership of HIMAA 10 per year

*Service to Other Relevant Associations/Societies*
Service on the National Board 10 per year
Service on the National Executive 7 per year
Service on the State Branch Executive 7 per year
Service on other committees 7 per year
Membership of the Association/Society 5 per year

*Points doubled for members in rural/remote localities

(More than 150 km [straight line distance] from the location of the activity [where appropriate]. The HIMAA Executive has authority to accept/reject a member's claim of rural/remote status.)

(HIMAA 2008, with permission)

## EXHIBIT 1.7 *BRITISH DENTAL JOURNAL* AND 'VERIFIABLE'[20] CPD

The UK General Dental Council (2002) required all registered dentists to engage in 250 hours of CPD over a five-year period with at least 75 of those hours being verifiable. Interestingly in that document they define verifiable as having concise educational aims and objectives, clear anticipated outcomes and identified quality control mechanisms. This led the *British Dental Journal* editors to include two papers in each issue with four multiple choice questions to each article. Completing the questionnaire grants dentists with one verifiable hour of CPD per paper. With 24 issues of the journal per year, this can account for up to 48 hours of CPD. There are other opportunities to gain verifiable CPD hours, particularly postgraduate courses and conferences.

400 of the 7242 people who were registered as having undertaken this verifiable CPD initiative were randomly chosen and sent a questionnaire. Of the 307 who returned questionnaires and who had undertaken *BDJ* verifiable CPD, 91 per cent agreed or strongly agreed that this had increased their knowledge. Furthermore 71 per cent agreed or strongly agreed that an element of their clinical practice had changed as a result of undertaking this type of CPD.

(Tredwin *et al.* 2005)

Perhaps the greatest divide is between those who regard CPD as courses, largely undertaken out of the workplace and formally assessed and those who consider practice itself as a source of learning and development that should be considered as valid CPD, if incorporated into a CPD programme. In a comprehensive review of academic literature on professional development and professional learning Webster-Wright found that the majority focused on programmes and content from the perspective of:

> learning as 'filling up' a reservoir of knowledge in a professional's mind that will run dry if left too long . . . the focus of much research and practice in PD [professional development] is atomistic, considering the professional and learning context as separate though related.
>
> (2009: 712).

This should not be surprising, given the source of this research: academics whose time, while not researching, is primarily spent delivering formal courses. Rothwell and Herbert (2007) found that some professional bodies, which include actual practice among valid CPD activities, find it difficult to convince some of their members that this is so.

A recent approach is to require certain activities or categories of activities to be based on the situation of the individual in relation to competencies required of the profession or more specifically of the role that professional performs. This can cut across the distinction between formal and informal CPD activities or even between distinct CPD activities and 'actual' practice. These competency frameworks usually include both generic and profession-specific competencies. Some specify a range of competencies from which members can select those most relevant to their particular role. Others prescribe a set of core competencies that must be covered. Use of these frameworks is more likely where CPD is conceived as proof of competence (Friedman and Woodhead 2008). However, competency frameworks can also help individuals to understand PDV, in particular how their learning can connect to their career in terms of stages of competency.

## 1.6 Actual activities regarded as CPD

Using survey methods it is difficult[21] to identify all activities that professionals recognize as CPD during their normal working practice. However, surveys are useful in distinguishing the extent to which informal activities that are considered by professionals themselves as time spent on CPD, compared with formal courses and events.

For example, from a survey of 582 qualified accountants who were members in practice of the four main accounting bodies in the UK: Association of Chartered Certified Accountants (ACCA), CIMA, Institute of Chartered Accountants in England and Wales (ICAEW) and Institute of Chartered Accountants of

Scotland (ICAS), 37 per cent reported doing more than 100 hours of CPD during the previous 12 months; that is in 1999 (Paisey *et al.* 2007: 389–90).[22] This was at a time when the minimum requirements were expressed in terms of hours for all these accounting bodies: between 30 and 55 hours for three of them and around 100 hours for one. For the 12 options offered in the questionnaire, the breakdown of hours spent on different activities is shown in Table 1.2.

Technical reading was reported as occupying most hours of CPD; 82 per cent reported doing some hours of this. However, adding up courses organized by professional bodies and educational establishments and in-house courses came to 27.2 hours on average. Hours spent on courses organized by their professional bodies far outnumbered those on courses organized by an educational establishment.

Comparing average with median it is clear that there were a few who carried out many hours of the different activities. More than half the sample only did technical reading and/or attended courses organized by the professional body. The small number who teach or examine spent many hours at it. A few reported more than 1,000 hours of CPD in the previous 12 months. One reported 2,400

**TABLE 1.2** Average hours spent on CPD activities in previous 12 months

| Activity | Average hours | Median hours |
| --- | --- | --- |
| Technical reading | 37.5 | 24.0 |
| Teaching/examining | 13.4 | 0.0 |
| Course organized by professional body | 11.8 | 8.5 |
| Computer-based learning not related to work | 8.9 | 0.0 |
| In-house course | 8.8 | 0.0 |
| Conference attendance | 8.4 | 0.0 |
| Self-study for a work-related qualification | 8.3 | 0.0 |
| Course organized by an educational establishment | 6.6 | 0.0 |
| Self-study for a non-work-related qualification | 6.3 | 0.0 |
| Writing technical material | 5.3 | 0.0 |
| Computer-based learning not related to work | 2.3 | 0.0 |
| Membership of technical committee of own professional body | 0.8 | 0.0 |

*Source:* Adapted from Paisey C., Paisey, N.J. and Tarbert, H. (2007) 'Continuing professional development activities of UK accountants in public practice', *Accounting Education: an international journal*, 16(4): 391. Reprinted by permission of the publisher, Taylor & Francis Ltd, http://www. informaworld.com.

hours of CPD in the previous year or over 50 hours per week. The authors pointed out that this member considered all work to count as CPD. They commented that this person clearly did not understand the guidelines on what their professional body counts as CPD, showing 'that professional bodies should be careful in their definition of what counts as CPD.' (Paisey *et al.* 2007: 392). Interestingly in recent years those professional bodies have been moving towards the other end of the spectrum, that practice itself can be regarded as CPD if it is incorporated into the CPD cycle: planned, reflected upon and evaluated in terms of learning and practice outcomes.

In a survey of 7,275 professionals in 23 professional bodies in the UK, Ireland, Canada and Australia undertaken in 2008 (PARN 2008a), respondents were asked what activities they undertook in the past 12 months as recognized CPD. Three out of the four most popular CPD activities were informal. Far less common were those reporting taking courses or modules leading to either a professional qualification or a university qualification. In effect most of CPD is informal activity that may be thought of as having become formalized through the label of CPD (Cheetham and Chivers 2005).

# 2

# CPD: WHO? WHO FROM? FOR WHOM?

## 2.1 Introducing players and stakeholders in and around a *field*

In Chapter 1 we discussed what CPD is in terms of what it aims to achieve, the process of undertaking it and the activities it involves. Here we concentrate on the people and organizations involved. CPD is not a profession (though it may become the knowledge base of one), but it affects most professionals; some would say all. It is also not merely an adjunct to various professions; it has a development path of its own. This path is affected by many different people and organizations, which we identify as players or stakeholders.

These include professional bodies – representative professional associations and regulatory bodies; specialists in designing and maintaining CPD policies and programmes; suppliers of formal CPD activities; academics; IT specialists; and ultimately those who rely on professional services – clients or patients and employers of professionals. Finally we must consider an even wider range of organizations and people: governments (both political parties and different government agencies or departments) and the general public.[1]

To comprehend this diverse range we introduce a term to describe CPD that allows us to think of it as a whole. That concept is a *field*. We view CPD as a *structured field of knowledge and practice*; connecting and influencing individuals, groups and organizations. Charting the nature and dimensions of the field will help us answer those difficult questions posed in the Introduction. What is really new about CPD? How is it changing? What are the consequences of CPD for professionals and professionalism, and more generally for the economy and society?

After introducing CPD as a field we examine separately active stakeholders who we call players in the field (who affect CPD and are affected by it) and passive stakeholders (affected by CPD, but having little influence on it as individuals or specific organizations). We further divide passive stakeholders into those who are aware and those who are unaware. It is possible to be affected by CPD without knowing it. Aware stakeholders are those who have some understanding of CPD and how it may affect them, though their understanding may not always be accurate.[2] Some groups of players[3] have a conscious interest in CPD and a strong opinion of what it is and what it should achieve. Some stakeholder groups, particularly clients or patients, are completely unaware of CPD; do not understand what it is or who does it. Many of those who are aware of CPD hold different views of its purpose and significance.

## 2.2 The CPD field

Field is a term used in general parlance to identify a branch of knowledge or an academic discipline: the field of medicine or environmental archaeology. Learned societies have arisen in support of fields. Some societies also developed representative functions for those in occupations using the knowledge base of the field, such as the Institute of Physics and the Royal Society of Chemistry.

CPD may also be thought of as a branch of knowledge, but the knowledge it embraces is mostly those of other fields. Some CPD involves the knowledge base peculiar to a profession (sometimes called specialist or technical CPD such as chemical formulae or how to decide which surgical instruments are appropriate for different tasks), some involves knowledge and know-how that is similar or the same for several professions and some is common to all professions: knowledge of the legal and social environment of practice, awareness of ethical dilemmas, knowledge of management techniques, use of IT and the internet, team working. These subjects are sometimes called generic CPD.

CPD also includes a branch of knowledge in its own right, separate from the knowledge base of particular professions. That knowledge base was introduced in the previous chapter. It concerns answers to questions such as:

- what should be accredited as valid CPD?;
- how should CPD be monitored and measured?;
- what is the role of planning and reflection and how should these processes be supported?;
- what should the role of CPD be for awarding higher levels in the profession?;
- how should the CPD cycle be formulated?;
- how should CPD be 'sold' to members?; and
- what should the consequences be of non-compliance with the CPD policy?

Figure 2.1 represents the CPD field in relation to relevant knowledge bases and different professions. The key distinction here is the degree of specificity of knowledge to the CPD field: between on one hand, knowledge of CPD policies, programmes and procedures (knowledge of CPD); and on the other hand the knowledge that CPD is intended to convey, the content of CPD. This distinction is similar to that between administration and subject disciplines at a

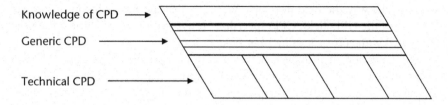

Knowledge of CPD ⟶

Generic CPD ⟶

Technical CPD ⟶

**FIGURE 2.1** Ways of classifying knowledge

university. Content of CPD can be further divided into generic and technical CPD.

Another way of describing the shape of the CPD field is terms of the positions of people within and around it. Are people part of its core or peripheral to it? We also distinguish a group between players at the core and unaware passive stakeholders on the periphery. Aware passive stakeholders may be regarded as potential players in the field (Figure 2.2). The nature of the core of a field like CPD is a combination of ways of thinking and acting or dispositions among players as well as the material and status resources that are available to active stakeholders. The shape of the field is moulded by how groups of players at its core are themselves influenced and how they influence others.

A field can be highly centralized and well defined if the norms of the core are strong and consistently held and many people are close to or part of the core, compared with the periphery. It will also depend on the extent of their power

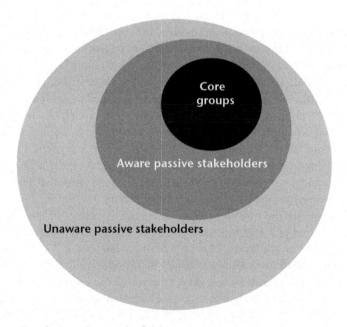

**FIGURE 2.2** People in and around a field

to shape the way the field develops. We argue that the most obvious group at the core of the CPD field, CPD specialists, is not strong and has little influence compared with core groups in other fields.

The gradation of influence between core and peripheral groups will also affect the shape of the field. Typically fields at early stages will have a small core and a very wide and diffused periphery of groups, who are affected by core ideas and activities but have little influence over them.[4]

An important influence on the shape of the field is the extent to which it generates institutions concerned with the field as a whole. Overarching institutions like learned societies, professional associations and regulatory bodies are important for developing norms within the field and also a strong sense of connection to it among players and stakeholders. Academics play this role in many fields. We will argue that for the CPD field, there are plenty of institutions within the core, but as yet, relatively few overarching institutions that focus on the CPD field as such.

Field is also a technical term in sociological theory representing the 'ground' or setting for the location of agents and their social positions (Bourdieu 1986, 1989). In the Appendix to this chapter we explore Bourdieu's idea of a field in more detail and identify ways that we use the term which are different from his.

## 2.3 Players in the CPD field

### 2.3.1 Core groups

*Professionals* have always developed themselves, often through activities and materials provided by professional bodies, but also through reflection in and on practice itself. However, CPD as a formally constituted set of practices is a product of *professional bodies*. CPD is therefore intimately bound up with the interests and policies of these organizations and those running them. CPD may be thought of as an 'institutional wrapper' provided by professional bodies around what most professionals had 'just done' in the past to keep themselves up-to-date and to develop themselves as professionals. In addition, there are *CPD specialists*, largely working for professional bodies, who set CPD policies and who design, maintain and develop CPD programmes. CPD specialists should be distinguished from individuals who run professional bodies, who would very rarely regard CPD as their main concern.

These three are the most developed categories of players in the CPD field. They are affected by CPD and affect the field. Virtually all professional bodies may be thought of as players. Not only do most have a CPD policy and programme, those without one must consider their position in relation to CPD. At least some of their members will expect them to have a scheme. Even if those running a professional body consciously decide not to have a CPD policy, or that they are not yet ready for one, they are likely to be challenged to show they have considered the issue. We argue in the next chapter that this became the condition of professional associations during the period from around the mid-1980s to the late 1990s, and since the turn of the century it has been becoming the situation of regulatory bodies. We also regard professionals to be players as a category. They may decide not to do CPD if their professional body has a voluntary policy, but it is an active decision they must take. They must choose to ignore the exhortations of their professional body to follow the offered programme. Even those in newly professionalizing occupations are likely to have heard of CPD, perhaps through statements on why their professional body does not yet have a policy. These we consider to be the core groups in the CPD field.

A *category* of people or institutions are players in the field when almost all of them must actively consider their position in relation to becoming seriously involved in the field. As a category, their actions will affect the size, shape and path of the field.

### 2.3.2 Peripheral groups and organizations

CPD is a form of learning. Some of that learning will be provided by *trainers, educationalists and educational institutions*; both private suppliers and publicly funded agencies. Private training organizations set up to provide professionals with CPD are clearly specialists and as such may be regarded as players. Others only provide CPD as a secondary activity. They may not consider CPD to affect them significantly. This is currently the situation for universities. Very few departments and some specialist units are players, but up to now hardly any universities have taken on CPD as a major activity. However, a few are beginning to take a more serious stance towards it, particularly the Open University (OU), but also some of the post-1992 universities. Those within universities involved in CPD often consider themselves isolated and unappreciated (Chivers 2006).

Another location of CPD specialists is among *employers* of professionals. Many employers are involved in CPD, but most not consciously as CPD. On-the-job training, induction into new job roles and performance evaluation are all activities occurring within organizations. These could be part of a formal CPD programme, but in most instances are not recognized as such. Rather they are regarded as organization policies or part of the organization culture. Some employers pay professional body subscription or registration fees for their staff and therefore indirectly pay for CPD. However, most do not use the term CPD for their training programmes and do not consider the implications of their training for the CPD of their employees. In fact many employers see CPD as something separate from professional development.[5] Therefore we consider employers as a category to be passive stakeholders, even though some individual employers do support CPD and a few integrate it into their organization policies.

Public provision of education brings *government policy makers* into play, both specific government policy towards the suppliers of publicly funded education, but also more general macro-policy towards learning and skills and the use of education to achieve broader policies such as innovation, economic growth, a fairer distribution of opportunities and social justice. The UK government has not addressed the issue of CPD in a substantial way. Political parties and government agencies are generally ignorant of the CPD field, though they have a great potential to influence it.

Other players must be taken into account if CPD is viewed as an assurance that professionals are up-to-date, that their expertise is relevant, that they are able to provide the latest and most effective advice and other services available. *Clients, patients and the general public*[6] are affected and so have an interest in CPD as stakeholders. *Consumer groups* (or patient or other user groups) are also stakeholders. Lack of publicity about CPD in general media has meant that very few in these categories are aware of the CPD field.

## 2.4 Individual professionals

CPD is huge. It is carried out by 3.4 million individuals representing 26 per cent of professionals and 12 per cent of the labour force in the UK (Friedman and Afitska, 2009).[7] While the proportions are smaller in other countries, CPD seems to be growing everywhere.[8] Those who do CPD are not only the traditional professionals, but also what some consider to be semi-professionals, para-professionals or aspiring professionals. Not only doctors and nurses but also a wide range of specialist health professionals such as physiotherapists, chiropodists and occupational therapists; not only lawyers but also para-legals and legal executives; not only chemists and physicists, archaeologists and architects, engineers, actuaries and accountants but also accounting technicians, occupational health and safety specialists, public relations specialists, fundraisers and a wide range of new therapists and counsellors, as well as managers of many specialities and levels.[9]

Most professionals can decide which activities to undertake for their own professional development. Even when a professional body limits which activities can be counted as valid, this leaves a wide range of choice. Professionals may have to clear certain formal activities with their managers or colleagues, such as taking courses during working hours, but by and large the particular activities chosen are up to the professionals themselves.[10] Those under a voluntary policy of their professional body can decide whether to participate in formal CPD at all. Why would they do it? What affects their disposition towards CPD? Let us begin by considering the reverse question.

### 2.4.1 Why would professionals NOT want to do CPD?

There is a literature on barriers or deterrents to adult education and some studies in the United States on deterrents to undertaking CPE courses. From this literature[11] four types of deterrents have been identified:

1  *Situational*: external barriers, beyond an individual's control. These include the costs of activities as well as work and family issues; such as the difficulty of taking time off work or lack of employer support and child care.[12]
2  *Dispositional*: based on personal attitudes. Doubts about likely benefits from any formal post-qualification learning activities, particularly among more experienced professionals.
3  *Institutional*: perceived poor quality of activities on offer, inconvenient locations or timing and difficulties of registration.
4  *Informational*: lack of information about availability and suitability of activities.

Perceptions of many of these deterrents were negatively related to a composite measure of perceived effectiveness of CPE courses by accountants in North Carolina, USA (Wessels 2007: 371–2). Significant relations were found for:

- situational (disagree that courses are good value in relation to costs);
- dispositional (finding courses less useful as experience is gained, can learn what's needed on the job or through in-house instruction, and a view that the requirement is too high);
- institutional (perceived low quality of courses, lack of relevance to needs, courses not right length); and
- informational deterrents (courses not well publicized, want to know satisfaction ratings of previous participants, hard to know in advance if a course is right and would provide professional benefits).[13]

Dispositional barriers have been important. CPD has not been universally welcomed, particularly by more experienced professionals in traditional professions and those not based in rapidly changing scientific disciplines (such as law). Normal practice provides sufficient opportunities to learn whatever is needed to maintain competence according to some. This view is perhaps understandable among professionals who do not need to impress superiors and particularly those who are 'winding down' their careers and practices in anticipation of retirement (see Exhibit 2.1).[14]

One respondent saw CPD as primarily supporting the Chartered title, and said that if you did not value the title, and people who are

> reasonably senior in the industry don't give two hoots about whether someone's got a title or not (as did our respondent), then CPD is an irrelevance.
> (Friedman, Davis and Phillips 2001: 156)

Barring major new concerns about CPD, we suspect this opposition will diminish as the older generation is replaced by individuals who are more attuned to the need to keep up not only their learning, but also formal evidence of that learning.

While some do not think they need CPD, others fear they may not be capable of developing their competence to higher levels.[15] Some are not particularly interested in developing themselves and their careers, as may be expected among any collection of individuals. A proportion will regard work as relatively unimportant compared with other aspects of life. They may simply want to put in the hours to make enough money to pursue other things. This proportion is likely to be lower in professions requiring long and difficult training for qualification, where the work is inherently interesting, and particularly where the consequence of what one does is palpable and important.

Evidence of negative motivation is strongest against the processes of recording, monitoring and assessment of CPD rather than the activities themselves: against the perceived bureaucracy of CPD. Ensuring you are *seen* to do CPD is regarded as a waste of time. Members of the CIPD regarded record keeping as a chore according to surveys commissioned in 2000 (Harris 2000a,b). Sankar (2003) claimed that resistance among doctors can accompany over-stringent requirements for CPD.

Another set of reasons for some not participating may be associated with self management according to writers from the CIPD (Megginson and Whitaker 2007: 10–14). These include:

- being fuzzy, not sure of what you should do next;
- being negative, thinking you are not the sort of person who will move on in your career no matter what you do;
- putting other people's priorities before your own;
- procrastination and avoiding difficult challenges.

These views concern not a lack of appreciation of the potential importance of CPD, or resentment of its bureaucratic elements, but rather an inability to fulfil personal ambitions. They are likely to apply more to newly professionalizing occupations.

Finally, Friedman, Davis and Phillips (2001: 156) report an interesting phenomenon. Some interviewees distinguished themselves from 'others' who were more negative about CPD than themselves. Being positive about CPD, they thought of themselves as atypical:[16]

I think I'm keener than the average.

I think there are other people though who have been here an awfully long time who are very comfortable and competent in the little box in which they sit [and CPD] is uncomfortable for them and they actually don't want to do it.

### 2.4.2 Why would professionals want to do CPD?

There are many different motives for doing CPD. Consider the CIPD definition in Exhibit 1.1. The authors go on to state:

> [CPD is] empowering and exciting and can stimulate people to achieve their aspirations and move towards their dreams . . . CPD provides the opportunity to soar like an eagle or a helicopter and look at our career progress from a wider perspective.
>
> (Megginson and Whitaker 2007: 3)

It can be motivated by self-interest, but there are also altruistic motives – the good of clients, patients and the general public. In a sense, in between these types of motives are ones expressed directly by many. CPD is something professionals just do. They do it out of interest or curiosity. Much like reading a novel for the enjoyment of it and to find out what happens next; many regard reading an article in their professional journals, going to a lecture or to a meeting in this light. It may promise something useful for practice, but it may also merely be of interest for its own sake: listening to a talk about the history of some aspect of the profession, or the details of the life of a famous practitioner. These activities are likely to be what is regarded as personal and professional development.[17]

In Exhibit 2.1 possible motives are arranged in a hierarchy: from higher level altruism to lower level self-interest; and from positive achieving good things; down to negative avoidance of bad things.

---

### EXHIBIT 2.1 HYPOTHETICAL SET OF REASONS WHY INDIVIDUAL PROFESSIONALS DO THEIR CPD IN ASCENDING ORDER OF MORALITY OR ETHICS

- Good of general public
- Good of clients/patients
- Good of the profession
- Good of employer
- Curiosity and a desire to pursue interest in the subject
- Personal accomplishment
- New job
- Career advancement within existing organization
- To maintain employment with employer
- Paid to do CPD by suppliers
- Obliged to do CPD by ethical code
- Forced to do CPD by employer
- Forced to do CPD in order to practise.

The higher motivations may seem theoretical, aspirational or even insincere or hypocritical (though there is evidence for them). Such motivations are not exclusive to those in traditional professions, but also occur in occupations that are professionalising:[18]

> their contribution is because they believe in the profession and they want to secure and support and encourage the future of the profession, a relatively small profession.
>
> (Friedman *et al.* 2008: 42)

We must also point out that for some professionals at some times, CPD is carried out primarily due to inducements from suppliers to encourage them to understand and to purchase (or request their organizations purchase) products. Conferences sponsored by pharmaceutical companies for medical practitioners have been identified as a dubious means for gaining CPD credits (Murray and Campbell 1997).

There are many strategies other players can use to motivate practitioners to do formal CPD. The professional way of motivating people is by inculcating values associated with the aims of CPD according to its definition: Professional Development Value. One of the more interesting ways professional bodies have motivated practitioners either to do CPD, or to do more than the minimum, is as a condition for promotion to higher status levels. In the UK, Chartered status or Fellowship status are common categories. Inclusion in performance appraisals by employers is another obvious way of motivating.

Exhibit 2.2 shows motivations for carrying out CPD from an online survey of 7,275 professionals from 23 different professional bodies in the UK, Ireland, Canada and Australia (PARN 2008a). Respondents rate eight possible drivers on a five-point scale from 'very important' to 'very unimportant'. The percentage

---

## EXHIBIT 2.2 MOTIVATIONS FOR DOING CPD[19]

1    I feel it is my duty as a professional to do it (87% important or very important/3% unimportant or very unimportant)
2    I do it to improve performance in my current role (83/5)
3    My professional/regulatory body requires me to do it (74/8)
4    I do it to develop as a person (71/11)
5    I do it to further my career in general (61/16)
6    I do it to further my position with my current employer (40/23)
7    It is explicitly included in my regular appraisal process (39/25)
8    I do it because I want to change careers (14/50)

(PARN 2008a)

ticking important or very important compared with those ticking unimportant or very unimportant is shown in parenthesis after each driver.

By far the most important were the top two drivers. Three of the top four may be regarded as aspects of a good professional (higher end of the list in Exhibit 2.1).[20] Considerably lower down the list in Exhibit 2.2 are aspects of career development. Inclusion in regular appraisals was important or very important for less than half of respondents, while personal development was for almost three-quarters. Only 11 per cent thought personal development was unimportant or very unimportant and more thought it important or very important compared with furthering one's career. These results indicate particularly worthy or high-level motivations.

This is not universally recognized; for example, according to Sadler-Smith *et al.* (2000) the main benefits of CPD are updating, competence and enhancing mobility. However, Rothwell and Arnold (2005: 29) found, of the following six reasons for undertaking CPD, that CIPD members confirmed the last as most salient:

1 avoid losing licence to practise;
2 it is enjoyable in itself;
3 make up lost ground;
4 maintain one's current position;
5 get ahead of the competition;
6 affirm one's identity as a good professional.

These motivations associated with what individuals consider to be the identity of a good professional or their duties as a professional are, as we will elaborate in the next chapter, only one way of commonly viewing CPD.

## 2.5 Professional bodies

Formal CPD is a creation of professional bodies. It is they who directly transformed professional development from something professionals just did, into its institutionalised construct: CPD policies and programmes. They still almost exclusively define what CPD is. They decide what counts as legitimate or valid CPD and provide support for the CPD cycle; though they do not always do this alone. The third most important driver for professionals to do CPD (Exhibit 2.2) was because their professional/regulatory body requires them to do it.[21]

The professional body/practitioner relationship concerning CPD is complex for several reasons:

1 The degree of control professional bodies attempt to exert over practitioners varies considerably. CPD compliance policies are analysed in Chapter 4.
2 Different grades of membership can have different CPD requirements and consequences for non-compliance.

3 There is a disjuncture, which is difficult to assess, between the expected professional body/individual practitioner relationship, and the actual relationship. The extent of this disjuncture will depend on the quality of recording and monitoring systems and the vigour with which instances of non-compliance are detected, investigated and disciplined. How seriously formal CPD is taken by practitioners depends on the likelihood of those transgressing being caught and punished, as well as the effort put into educating the membership about the policy.

4 Different types of professional bodies will have different relations to practitioners. Professional associations will normally support member CPD and often will set the CPD policy (see Chapters 4 and 5). Regulatory bodies will monitor the policy and impose disciplinary action for non-compliance if appropriate (see Chapter 6). Chartered professional bodies in the UK tend to carry out both functions, but many are subject to separate oversight bodies (such as the Professional Oversight Body for accountants, auditors and actuaries). They may set the compliance policy themselves and they may provide some support for CPD as well as, or in collaboration with, the relevant professional association. Some regulatory bodies do not deal with CPD per se; that is, they only deal with complaints and discipline following a complaint about incompetence, but not with policies to maintain competence beyond maintaining entry standards.

Professional bodies are definers and controllers, supporters and champions and also suppliers of CPD activities. Many of these activities have been part of the normal working of a professional body long before CPD.[22] Also with the coming of CPD a new source of revenue has emerged for professional bodies. Counting as part of CPD requirements makes it easier to charge for activities provided for free in the past. In addition, professional bodies can charge other suppliers of CPD activities by accrediting offerings as valid according to their CPD policy.

## 2.6 CPD specialists and CPD aficionados

Those in professional bodies who work on CPD are part of a new occupation. Roles within it range from strategic (designing and advising on policies and programmes), to low-level administrative (checking records, communicating with practitioners about the programme) with many tasks in between (organizing CPD events and activities and making adjustments to the programme). Reflecting this range of roles, those involved come from a range of backgrounds.[23] In 1999, 35 per cent of those running CPD were members of the profession itself; 28 per cent came from a background of education and training; 18 per cent had been administrators and 5 per cent came from a marketing background.[24] In smaller professional bodies whoever is responsible for CPD is likely to carry out other duties as well.

This diversity of backgrounds reflects how recent CPD is, but also how slow the field has been to develop what would be recognized across professions as a common knowledge and competency base. There is no specific qualification to become a CPD specialist, though this is likely to emerge. As the occupation develops we expect more who lead CPD in professional bodies will come directly from a CPD background, either with a specialist CPD qualification or lower level CPD experience in that professional body, or from CPD roles in other professional bodies or at other institutions. In 1998/99 many were anxious, particularly those with educationalist backgrounds, because they felt isolated. Some thought their background qualifications were not appreciated (Friedman *et al.* 1999: 116).[25]

There are two further substantial locations for CPD specialists: with CPD suppliers and with employers of professionals. In these locations CPD specialists are just emerging from other specialisms.

Suppliers of CPD activities are generally specialists in the subject they are teaching rather than in CPD per se. They are likely to provide the same material and deliver it in the same way with perhaps minor adjustments to comply with CPD recording requirements of particular professional bodies. They are not by and large CPD specialists. Some who were involved in the profession and the professional body set up independent training organizations for that profession. Some suppliers of materials or technology to professionals develop training materials to support sales. Often it is the administrators in these training and supply organizations who become specialists in understanding CPD.

CPD trainers often present CPD on their websites in similar terms to those of professional bodies. Some appeal directly to professionals, some to employers of professionals and some work with professional bodies. In addition, many are accredited by professional bodies and produce outputs in formats required by them or support those taking their courses to produce outputs in required formats. This can be a powerful marketing tool as often accreditation is necessary or it carries extra benefits, such as counting for double CPD 'points'. The Association of Reflexologists (AoR) charged trainers £125 per event and £40 per listing in its approval scheme for CPD events in 2008 (see Exhibit 2.3).

There are CPD specialists in universities, but as described below (Section 2.9), they are rarely identified as CPD specialists. They may be called members of education faculties or continuing education departments or Vocational Lifelong Learning (VLL) specialists (Chivers 2006). This reflects the immature condition of the CPD field.

CPD specialists can be found in other institutions, though usually they too will not have job titles that identify them as CPD specialists. There are trainers with companies supplying products to professionals such as drugs or equipment. They educate professionals on how to use these products, though many also use the training to sell products. Another group are suppliers of information technology and internet support to professional bodies, which either produce general systems that can also support CPD, or provide stand alone systems aimed

---

**EXHIBIT 2.3 AoR APPROVAL SCHEME FOR CPD EVENTS**

An event is defined for AoR CPD purposes as an organized activity such as a course, lecture, seminar or workshop that is made available to participants by a training provider. The training provider may be a college, private centre or an individual.

Benefits to providers of AoR approval for CPD Events:

- The AoR is respected throughout the UK and overseas. Approved CPD events will attract kudos from AoR approval.
- As the largest reflexology organization in the UK, AoR approved CPD events will reach a large number of members.
- Approved events are listed on the AoR website.
- Significant numbers of non-member reflexologists also visit the website in search of CPD opportunities.
- Approved events can be advertised in *Reflexions* within the AoR approved CPD section, subject to meeting relevant deadlines.
- Demand from members will be increased due to double points earned by being an AoR-approved CPD event.
- Providers can offer promotional rates to AoR members to increase uptake.
- CPD providers that are members also earn double CPD points.

(AoR 2008, with permission)

---

at CPD, such as online courses. The most numerous are training specialists and administrators in human resources (HR) or personnel departments among employers of professionals. A few of these are coming to be CPD specialists, but these are largely confined to professional services firms.

Finally, there are academics who research CPD. Compared with education researchers investigating young people, they are few. Some specialize in adult education or lifelong learning, but very few of them work on professionals.[26] Additionally there are academics beyond those specializing in CPD, who are concerned with a variety of subjects that CPD could impact on, such as socio-economic effects of the professions, public welfare policy, competition policy and support for economic growth and trade balance.

It is difficult to estimate the proportions of CPD specialists coming from these very different organizational settings, especially as most of them do not carry job titles that identify them with CPD.

CPD specialists *should* be the most important group to develop the CPD field, raise the value of resources to be had in the field and spread its influence. Indeed CPD specialists have led certain developments in the field which we will discuss in later chapters; however, the key group to raise the value of resources in the field and to spread its influence has been professional bodies, or those running them. If the CPD field is to expand and develop further, certain other groups of stakeholders will have to become players, or at least the ranks of CPD specialists will have to grow from those ranks.

## 2.7 Employers of professionals

CPD is not recognized by most employers or widely in the literature on employer training. Other labels are used – human resources development (HRD), training and development, learning and development, workplace learning, management learning – though these terms have been linked to CPD by some academics (Smith, I. 2004).

CPD can give employers appropriate training with considerable cost savings. Some CPD is provided free by professional bodies and much will be paid for by individual professionals themselves. In addition, having CPD activities accredited by a professional body can save employers search costs. CPD can contribute to employee performance appraisals, though not without some twisting in most cases. On the other hand, professional bodies can recognize training provided by employers as CPD. Some employers encourage reading groups among staff to consider how journal articles and other materials relate to ongoing work. Some have outside speakers come to lecture staff or expect employees to report to other internal staff on conferences they have attended. In this sense some companies, particularly high tech and professional services firms, operate a little like academic departments.

A few employers place a portion of their professional staff training under the CPD banner in order to benefit from professional body support. However, most run their training of professional staff under other labels as noted above, or under a company branded label (see Exhibit 2.5). We surmise the sorts of professional services firms likely to link with professional body CPD schemes to be mainly middle sized with a strong professional culture, but not a well developed internal training function beyond taking on individuals for initial training contracts.

Links will also be of value to companies not primarily providing professional services, but large enough to have substantial numbers of staff of a particular profession such as is the case of UK Bus Company, part of First Group (Exhibit 2.4).

Some larger companies providing in-house training find it useful for their training to be accredited by outside bodies in order to offer it to the outside world. Also some professional bodies have come to involve employers in the design of their CPD programme and some include employer provisions in their programme. CPD may be understood by some employers as a way of encouraging staff to take control of their own training and development.

---

### EXHIBIT 2.4 CPD SUPPORT SCHEME FOR EMPLOYED FINANCIAL PROFESSIONALS AT UK BUS

UK Bus employs 70 qualified accountants in 20 area businesses across the country. In co-ordination with the company's learning and development team the CPD project manager adopted the CIMA (Chartered Institute of Management Accountants) CPD Planner and Harvard ManageMentor Plus as their online platform. They fully integrated this CPD into the performance management processes at UK Bus. The project was stimulated by senior management awareness of finance professionals' isolation within the company.

> The planning tools were implemented quickly, with CIMA's CPD team providing excellent service . . . For the first time, a diverse group of accountants began to think seriously about their roles and the skills required to execute them well. This is why the six-step CIMA professional development cycle has been so successful within UK Bus.

According to the project manager, six months into the initiative 'the biggest result has been a real sense of motivation among the finance teams.'

> As part of the performance management culture, CPD can become a focal point for management discussion, allowing individuals to tie their development to specific skills that will help them then achieve organizational objectives.

UK Bus plan to get CIMA accreditation for the CPD process so their financial professionals can use it for compliance with CIMA policy. This they believe will 'enhance their reputation as an employer of choice.'

(Crompton 2007: 29–30)

---

Consider why employers may *not* want to connect to CPD. CPD is not *coincident* with employee training and development and an employer, particularly a professional services firm, may regard their unique in-house approach to training and development as a draw to attract a better pool of recruits (Exhibit 2.5).

Another reason for employers to be wary of CPD is that some of what is covered by professional bodies is aimed at helping professionals to leave current employers and find new jobs. Some employers are not keen for staff to do any more than is necessary to keep up their competency in their current role, or they wish all training to be stamped exclusively with the culture of their organization.[27] Recently, large employers have been trying to get staff to think and act across the organization, with a greater sense of what is needed for the

---

### EXHIBIT 2.5 KPMG ON TRAINING AND DEVELOPMENT OF STAFF

Each KPMG member firm has its own range of national training and development programs and this is complemented by our global learning and development initiative, Compass. We believe we have developed one of the strongest learning and development packages you will find anywhere – a powerful combination of technical training, coaching and mentoring, skill building programs [and] industry secondments.

(KPMG 2010)

---

organization as a whole rather than furthering their own departmental aims. Traditional departmental 'silos' they aim to break down are often based on traditional professions.[28]

A particular problem for large companies employing a variety of professionals is the bewildering differences in CPD requirements. As will be explained in the following chapters, for some CPD is compulsory, for others it is voluntary; some require a minimum number of hours of CPD spent per year, others measure CPD by criteria based on what is learned or how practice is affected rather than by time spent. For some particular courses are accredited and/or provided by the professional bodies, but not for others. This raises the costs of linking employee training to CPD and discourages many from even attempting to familiarize themselves with this landscape.

Finally, there is a new and radical tendency for employers to provide training for their employees (and others), which has the status of university courses. Employers can take on university functions, accredited as outposts of existing universities. More radically certain large employers have been developing 'professions' based on themselves, through establishing their own 'universities'. This is already coming to be established in the information technology (IT) world with Motorola (Motorola University[29]), Microsoft (Microsoft Partner Network, Training and Events[30]) and SAP (SAP Training and Certification Shop[31]). It is coming to lower-level qualifications as well (Exhibit 2.6).

### 2.8 IT intermediaries for recording, supporting and delivering CPD

A new speciality within the IT field has developed to provide electronic delivery, recording, guidance and other forms of support for CPD. Some of these companies have arisen to intermediate in the IT market, providing systems to support private companies or member databases in the member association sector (trade and professional associations). Examples of these who are active in the UK at the time of writing are *Premier IT, Skilsure* and *Echelon*.[32]

---

**EXHIBIT 2.6 TOWARDS MCDONALD'S UNIVERSITY?**

In January 2008, McDonald's became the first commercial organization allowed to award nationally recognized qualifications. These will exist at two levels. They are piloting a 'basic shift manager's' course, which will cover marketing, human resources and customer service skills. The Qualifications and Curriculum Authority have authorized the company as an exam board and the course, which is an in-house training scheme, will be accredited as the equivalent of an A-level. UCAS are considering whether this can be used to qualify for university admission. John Denham, the Secretary of State for Skills, said:

> This is an important step towards ending the old divisions between company training schemes and national qualifications, something that will benefit employees, employers and the country as a whole.

(Pidd 2008)

---

## 2.9 (Potential) suppliers of CPD activities: higher and further education institutions

Higher education institutions (HEIs – primarily universities) are stakeholders in the CPD world as suppliers and potential suppliers of CPD activities. Potentially, they are also players by becoming thought leaders in defining and reflecting on what CPD is and its implications. We believe these institutions have not come anywhere near fulfilling their potential for these roles.

Some CPD may be provided by traditional individual subject departments based on fields of knowledge, particularly those providing initial qualifications recognized by professional bodies (such as in engineering subjects). These departments are likely to have established reasonably good relations with particular professional bodies, though often the relation will be confined to particular academics who are active volunteers in their professional body (Exhibit 2.7).

A second location for provision of what is now labelled CPD are specialist departments originally designed to provide different kinds of non-traditional university education. In some universities CPD courses are organized and taught in continuing education or lifelong learning departments. These would previously have been labelled Department of Extra-Mural Studies or Department of Adult Education, or some other designation that distinguished it from the main business of the university based on subject fields of knowledge. These departments contain relatively few academic staff. Rather their staff would organize academics in subject-based departments to do the teaching. These academics tend to regard this as 'spare time' activity, not part of the normal (and

## EXHIBIT 2.7 LINKING DEPARTMENTS AT HIGHER EDUCATION INSTITUTIONS AND PROFESSIONAL BODIES

The senior professor there is a [professional body] member, so the university approached us and we became involved in the development of the course . . . professional bodies need to develop good relationships with the relevant individuals at universities.

I was working at [one HEI] so I obviously know all the Heads of Departments in the Business School there and could speak to any of them, and it might be the same in [another HEI] because I was their external assessor so there are certain unis where I could pick up a phone and speak to the person who taught X . . . when I started here I was told very clearly that the first thing I had to do was to establish a decent business programme so I had worked in [one HEI] and I knew the people in the Business School there so I went back to them and I said 'this is what we need, can you do it?' so they developed us a course . . .

(Friedman *et al.* 2008: 95)

more legitimate) teaching of courses directly bearing credit towards a degree. Practitioners are also brought in to teach. In the last 40 years, as universities have become more and more research oriented, and as teaching and research has become subject to direct assessments by government agencies, these departments have lost favour.

Consider the negative: why *not* become involved in CPD. Traditionally universities were set up as communities of scholars. Their primary social role was to admit appropriate young people into that community and to pass them out to the wider world with degrees as a mark of their success at learning and of their suitability to be admitted to work; originally in the Church, the top levels of the military, the law, politics or as physicians (Jarausch 2004). Universities still represent well defined communities and most students at most universities are still full time and stay for at least three years (though this may be reduced to two years in the near future). Staff are attuned to and rewarded for research first and teaching full-time students (often a long way) second. 'Publish or perish' is a common warning given to new academic staff.

To the outside world it may seem a small adjustment to teach professional practitioners short courses and provide workshops for them, even to link to the CPD requirements of professional bodies. But this has hardly occurred. Academics have resisted turning their attention to supplying CPD activities. Reputations are based on research. Teaching, particularly of postgraduates, can be linked to research as the latest thinking in the field is imparted. Practical knowledge is generally regarded as inferior to theoretical or academic knowledge.

There are also fewer economies of scale in teaching CPD compared with undergraduate teaching. A large set of lectures on a particular theme can be worked up in less time per lecture than a collection of CPD hours on different and less closely related topics. Textbooks are not often available. It is also easier to repeat undergraduate lectures from one year to the next with minor adjustments as the core of knowledge in academic fields changes slowly compared with practice.

Academics are also not particularly well equipped to provide CPD. Most CPD requires knowledge of the practitioners' world to link technique with how technique should be applied. Few academics have their feet in both camps. Practitioners can be a much tougher audience than undergraduates owing to their age and experience as well as the likelihood that they will be paying for the service themselves, or if paid by others it will be employers rather than parents. They will expect what they receive to be useful in practice as attested by first-hand knowledge.

Apparently universities account for only 8 per cent of the CPD market.[33] This is changing. UK universities are becoming more sensitive to market opportunities where they can charge the full cost of what is provided. Full-time postgraduates from abroad, particularly from China and South-East Asia, have been a welcome source of full cost fee-paying students in the last 20 years, but numbers have been declining in the past decade as those countries build their own universities.

In addition, the UK government has been acting under the general presumption that universities do not provide graduates with the skills employers want. This has led to a range of policies to encourage universities to provide transferable skills, especially in postgraduate courses (HM Treasury 2002; Department for Education and Skills 2004). The general aim has been to bring them into communication with employers, both directly and through intermediaries set up and developed by the previous Labour governments, such as Regional Development Authorities and Sector Skills Councils. Universities have responded by developing units off-line from traditional departments.

This has led to a third, more recent, location for CPD activity: specialist units focusing on enterprise or employer engagement often located within the central administration.[34] Those who develop programmes for CPD there are administrators and often entrepreneurs who bring together expertise both from within the university as suppliers of knowledge, and from the professions as demanders of CPD and employers of professionals as demanders of custom-designed training labelled according to the desires of those companies.

All three locations for CPD activity are as yet peripheral to the main business of universities, particularly the more traditional ones. Future development of universities as suppliers of CPD will depend on further changes to their cultures and structures.

Further education colleges (FECs)[35] are somewhat different.[36] In the UK they have been involved with professional education and academic subjects as well as vocational training and education, while in other European countries it is only for the latter. Most full-time students are 16- to 19-year-olds, the intention of FECs being to take young adults from compulsory education through to the training needed for employment. However, the majority of students are part time, most with jobs, who are improving their skills on day release from their employers. The distinction between FEC and HEI is becoming more blurred in the UK, with FECs offering some higher education and many of the post-1992 universities offering further education.

## 2.10 Government

Governments have a potential interest in CPD policy through its possible effect on:

- general aims of all democratically elected governments such as: the competitive position of the country, general social welfare, the likelihood of strain on criminal courts if CPD is not pursued;
- particular interests of the government in power to remain in power: bad media arising from suspected incompetence of professionals can implicate the government of the day;
- political or ideological positions of the particular party in power.

One way to illuminate interest in CPD is to examine government policies that may impact on it. The extent of direct government policy intervention and the level of public investment in education, for example, can be roughly aligned to the age of learners at three levels:

1 a highly focused approach with direct involvement in education of young people, largely funded by the public purse;
2 a somewhat more laissez faire attitude towards higher and further education, for which almost all institutions receive substantial but falling public funding in the UK;
3 patchy, initiative-led, involvement in adult education with much of the actual teaching left to unsupported private agencies and government funds primarily used to fund brokers and advisors (such as the Small Business Services and the Sector Skills Councils).

In the past higher and further education institutions have been allowed to design courses and develop quality assurance procedures for themselves. Recently, government has funded a more interventionist approach to quality assurance through the research assessment and teaching assessment initiatives, much to the concern of many academics (Elton 2000). However, government quality assurance initiatives have not applied to activities unconnected to degree awards.

Most recently, the UK government has been trying to get higher education institutions to become more focused on providing graduates with skills that business wants, to develop their 'third strand' of activities (after teaching degree courses and research); services for business and communities. The Lambert Review (2003: 26) states:

> Part of the answer to increasing the demand from business lies in enhancing the role of the development agencies in developing links between business and universities. Development agencies should act as facilitators of business–university relationships by actively seeking out companies in their region which could benefit from working with universities.

However, the government is also keen that these interactions fit both with challenges communities face and with the aims of universities:

> universities work to a variety of missions . . . such as internationalisation, a civic role or regional engagement. The role of collaborative activity is. . . important in shaping the mission and focus of an institution. We would not wish to narrow down the contribution of universities and college by focusing on a small number of policy areas . . .
>
> (Higher Education Funding Council for England; HEFCE 2008: 6)

A second strand of government policy impacting on CPD is directed at citizens rather than institutions. Dealing with CPD directly has not been a priority of UK, EU or other governments, but there have been policies aimed at concepts that could be interpreted as containing CPD: lifelong learning and adult education. Connections between the history of CPD and these concepts are discussed in the next chapter.

The UK government, along with many others as reported by the Organisation for Economic Co-operation and Development (OECD) have been increasing support for adult education for some years. Recently in the UK this has been labelled the 'skills agenda'. There are two types of people these initiatives have been aimed at: those who 'missed out' on gaining employment enhancing skills or higher education when young, and those who have lost their jobs and need retraining to skills that are employment enhancing. The former seem to have been more strongly supported in the UK, the latter in other OECD countries (OECD 2004). However, these initiatives are generally concerned with lower level skills (except for IT and internet skills). The (generally unstated) presumption is that professionals had already received their 'share' of higher education. Also, professionals who lose their jobs are apparently presumed to be able to afford their own retraining, or they may be presumed to receive support from former employers through redundancy packages.[37]

Governments have also dealt with CPD indirectly through regulatory bodies they have set up or encouraged others to set up (see Chapter 6).

## 2.11 Broadcast media and public commentators

CPD has hardly been taken up by the media. Those editing and writing for traditional mass media have an interest in whatever sells newspapers or boosts listening or viewing figures. This can also be so of broadcast aspects of the new social media, particularly blogs and Twitter. In general, bad news seems to attract more followers, especially spectacular failures or stories of great harm done to figures that either the public is sympathetic to, or that represent the public itself.

The media, particularly the general media – daily newspapers, national radio and television – are potentially important players in the CPD field. Up to now they have had little direct impact as they have hardly registered its existence. However, CPD is affected by the media approach to professionals and particularly to incidents of professional misdeeds. The media influences government and galvanizes public opinion. In this it can encourage regulatory rigour in CPD. It can also influence professional bodies to counter bad reputation effects by investing in CPD.

The media has not taken up stories indicating the positive value of CPD. There are stories demonstrating the value of education for young people and of how those who did not get a good education when young can benefit from education. There are stories of how older people may or may not fit so well into the young person's world of academia (e.g. *Educating Rita*). Why are there no stories about CPD?

Perhaps it is because CPD is not associated with institutions as concrete as universities; perhaps because professional bodies have traditionally been rather secretive about their inner workings; perhaps because CPD is carried out in such small chunks; perhaps because the cement that holds these chunks of CPD together is not yet well understood and is not yet stable. Finally, perhaps it is because CPD is a way of supporting and ensuring something that has been expected by definition in the past: that experts know what they are talking about and that professionals are trustworthy. A *story* would be an instance of these expectations being disappointed (even if many do not hold them), rather than what is done to encourage the fulfilment of those expectations.

## 2.12 The players/stakeholders and governance of CPD

Figure 2.3 shows how the different players and stakeholders are *placed* in relation to the CPD field at the time of writing. It is rather speculative, but provides what may be a useful perspective or bird's eye view of the field. We shall use this map in Chapter 10 to chart our views on how the field is changing.

We are mapping the various player and stakeholder groups according to their power to influence the CPD field, indicated by how high they are on the map,

FIGURE 2.3 Map of players/stakeholders' power to influence the CPD field

and the extent of their involvement or their dependency on the field, indicated by their position to the left or right side.

Those at the right-hand side are most involved, in that they are more dependent on the field for access to the resources they need.[38] Those who specialize in CPD at professional bodies, particularly those who implement CPD programmes, may be regarded as very highly dependent on CPD for their livelihoods. Similarly, specialists in CPD at training organizations, further and higher education institutions and at employers will be keenest to track developments in the field and will have strong opinions on what CPD really is.

Professional associations have also been very involved in CPD, though clearly only those with a policy and those with a substantial programme of activities and support, and particularly those who draw significant income from CPD. As professional associations put more resources into their CPD programmes, their reputation with their members in particular becomes more dependent on how members regard CPD. Regulatory bodies are overall much less dependent on CPD. For them it is less an income source and more a potential plank or 'pillar' of professional standards and regulation (Friedman and Hanson 2010). However, as yet, some regulatory bodies do not see CPD as a third pillar of regulation along with initial qualifications, and complaints and disciplinary procedures. For this reason we place them in the passive stakeholder zone, though we seem to be on a cusp of a change towards regarding professional regulation as having three rather than two pillars. Regulatory bodies as a group are becoming players rather than passive stakeholders.

Passive stakeholders in the field are much less dependent on it because their missions or their sources of resources are much wider than CPD. CPD forms only a small part of their activities and concerns.

Power to influence the CPD field is even harder to assess than the degree of involvement or dependency. Power to influence the CPD field relates both to whether one can impose one's own definition of CPD on others in the field, and the extent and ease with which one can turn resources available in the field to one's own favour. Though individuals may act to achieve this, it is the group categories we are particularly interested in. The distribution of power within each of the categories of groups in the figure is not investigated here. In addition, there is the problem of separating actual influence from potential influence and assessing the length of time before potential influence could be exercised. Figure 2.4 shows potential power to influence against dependency.

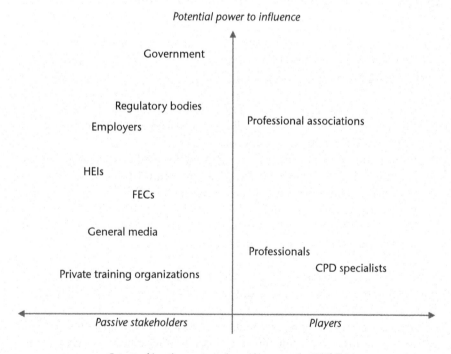

**FIGURE 2.4** Map of players/stakeholders potential power to influence

Clearly the government has enormous potential power to influence CPD; however, if governments do not recognize the significance of CPD for achieving their broad aims, the potential will be a long way off being realized.

In the diagram we distinguish five sets of institutions (professional associations and regulatory bodies, government, different education providers and the general media) and two categories of individuals (professionals and CPD specialists). Of these sets of institutions, all of which have great *potential* power to influence the field, only professional associations have to date exerted strong influence over the field. It is they who have defined CPD, decided on how it should be governed and supply much of the activity. They are of course influenced by the perceived desires of their members, but during the earlier years of CPD they have taken the lead. For this reason Part II is primarily concerned with their policies and programmes. In Part III we consider employers and HEIs as groups who may yet realize their potential to influence the field.

## 2.13 Appendix

### Using the term field for CPD compared with Bourdieu's field concept

For Bourdieu, a field is a social space or arena in which people behave strategically in order to exercise power and pursue or augment resources they desire. These social positions depend on three factors:

1 Commonly held rules or norms for interaction in the field.
2 Resources that are available to individual agents; these are combinations of social, economic and cultural 'capital'.[39]
3 Dispositions of individual agents that may be attributed to their regular habits or what Bourdieu calls their 'habitus': acquired schemes of perception, thought and action that persist. One aspect of habitus we emphasize is the different visions groups in the field have of what CPD is to them. These ways of perceiving CPD have an effect on norms for interaction and resources available in and through the field.

In applying this technical term to CPD we must point out certain adaptations and developments that are required, principally because CPD is an emerging field.

First, all actions cannot be captured by the idea of people operating strategically if this means actively pursuing resources or other objectives. Many act in a field and influence others in the field without operating strategically. Some fields are peripheral to their interests. They may act in relation to these fields without even being consciously aware of how they are operating. For example, in the past most did not attend to the natural environment. They would not have noticed the few recycling bins that were around; they would not attend to news items about environmental damage and would have regarded others around them who did take the issue seriously as cranks, as not of them. This has changed for most people. Thus, the extent to which the field is regarded as important enough to an individual in which they may wish to act strategically can change.

Strategic activity becomes a variable; individuals sometimes attend to what they are doing, and sometimes operate on a kind of auto-pilot. As an emerging field we must allow for this dimension of strategy as it encourages us to consider certain questions. Why do some attend to CPD and regard it as a focus for their strategic attention, while others do not? Why and when do some people change and come to take a more active strategic approach to CPD? What are the barriers to more making such a change? We emphasize this distinction by labelling people and groups who do regard CPD in a more strategic manner as players in the field. Those who rarely, if ever, regard CPD in this way we label passive stakeholders.

Second, we allow for fields to support the achievement of 'inner life aims' not directly connected to resources identified in factor two: a balanced life, a calling, or other ways of achieving aims in life that need not involve (though could come with) accumulation of material or cultural or social resources. This aspect of professionalism was emphasized by early sociologists of the professions (Marshall 1939), but has hardly been referred to by sociologists since the 1970s. It is important to recognize that some professionals do CPD and behave in other ways expected of them, not necessarily for personal material gain or for status, or even out of a sense of altruism. Rather they, in Bourdieu's terms, have a disposition to carry out CPD; it is part of their habitus. How does this arise?

It is our contention that professionals act (in part and not at all times) out of a sense of having a calling based on an inherent personal interest, even fascination with the subject – a sense of curiosity about aspects of practice and the knowledge base behind it. In addition, this sense of calling may be based on a sense of duty to their profession. 'I am a professional and I owe it to my profession, to my sense of what it is to be a professional, to keep up-to-date, to read the professional journal', and for many, to participate in activities organized by the professional body, such as going to branch meetings or to lectures. This is not to ignore two common polar positions in the debate about the professions: that professionals are motivated either by material self interest (like the rest of us?) or by a sense of altruism towards their clients/patients and a general sense of public duty. Rather, we contend that some professionals act for neither, at least at certain times. Many act out of a commitment to what they regard as a worthy calling: to leave one's mark on the world, to live a 'good' life, to exercise one's talents. This does not preclude self-interest or altruism.

When a professional decides what to charge for services rendered, self-interest and altruism are likely to be the best ways to understand the different outcomes. However, these polar positions are not adequate for understanding a professional deciding whether to undertake a CPD activity, or whether they reflect deeply on a service they are about to deliver or have just delivered. Much confusion and controversy over CPD arises from a lack of appreciation of these other types of motivations or dispositions.[40]

The size of the field depends on how many practise CPD and how intensely they do it, as well as how many supply CPD activities and develop CPD programmes, and the resources this entails: economic, cultural and social. It also depends on how many are influenced by the idea of CPD and are recognizably affected by the practice of it. This in turn will affect the cultural capital to be had from doing CPD, supplying it and otherwise being involved with it.

There are many fields in a society, interacting and overlapping with each other to varying degrees. Some will dominate others for generating and distributing power and resources. A further complication is that the way fields may be regarded can be at different levels of abstraction or detail. Some will be committed to what they regard as the field of small particle physics, some to physics, some to science; in addition, some will think of themselves primarily as physicists, some as scientists and some as professionals. Most will think of themselves as all three, but in varying proportions at different times. At different levels there will be different sets of institutions and organizations, and therefore different resources available and possibly different norms. The Institute of Physics (IoP), the Science Council and PARN are organizations aimed at these three different levels.

We may think of the professions all together as a single field in modern society, comprising the individual professions connected to knowledge bases that are usually considered as particular fields. Here we are concerned with a particular habitus that cuts across all these fields; that is, the basis of the disposition to trust professionals and the disposition among professionals to regard their particular knowledge base and practice as something they wish to and 'ought to' maintain and develop: the disposition towards professional development.

# 3

# VISIONS OF CPD

*CPD has no written history. It has evolved through a series of trajectories within individual professions only weakly relating to each other. Also developments since the inception of formal CPD are viewed differently by different players and stakeholders. What will come to be regarded as the true or accepted history of the early development of CPD?*

## 3.1 Introduction

Formal CPD has been around for 30 years in the UK. In the context of the origins of the professions, it is relatively new. Professionals have been developing themselves since professions were formed.[1] The youth of CPD is remarkable in the sense that humanity is new in reference to, say, the age of the earth or the span of life on earth. One may well wonder why CPD is not as old as the professions, or at least as old as formal professional qualifications.

CPD is also new in a second sense; as a broad concept that is widely associated with professionalism. Some professions have had CPD policies and programmes since the 1980s, but for most it is more recent. Only in the twenty-first century have a clear majority in the UK had CPD policies. For other countries with similar traditions of professionalism to the UK, the spread of CPD is more recent.

No one yet has written a history of CPD. This is remarkable because of the vast numbers who follow a CPD programme, the substantial resources that go into its practice, and especially, because of the potential effects of CPD on social and economic life, and the potentially harmful effects of some professionals not carrying out CPD. This is the mystery of CPD. Why has this important phenomenon received so little public attention?

We aim to contribute to a general history of CPD here by answering specific questions about its early years. What were the precursors of CPD? Why did CPD emerge in the 1980s? What was new about it then? Answering these questions leads us to confront the potentially contested nature of CPD. To do so we explore different visions of what CPD might be, associated with different players and stakeholders. This will help us to understand how the field is changing. Five different visions are elaborated in this chapter.

## 3.2 Prehistory of CPD: what professionals just did (Vision 1)

Most professionals have always developed themselves after qualification. Many who resisted CPD in the early days declared 'I am a professional, I am always learning and developing myself' (Friedman, Davis and Phillips 2001: 64). Why would such a statement be a justification for resisting CPD? What is the nature of the activities or processes that these professionals might be thinking of as learning and development? How might they be opposed to, or a duplication of, what these professionals are being expected to do for CPD?

Learning and development may mean:

1 Formal educational activities undertaken after initial qualification such as courses in specialties within one's profession or courses in management in order to progress.
2 Individual lectures, seminars and other short training activities including, more recently, online training on specific subjects.
3 Observing others and discussing problems and cases with more experienced practitioners within one's own practices or employing organization (French and Dowds 2008). Also discussions with professionals encountered during work but not in one's own organizations.
4 Learning from activities off the job, but not necessarily constituted formally as education or training; reading out of interest, attending social events and in the course of volunteer activity such as attending branch meetings or special interest group activities or other administrative roles connected to their professional bodies.
5 Learning from practice itself. Successful professional practice may be interpreted as accumulating context-specific understanding of what is required; not only which aspects of the codified knowledge should be applied in particular situations, but also other kinds of knowledge, such as the language of practice (both verbal and visceral) by which professional advice and other services are effectively conveyed.

The first two of these are what would logically seem to be the primary stuff of CPD.[2] However, one reason why CPD is widely misunderstood is that those expressing the vision of CPD as something they have always 'just done' are likely to have in mind all of these activities. Let us examine the last three in more detail.

### 3.2.1 Learning and developing from practice itself

This is obvious to common sense, but was ignored by most early CPD schemes.[3] Nevertheless, for some it is the very essence of what it is to be a 'true' professional. Learning and development derived from practice can be viewed as the actual learning and development of virtually all professionals.

Donald Schön (1973, 1983, 1984) is the key figure who drew attention to the nature and significance of context-specific understandings in professional practice. For Schön, and many others following his lead, the essence of professionalism is 'reflective practice'. How did he come to this conclusion: that to be truly professional is to be a 'reflective practitioner'?

Schön begins with the observation that people who act in a skilled or intelligent manner in ordinary life tasks cannot be thought of only as *applying* knowledge acquired in an educational setting or as applying theory to practical decisions or activities (1983: 50). However, this is the prevailing view. Schön refers to it as 'Technical Rationality'. Instead people acting with skill or intelligence exercise know-how embedded *in* the action – implicit in the pattern of action – according to their 'feel for the stuff' with which they are dealing. This is how a golfer or a football player judges distances or how we recognize a face we know, or how we read a mood on someone's face. Schön does not deny that we sometimes think about acting before we act, however more generally we act intelligently; that is, we act in our minds, knowing more than we say or can say.[4] This he calls *knowing-in-action* – 'actions, recognitions, and judgements which we know how to carry out spontaneously' (1983: 54); things consciously learned in the past, but which we may not be aware of having learned.

The next step in Schön's argument is to recognize that sometimes people think about what they are doing while doing it: 'thinking on your feet', 'keeping your wits about you', 'learning by doing'. Schön suggests the phrase, *reflecting-in-action*. This is different from knowing-in-action. It is learning to adjust while acting. It involves noticing what you have been doing, the situation you have been doing it in and its effects; all at the same time as acting. This is often called improvising. Much reflection-in-action is associated with experiencing a surprise. When knowing-in-action leads to the expected result, it does not lead to further thinking, but if the result is unexpectedly 'pleasing and promising or unwanted' reflection-in-action may occur. Reflection-in-action focuses on several things at once: 'outcomes of the action, the action itself, and the intuitive knowing implicit in the action' (Schön 1983: 56).

Next Schön connects this to professional practice. *Reflection-in-practice* is the application of reflecting-in-action to professional practice. It is the distinguishing characteristic of the reflective practitioner.

Professional practice involves:

- repetition of certain situations and actions over and over again; practice in the sense of preparation for performance as for a musician;
- dealing with situations or 'problem settings' that are of varying degrees: complex, uncertain, unstable and unique;
- dealing with value conflicts, that is, demands to achieve at the same time: adherence to professional codes, efficiency, satisfying different stakeholders;
- a creative process of pattern recognition derived both from acquired knowledge and experience and from the specific problem situation.

By 'practising practice', a specialist professional experiences many minor variations of a few types of situations; for example, many different property boundary definitions for a solicitor specializing in property conveyance, or many different answers to set interview questions for a human resources manager. This encourages efficiency and effectiveness so long as the practice remains stable. The professional 'develops a repertoire of expectations, images, and techniques. He learns what to look for and how to respond to what he finds' (1983: 60). *Knowledge-in-practice* deepens – the solicitor can recognize a boundary definition that is likely to lead to dispute and requires clearer definition, a human resources professional recognizes specific answers to her questions as indicating a better candidate overall, even if the answer is not exactly what was expected by the interview panel.

Schön (1983: 60–1) recognizes that repeating a narrow range of situations or problems to solve over a long period can have negative consequences. It can lead to a deterioration in a professional's appreciation of wider aspects of the situations she faces – 'selective inattentiveness to phenomena that do not fit' – specialist doctors who do not attend to the whole patient, solicitors who do not attend to their client's time constraints in deciding how far to pursue a potential boundary problem, the human resources professional who regards the name on an application form as a signal not to interview without looking carefully at the rest of the form. Complacency with knowing-in-practice will limit a professional's reflection-in-practice.

Also, one can become bored, or burnt-out. In these circumstances 'reflection-*on-practice*' can be of crucial importance. For most professionals reflection-on-practice and reflection-in-practice occurs as different phases of professional practice. Schön gives numerous examples of how professionals reframe the problems they face in practice through reflection-in-practice and reflection-on-practice. They come to see that certain ways of looking at practice situations could and should change in consequence of how actions are panning out, in consequence of noticing patterns and unexpected variations in practice. Perhaps the doctor comes to recognize that a patient has more than one disease and treatment for one is exacerbating the symptoms of another; perhaps the solicitor sees that delay is likely to lead to the collapse of an otherwise advantageous transaction for a client; perhaps a human resources specialist finds an excellent candidate who has had their surname anglicized or Americanized.

Where does this reframing come from? Schön concentrates on emergence of reflection-on-practice arising from reflection-in-practice. However, the likelihood of this occurring varies according to the nature of professional practice and the mindsets or dispositions of individual professionals. It is more likely to arise where professionals have sufficient autonomy to alter practice based on their own judgements and where professionals regard the situation as important enough to be worth the effort. This is particularly so for contested advice and services such as are provided by barristers and some solicitors (see Gold *et al.* 2007),[5] or for those involved in competitive bidding to win professional services contracts. In most circumstances practice may be regarded as a continuous stream of events that involve actions and possible challenges. It is from acting in these situations that professionals learn as part of their daily practice. Seeing professional development in this way it is easy to understand why certain professionals say they do it every working day of their lives, and always have done so.[6]

Reflection-on-practice can be encouraged or discouraged by broad philosophies about the relationship between theory and practice. Following the technical rationality model, professionals can conceive of their practice as following a logical line from:

- basic theories, to
- broad principles of analytical techniques for applying theories, to
- analysing concrete situations in a manner informed by this knowledge.

This for Schön is the dominating approach from educational institutions. He regards it as a hindrance to reflection-in-practice. It encourages some professionals to be satisfied with their knowledge-in-action and in consequence 'find nothing in the world of practice to occasion reflection'. By 'selective inattention' they 'preserve the constancy of their knowledge-in-practice'. They regard uncertainty as a 'threat' (1983: 69).

Others, who may be more favourably inclined towards reflection-in-practice, and perhaps better at it, may still feel uneasy about relying on it because of their inability to articulate what they know how to do. They doubt its quality or rigour. Those who engage in reflection-in-practice face a 'dilemma' of rigour versus relevance if they are steeped in technical rationality. They experience this dilemma if a rationality that prizes or at least that legitimates reflection-in-practice is not in place to support them.

Reflection-in-practice is primarily conceived by Schön as a process interior to the individual professional: a kind of reflective conversation between the individual professional and his or her situation. He has been criticized for this emphasis on the individual (Thompson and Thompson 2008). However, towards the end of his book he does consider how reflection-in-practice can be increased[7] by involving others.

### 3.2.2 Learning and developing from others in the context of professional practice

The others Schön primarily considers are clients. He proposes a 'reflective contract' as a radical improvement to what he calls 'traditional contracts' (1983: 295–307).[8] Rather than the expert presuming to know everything, to hide her uncertainty, keep her distance from the client and expect deference and status recognition from the client, the reflective practitioner is presumed to know important and relevant things, but not to have exclusive knowledge and not to be devoid of uncertainty. The reflective practitioner also should be keen to seek connections to client thoughts and feelings and to make real connections to clients. The client, rather than gaining security based on faith in the professional and in her correct advice, joins with the professional and exercises some control over the situation, expects to be responsible for providing certain information and taking certain actions. The client tests judgements about the professional's competency through experience of the relationship.

Moving out from the direct professional–client relations are a host of other professional–stakeholder relationships. Conversations with, and observations of, direct managers and peers or work colleagues may stimulate reflection. Reflections may also be stimulated by interactions with: higher level managers; judges for lawyers; hospital administrators for doctors and nurses and other health professionals; planning department officials in local government for architects; various inspectors and quality assessors for teachers and academics.

Quite apart from reflection-in-practice and reflection in and around practice undertaken in an informal manner, which are more or less directly thrown up by practice activity, professionals undertake more focused learning activities that can be either self-generated or presented to them as an opportunity for development.

### 3.2.3 Learning and developing from informal activities and from others apart from the action of professional practice

Many professionals avidly read technical journals and practice-oriented magazines and newsletters produced by their professional bodies. Most would regard these, particularly the former, as learning and development activities. However, there are also activities that professionals undertake out of the setting of practice, which may be regarded as infused, at least potentially, with opportunities for reflection-on-practice and reflection-in-action. Working alongside fellow professionals on activities such as committees of their professional bodies or in consultations for government bodies, are 'serious' off-the-job learning opportunities. Attending social events where other professionals will be present also provides opportunities to learn, even if in a casual manner. This activity, too, would have been presumed to be part of what was expected of professionals. It would have been a major component of their social capital. Circles of friends and colleagues overlapping with communities of practice[9] would lead to key advantages.

It is largely these middle-range activities, not specifically part of gaining further qualifications or other formal training, and more organized than merely on-the-job experience, that were the precursors of CPD. It is difficult to say precisely how much time professionals would have spent on these activities, or to what effect. Records will exist in some professional bodies to indicate the extent of branch activity. Attendance records for head office functions would have been kept by some. Professional bodies are likely to have good records of how many copies of their journals, magazines and other promotional materials had been sent out, but few surveys of how many read this material.

The point to emphasize here is that all this activity was not considered by most to be separate from being a professional. It was what professionals 'just did'.

> The vast majority of doctors are good learners and have always just got on with their own continuing medical education and professional development – that is what being a professional means.
>
> (du Boulay 2000: 393)

These aspects of professional practice, leading to learning as something professionals 'just did' together made up what Houle (1980: 124) called 'the zest for learning' of professionals.

The question that needs answering from this perspective is: how did what professionals just did come to be reconstituted as formal CPD? For this we need to consider what professionals just did from the perspective of the organizations that represent and regulate them: professional bodies.

## 3.3 Prehistory of CPD: the trajectory of member services from professional associations (Vision 2)

CPD may be viewed as a service or benefit that professional bodies, mainly professional associations, provide for their members in return for subscription fees. The CIPD defines CPD (Exhibit 1.1) in terms of the benefits professional development can bring members in the 'real world'. CPD is how members take control of their own learning and development, and their careers. The Royal College of Physicians' definition states that CPD ensures that members continue to develop and enhance what is required to be successful in their working lives.

Long before it was called CPD, professional bodies provided opportunities for professional development; networking opportunities through branches, dinners and awards, as well as offering meeting rooms and a library for members. This was in addition to directly spreading information about new developments through journals, lectures and workshops. These services were provided to members when professional associations were formed either from learned societies around common interest in a subject, or from practitioner clubs within a particular city or region.

The formalization of these activities as CPD has tied members more closely to their professional associations. Those running professional associations have long been concerned that the majority of members (for some the overwhelming majority) were not involved and therefore vulnerable to not renewing their membership (Friedman and Williams 2007). CPD can be a strong reason to continue membership where membership is optional. CPD need not rely on member activism. In addition, there is money to be made from CPD. Many professional associations charge members for provision of CPD. Other suppliers of courses or events can be charged fees for the professional association to accredit their offerings as suitable to count as CPD.

From this perspective the emergence of CPD may be illuminated by asking why professional associations would choose to formulate certain services they had always provided as CPD? Why would the numbers going to branch meetings be transformed into numbers of hours of CPD of individual attendees? The answer is manifold: to bind members more closely to the association; to raise revenue; to raise the professional body's reputation and that of the profession as a whole.

We regard CPD as a 'killer application' for professional associations:[10] not merely because it can achieve different aims, but because they are mutually reinforcing aims: positive feedback loops. The more a professional association invests in CPD, the more its members will want to do it. The more members who do it (and are seen to take it seriously) the more revenue will be raised and the higher will the reputation of the profession become.[11] In addition, this will encourage members to request that it be done by all in the profession. This process can become irreversible, that is, a profession cannot abandon CPD and go back to where its reputation may have been before CPD.[12]

## 3.4 Prehistory of CPD: maintenance of professional standards (Vision 3)

Consider a rather different definition of CPD from Exhibit 1.1. The Health Professions Council, a regulatory body, defines CPD as a way to ensure that registrants retain their capacity to practice safely, effectively and legally. CPD is viewed as a way of ensuring practice accords with expected professional standards. Notice from Rothwell and Arnold's (2005) list of reasons for undertaking CPD given in Chapter 2 that 'to avoid losing licence to practise', is very different from most of the other reasons, such as 'to get ahead of the competition' or 'because it is enjoyable in itself'.

Regulatory bodies have been slower to embrace CPD than professional associations, reflecting in part the long-standing presumption in the past that individuals are fully fledged professionals once they have passed the qualification bar. This is the power of credentialism and reflects what Schön called technical rationality.[13] The presumption had long been that individuals graduating from universities or professional colleges may be expected to understand basic and applied theories and techniques that lie behind professional practice, and that after a brief period of supervised practice, these individuals would be qualified to apply their knowledge to practice situations throughout their working lives. Widespread appreciation of acceleration in the pace of technical and social change has challenged this view.

Long before CPD it was assumed that on qualification individuals were also inculcated with relevant professional ethics. They were trustworthy. This was connected to the idea that only gentlemen could be professionals. What distinguished gentlemen was that they could be trusted.[14] This may not have been true in all cases, but it was a widely recognized norm. This seems now to be part of a bygone era of blind trust in authority and in traditional professions (O'Neill 2005).

Contemporary views are coming to regard trust as a product of professional activities, such as CPD (Gilbert 2005; Owen and Powell 2006). CPD makes informal and semi-formal professional development activities visible and thereby not only legitimates them and renders them useful for career development records, but also has the potential to underpin more informed trust in professionals by showing to clients, patients and employers that professionals are actively developing and maintaining their competence. The emergence of CPD can then be envisioned in terms of conditions that led to diminishing confidence in professional standards regulation that focused on initial education and training.

## 3.5 Prehistory of CPD: yet another of a stream of trappings to legitimate professionalism (unjustifiably) (Vision 4)

Professionalism is a contested concept and has been throughout its history. There have been those who have thought of the professions as a primary force for good in a flawed society:

- 'moral milieux' that bring cohesion to society through professional ethics (Durkheim 1957: 29);
- a major force to temper rampant individualism to the needs of the community in an acquisitive society (Tawney 1921);
- motivated by the common good (Parsons 1954).

These views of the professions dominated academic thought from the late-nineteenth century to the 1960s.

However, from the emergence of the professions in the late middle ages, there has been another view of the professions, which has been expressed by certain well known and outspoken commentators and academics. This regards the professions as perversions of the legitimate sources of power and authority in society. As George Bernard Shaw famously quipped: 'All professions are conspiracies against the laity' (1911). While he may not have thought of it as such, his comment accords with strong neo-classical economists' views that professions are an impediment to competition and so subvert the proper working of markets. This view was particularly expressed by Nobel Prize winner Milton Friedman (Exhibit 3.1).

Behind these views is a belief that professionals are motivated not by altruism, nor to act in the interests of their clients or patients and even less so in the

---

## EXHIBIT 3.1 MILTON FRIEDMAN ON PHYSICIANS

When all this is said, many a reader, I suspect, like many a person with whom I have discussed these issues, will say, 'But still, how else would I get any evidence on the quality of a physician? Granted all that you say about costs, is not licensure the only way of providing the public with some assurance of at least minimum quality?' The answer is partly that people do not now choose physicians by picking names at random from a list of licensed physicians; partly, that a man's ability to pass an examination twenty or thirty years earlier is hardly assurance of quality now; hence, licensure is not now the main or even a major source of assurance of at least minimum quality. But the major answer is very different. It is that the question itself reveals the tyranny of the status quo and the poverty of our imagination in fields in which we are laymen, and even in those in which we have some competence, by comparison with the fertility of the market . . .

(Friedman 1962: 158)

---

interests of the general public. Rather they are motivated by self-interest (like all others). In addition, the trappings of professionalism are ways of preserving and extending that self-interest by what is in effect sham branding. Branding themselves as trustworthy experts, professionals stimulate demand for their services. At the same time they use the badges of professionalism (high education and lengthy periods of apprentice-like supervised practice) to limit their supply. Both support high prices for their services or high wages for those employed to provide such services.

There may be asymmetry of information in the provision of services that have become professionalized, and this would justify some sort of guarantee that those services are of a certain quality. However, it is contended that professions provide such guarantees on two false premises:

1  that such guarantees actually bind the members of the profession to behave in a certain way;
2  that it is necessary to go through all the hoops professional bodies require in order to obtain the expertise necessary to provide a service of sufficient quality.

The coming of CPD, from the perspective of this vision, is yet another prop to convince the general public that the professions are competent and ethical. CPD is yet another way of limiting supply of professionals by placing another barrier, perhaps not to entry, but to continued membership in the profession.

professional bodies have been drawn towards continuing professional development (CPD) as a means of demonstrating they remain up-to-date and, by doing so, they protect their professional autonomy, maintain their privileged status as an occupational group, and concomitantly their position in society more generally.

(Gold *et al*. 2007: 236)[15]

This vision may be thought of as a potential forerunner of anti-CPD opinions. It is potential in that it is premised on CPD becoming widespread. Once this occurs CPD may be regarded as a limitation to the continued supply of professions. However, this vision could be a brake on widespread appreciation of CPD as an important and valuable phenomenon.

Paradoxically, the very reasons for CPD emerging are also reasons why this vision of CPD could become widespread. Although CPD might make professionalism less of a sham in the eyes of some,[16] it could also be further evidence that professionalism is a sham to others, particularly if CPD is not taken seriously by individual professionals, if it is perceived as aspirational only.

## 3.6 Why did CPD emerge?

Why major events in history have occurred, and why at the particular time they did, will always be controversial. Volumes have been written on why wars have been fought or why certain technical advances or social movements emerged. Generally these histories are written after the recognized event or change, when how it 'turned out' can provide a focus for the history, even if it may seem unfair to do so (because the winners get to write or re-write history). Here we are beginning to write the history of a change that is still emerging. Also, the phenomenon itself is changing as it emerges. It may be that in decades to come the emergence of CPD will be viewed as a clear event with particular consequences, but from our perspective within the maelstrom of emergence, it is difficult to do more than indicate a number of ways this story may be written.

We can think about the coming of CPD in terms of factors that would encourage groups who would become players in the field to turn to this formal and structured manner of organizing the learning and development of professionals.

Consider four reasons for the emergence of CPD:

1 The most direct and logical reason has been because initial professional qualifications were no longer being regarded by *professional bodies* as sufficient. They came to recognize that professional competence requires systematic effort throughout a professional's career. More than this, professional bodies came to recognize that professionals must be *seen* to do so; that is, their efforts came to be subject to scrutiny as well as systematic support by professional bodies (as have professional bodies been by government and the media). Individuals are increasingly expected actively and

continually to develop themselves as professionals and to demonstrate to their professional bodies that they are doing so. This is not obvious from many of the definitions of CPD discussed in Chapter 1.

2   Recognition among certain *professionals* not only that post-qualification learning and development was important (as most recognized this without wanting something like CPD), but that it was important to pursue this more systematically and more visibly. This would have been stimulated by white collar lay-offs.

3   Professional associations regarding CPD not only as a new and important member benefit, one that they can easily provide by rebranding much of the things they already did, but also that by doing so they could encourage members to partake of activities provided by the professional body. If members get 'CPD credit' for participating in association activities more will do so.

4   High-profile cases of misconduct or incompetence on the part of individual or groups of professionals encouraged the belief that more should be done to prevent such outrages. Just as the criminal justice system is criticized for relying entirely on the deterrence effect of visible punishments for convicted offenders; that is, for neglecting positive factors such as teaching citizenship in schools, supporting single parents, providing sports and activities clubs for young people to let off steam, encouraging offenders to face up to their victims, so the reaction to high-profile cases of professional misconduct can lead to calls not only for harsh punishments (and criticisms of professional bodies for not meeting out harsher punishments more speedily), but also for policies to ensure that fewer professionals will stray either through stricter entry requirements or for positive supports for competence and ethical behaviour after entry.

## 3.7  Why did CPD emerge in the late 1970s and 1980s?

Though there is a clear line of argument for each of the suggested reasons for the emergence of CPD listed above, why did they become compelling in the 1970s and 1980s? Why did professional bodies come to react to technical and social change, to scandals and to the need to develop stronger ties with their members, with so strong a change as to introduce CPD policies and programmes at that time and not decades earlier?[17]

The answer lies largely in the radical upheaval of the late 1960s and 1970s, in the general rise in scepticism about authority in the West at that time. CPD as a response to these problems emerged with a lag, in part because it is not an obvious solution – it required a change in vision of what professional bodies do – and in part because the formality of CPD is not obviously in the interests of professionals.

Schön (1983: 5–6) identified 1963 as a high watermark of regard for professions in the United States, marked by an article in the American Academy of Arts and Sciences journal, *Daedalus*, which began: 'Everywhere in American life, the professions are triumphant' (Lynn 1963: 649). Since then he recognized a crisis of confidence in professional knowledge, which he linked to the role of professionals in pursuit of the Vietnam War (Schön 1983: 9–20). This period of social unrest was particularly associated with dissatisfaction among educated youth.

In the 1950s and 1960s huge investments were made in further and higher education in the UK, the USA and most other developed countries, reaching a high point in America at 1 per cent of GNP (*UK Public Spending* 2009, *US Government Spending* 2009). The demand for places in higher education had grown enormously since the end of the Second World War, reflecting a growth in demand for professional jobs that in turn reflected aspirations of those who fought in the war, and those who were displaced by the war and who migrated particularly to the UK, the USA, Canada and Australia, seeking a better life. Some believed that this could be achieved through education leading to professional work, but most worked hard in jobs that they could immediately take up, saving the idea that investment in long-term education could be made for their children. By the early 1960s children born during the war and just after, the baby boomers, were coming up to higher education age.

Governments in those countries responded not only to this new demand for higher education, but also to an idea that emerged from the wartime experience, fuelled by the continuing experience of the Cold War and intensifying global competition. The idea was that economic prosperity depended critically on a country's technological base (rather than the inherent industriousness of their people, the astuteness of their political leaders or availability of natural resources). In the UK the Robbins Committee (Committee on Higher Education 1963) recommended expansion of higher education, and in that year Harold Wilson spoke to the Labour Party conference of the coming white-hot technological revolution that would lead to the removal of restrictive practices and the development of a more interventionist government run by planners and professionals. Wilson won the subsequent election of 1964 and established 16 new universities.

The wave of radical upheaval of the late 1960s was carried by this rise in students and by the particular trigger of the war in Vietnam, but there was something deeper affecting the main group of protesters, university students and other young people. That was a questioning of all forms of authority and also a questioning of the values of their parents' generation. Broadly the targets of protest and revolt were American foreign policy, consumerism and capitalism. More particularly it was the draft in America and the way universities were run. Why should old professors and distant administrators run universities? Why should the students themselves not have a say? At many universities there were sit-ins and occupations. A phrase common in the United States at the time was, 'don't trust anyone over 30'.

It was inevitable that other sources of authority would also be questioned. In a pluralist society, many of the plurality of authority sources would be challenged, including the professions. Medicine in particular came in for strong criticism as new or non-traditional medicines were revived or elaborated,[18] but all came under criticism as the 'disabling professions' (Illich 1977; Illich et al. 1977a). Academics in America and the UK were also influenced by a wave of social criticism arising from French intellectuals who had been disillusioned with socialist and communist parties in the 1960s. Michel Foucault led a devastating critique of the medical profession (Foucault 1963).

As the global economy began to stutter in the early 1970s and again in the early 1980s, public sector finances suffered at the very time of pressure on them from rising unemployment. The 'fiscal crisis of the state' led to government cutbacks at national and local levels (O'Connor 1973). New public sector professionals did not have the answer to social problems, which were part of far broader social changes. The global recessions of the early 1970s and early 1980s discouraged employers from allowing their professional employees time off to attend branch meetings of professional associations or to carry out work for the professional bodies in office time using office resources (see Abbott 1988: 154 and Putnam 2000).

Finally, in the 1980s there were a series of environmental revelations and disasters of such proportions as to lead to widespread questioning of expert judgement. Recognition of acid rain, global warming and the depletion of the ozone layer in the early 1980s, combined with serious accidents, notably the Union Carbide Bhopal chemical leak of 1984, in which 3,800 people were killed (Weisaeth 1994); Chernobyl in 1986, the most serious nuclear accident ever, (UNSCEAR 1988) and the tanker Exxon Valdez oil spill in 1989 (Piatt et al. 1990; Cohen 1995).

These revelations and events were not seen as merely the failures of policies and politicians, but rather the finger of responsibility was also pointed at scientists and technologists. These were failings of experts, who were either incompetent or too amenable to financial or political pressures, or who were viewed as incapable of, or uninterested in, exercising independent professional judgement (Unger 1994).

In addition, the decline in trust in professionals may be connected to a decline in the sense of calling among them since the 1960s. Society as a whole has been affected by changes in expectations of working life and a reduction in senses of duty and self-sacrifice. Professionals expect career advancement. There is pressure on professional associations to provide their members with opportunities to develop themselves and for systems that will allow them to demonstrate to current and future employers that they have been developing their competence.

We believe these criticisms of a broad range of professions have led the professions to respond, through their professional bodies. The response is taking several forms. For one thing a number of professions are becoming less secretive about their practices, more willing to use open access parts of websites to let the general public know what they stand for (though there is still a long way to go in this direction). Arguably the most significant, and potentially effective response has been the development of formal CPD policies and programmes to show that professionals are keeping up-to-date.

## 3.8 Prehistory of CPD: educationalist ideas and ideals for lifelong learning (Vision 5)

It is possible to write a very different history of the coming of CPD based on different players and a very different vision of what CPD 'really' is. CPD may be thought of not as a way professionals behave as part of a community of practice, not as a service provided by professional associations and not as a positive way of ensuring technical and ethical competence of registrants of a regulatory body, but rather as a set of educational practices based on progressive (even idealistic or revolutionary) ideas and ideals. From this perspective CPD may be thought of as arising out of adult education and lifelong learning.

The purpose of education has been debated for centuries. Is it to prepare people for work or to prepare people for life (Holmes 1995)? Connected to this is controversy over the relative importance of theoretical versus practical knowledge. Also where should education take place, in formal institutions or in less formal settings? How important should education be at different life stages? Should resources be concentrated on children and young adults?

In the 1950s these debates seemed to have been well settled in the UK and the USA. Education was associated overwhelmingly with formal institutions, schools and universities. Education institutions were to prepare children and young adults for life as well as work, and universities in particular were to develop new knowledge that would maintain the edge of the West over the Communist bloc and ensure future prosperity. Advances in science and technology had been shown to be the key to winning the war against Hitler. New fields of social sciences could also contribute to understanding individuals and groups as well as the economy itself. Pursuit of academic excellence became oriented more to research than to teaching.

### 3.8.1 Lifelong learning

Lifelong learning is a philosophy, not merely a view that learning should occur throughout one's lifetime. At the beginning of the twentieth century the philosophy was set out by Dewey who suggested:

> The inclination to learn from life itself and to make the condition of life such that all will learn in the process of living is the finest product of schooling.
>
> (1916: 51)

Dewey believed that education is the foundation of a rich life and that such a foundation can be made at any stage in life and then built upon. However, learning from life and schooling or formal education are different. Schooling should prepare people for lifelong learning, but lifelong learning was not provided by education institutions. Clearly this is an ideal, an aspiration. Dewey has been influential mainly in the USA, though in the UK there has been a strong tradition of worker education and general self-improvement and group learning from the nineteenth century (Smiles 1860). Many of the new professions of the nineteenth century arose out of societies for group learning or 'learned societies'.

As a policy, lifelong education emerged in the 1970s. The Faure Report (Faure *et al*. 1972) suggested that education prepares people for a society that does not yet exist but which may within their lifetime.

> If all that has to be learned must be continually re-invented and renewed, then teaching becomes education and, more and more, learning. If learning involves all of one's life, in the sense of both time-span and diversity, and all of society, including its social and economic as well as its educational resources, then we must go even further than the necessary overhaul of our 'education systems' until we reach the stage of a learning society.
>
> (Faure *et al*. 1972: xxxiii)

Some would say a learning society cannot be achieved by education systems unless those systems break out of education institutions.

The model of lifelong education was adopted as an ideal by UNESCO, influenced by writers such as Lengrand (1976). According to Cropley (1979: 101–4, see also more recently Knapper and Cropley 2000: 170) it is meant to:

- involve learners as actors in their own learning;
- foster people's capacity to be active learners, rather than passive recipients;
- lead to the democratization of society, and
- improvements in the quality of life.

Since the 1970s the terms lifelong learning and the learning society have become increasingly popular. One scheme for summarizing lifelong learning and lifelong education is as follows:

- Learning from life; that is, an attitude or inclination, spilling over from formal schooling as an ideal; that learning should come from all experiences.
- Learning throughout life, that learning is not confined to youth and does not stop with the attainment of any notion of maturity.
- Learning without instruction. Learning as an active, rather than a passive process and therefore not requiring being taught in a formal manner.

- Learning with society. This is not obvious from the term lifelong education or learning, but proponents imply that lifelong learning should not be confined to an individualistic activity. Learning comes from interactions with others, rather than from specifically designed education materials.
- Learning throughout society. Learning is part of the democratization process in that the exercise of democracy requires people to make informed choices. Informed participants in a truly democratic society must not be confined to an 'educated' elite.

(Friedman, Davis et al. 2000: 30)

Occasionally CPD is described in terms of lifelong learning for professionals (such as lifelong learning for engineers – see Padfield and Schaufelberger 1998; Guest 2006), but the other way round is rare; that is, discussions of lifelong learning rarely mention the tremendous proportion of lifelong learning that is undertaken by professionals under the label of CPD.

While lifelong learning had been a philosophical and a policy ideal, actual policy for learning after initial training or qualifications has gone under a number of headings: adult education, recurrent education and continuing education. Each of these has attracted policy initiatives and some institutional backup.

### 3.8.2 Adult education and other labels for education for adults

Jarvis (1995: 22) offers the following definition of adult education:

> any education process undertaken by adults, whether liberal, general or vocational, and located in the spheres of adult, further or higher education or outside the educational framework entirely.

He notes that the term adult education carries negative connotations in the UK. It implies liberal education undertaken by middle-class people during leisure time; an indulgent, self-centred activity, which is not connected with social purposes; a frivolous activity with little concern for its quality.[19] Therefore other labels have been eagerly embraced, such as recurrent education and continuing education.

*Recurrent education* was defined by the OECD in 1971 as 'formal, and preferably full-time education for adults who want to resume their education, interrupted for a variety of reasons' (Kallen 1979). From the mid-1970s it was supported in the UK by the Association of Recurrent Education. Some believed a specified amount of full-time formal education during one's lifetime was a moral right that could be used to redress not only educational inequality, but also occupational inequality (Gould 1979). It is important to recognize this aspect of recurrent education that connects to the meaning of lifelong learning as learning throughout society. Others regarded this to be a limited or even conservative approach, because it focused on formal education (Cantor 1974). Being associated with formal and full-time education, recurrent education could be viewed as a barrier to certain aspects of lifelong learning listed above: learning from life, learning without instruction and learning from society. Viewed as attempting to impose learning 'from above' and sacrificing radical education content for political gain, recurrent education could become a target of radical educationalists such as Illich (1971), who called for the 'deschooling' of society. Recurrent education is still important in Scandinavian countries where it refers to policies on paid educational leave. However, recurrent education has waned, particularly in countries where the early 1980s brought both economic recession and Conservative governments. The UK Association of Recurrent Education changed its name to the Association of Lifelong Learning.

*Continuing education* may be simply defined as post-initial education (McIntosh 1979: 3). It was considered broader than adult education, incorporating personal, social, economic, vocational and social aspects of education (Venables 1976: 23–4). During the late 1970s it 'gradually worked itself up the national education agenda' (Sockett 1981: 5). University extra-mural classes came to be regarded as continuing education and changed their names accordingly.[20] Part of the gathering success of continuing education came from the introduction of *Continuing Professional Education* among professions in the UK and even more so in the United States (Jarvis 1995: 28). Jarvis also suggested that continuing education became more popular than recurrent education in the UK because it:

> is a much more nebulous concept, having no undertones of radicalism, it is hardly surprising that it has gained so much support and that it is incorporating elements of recurrent education within it.
>
> (1995: 33)

Continuing education includes vocational and non-vocational education, but UK government support for it has had a vocational bias. The definition provided by the Accrediting Commission of the Continuing Education Council of the United States refers to:

> the further development of human abilities after entrance into employment or voluntary activities . . . [It] includes that study made necessary by advances in knowledge. It excludes most general education and training for job entry . . . Most of the subject matter is at the professional, technical and leadership training levels or the equivalent.
>
> (cited in Apps 1979: 68f)

Here a further aspect of lifelong learning is emphasized: continuing education is required or 'made necessary' by advances in knowledge. This has been an important stimulus for Continuing *Professional* Education.

### 3.8.3 Emergence of Continuing Professional Education and transition to CPD

Evidence that a concept of CPE was beginning to emerge in the late 1960s in the UK is provided by research and consultation papers produced throughout the 1970s for particular professions. The Ormrod Report (Arthurs 1971) referred to the value of 'continuing legal education' enabling lawyers to become fully equipped members of the profession. Acheson (1974) conducted a survey of the opinions of GPs in England and Wales about the organization of continuing education. Gardner (1978) was carrying out research at the University of York to develop continuing education for the building professions.

CPD can be viewed as emerging from CPE in three logical steps (Exhibit 3.2).

CPE in the USA and Canada seems to have in many cases transformed into what is called CPD in the UK without a change in label. However, in more highly regulated professions, it is likely that in the USA in particular, regulators

---

**EXHIBIT 3.2 THREE STEPS TO CPD IN EDUCATIONALIST TERMS**

Step 1   *Completing Professional Education.* Professionals need further education after initial qualification to become fully qualified because of the difficulty in providing specialized education required to get a professional up to speed in their chosen area of speciality. Many will find it difficult to choose a specialism until they have some experience of practice. The set of well defined specialisms can be too large for most colleges or universities to cover adequately and newly qualified professionals will have to go elsewhere.

Step 2   Courses might be needed throughout a professional's working life to keep up to date while working within a chosen specialist path one is formally qualified for. This is *Continuing Professional Education*, at least in the UK. There is a long history of formal Continuing Medical Education (CME) in the USA.[21]

Step 3   Genuine *Continuing Professional Development* means more than attending courses, which are by their very nature pre-designed and perhaps prescribed by agents other than the practitioners themselves. It is about being strategic and systematic and taking personal responsibility for maintaining and developing your knowledge base and your techniques. In this it embraces the philosophy of lifelong learning.

do not 'count' reading and other informal activities. In these instances the CPD cycle would be less important. CPE is exclusively formally examined activities. Planning of such activities and reflection on them are incidental to the 'results' of examinations. In these instances CPE in the USA is like CPE in the UK and CPD either does not really exist or it is clearly regarded as something else.[22]

Step 3 can be difficult to understand. It involves a very different view of knowledge acquisition and practice support from what had become very strongly entrenched in the educational system in Western society during the twentieth century and particularly strongly developed in the two decades after the Second World War.

Continuing professional education received a boost from the UK Conservative government in the 1980s and early 1990s. In 1982, they introduced the Professional, Industrial and Commercial Updating Programme (PICKUP) designed to increase competitiveness in the UK, through funding short courses and customized company training programmes provided by further and higher education. PICKUP also funded continuing education programmes of the Engineering Council and other professional associations. While modest in comparison with Manpower Services Commission support for the young unemployed, PICKUP funded short vocational courses aimed at new management methods, new technologies and recent legislation for employees. Universities became more involved in 1985 with the launch of the PICKUP in Universities scheme. This funded training co-ordinators at universities outside the normal department structures (often the first person to be employed to work across departments). National PICKUP in Universities conferences were organized annually from 1986 into the 1990s. The name PICKUP was changed to Continuing Vocational Education in 1992. By the end of the 1990s the label had changed again to Vocational Lifelong Learning (VLL) (Chivers 2006).

VLL professionals may be regarded as CPD specialist professionals, but located in universities rather than in professional bodies. Some are located inside university central administration along with other outreach activities such as consultancy or applying for industry research contracts. Some are in continuing education departments. Some are in small specialist vocational learning units (short course centres) and a few have directly entered academic departments. Chivers (2006) notes 'considerable attrition' of these posts as some universities closed down continuing education units with the decline of funding for VLL work from central government and as demands for stronger research and traditional teaching performances rose. Also, he found that VLL professionals had been resigning or moving on to other work at the university because they found VLL activities were not prized or well supported.

Perhaps because academics are more likely to record their activities publicly, we find earliest references to CPD as an educational concept. According to Todd (1987: 4–5) the term continuing professional development was coined by Richard Gardner at the University of York in the mid-1970s. He introduced the term to signal his belief that there is more to continuing education than formal courses. CPD was intended to signal inclusion of informal or incidental learning arising in practice.

Though the CPD concept originated in the UK in the late 1970s, it was only formally adopted and defined by professional bodies during the 1980s. Before then many terms specific to particular professions were used to describe post-qualification education or learning: in-service education for teachers (DES 1972), continuing formation for engineers (Cannell 2008), Continuing Medical Education (CME) for doctors (Rogers 1982). Some of these terms, such as CME, continue to exist alongside CPD (Standing Committee on Postgraduate Medical and Dental Education; SCOPME 1999). However, the term CPD has generally replaced CPE and other similar terms in the UK.

## 3.9 Picture of CPD in its early years

According to a survey of 123 professional bodies in the UK carried out in 1987, 47 per cent had a CPD policy and a further 31 per cent reported that they were considering introducing a policy (Welsh and Woodward 1989). It is likely that this was an overestimate as the survey would have certainly been biased towards larger professional bodies, which were more likely to have a policy.[23]

Early CPD programmes concentrated on explaining what CPD was, what could count as CPD and how to record it. Almost all professional bodies issued a record card.[24] Most introduced it on a voluntary or obligatory basis (see Chapter 4 for an explanation of these terms). Policies on CPD were generally defined in terms of expecting a certain number of hours to be undertaken within a year or some other period of time.

A particularly interesting early example of CPD came from the Construction Industry Council, whose 1986 definition of CPD was widely used throughout the engineering and construction industry sectors, and spread to others by the late 1990s as noted in Chapter 1. In addition, through the European Project for the use of Standards of Competence in CPD for Construction Industry Practitioners (EUSCCCIP 1998), these sectors led the way in promulgating the use of the CPD cycle to help organize guidance and the support professional bodies gave to their members, as well as emphasizing to members that CPD was a cyclical process, both continuous and neverending.

The distinction between Vision 2 and Vision 3 – CPD as a member service and CPD as a means of controlling professional standards – can be clearly seen from a study in the early 1990s. Rapkins (1996) distinguished two models of CPD policy and practice: the sanctions model and the benefits model (Table 3.1). According to Rapkins the benefits model aimed to raise the status and profile of the professional body. The sanctions approach served to demonstrate that members were up-to-date. Newer professional bodies tended to adopt a benefits model; older, more established organizations, particularly regulatory bodies, tended to the sanctions approach.

**TABLE 3.1** Early view of CPD policies and programmes

|  | *Sanctions model* | *Benefits model* |
|---|---|---|
| Type of professional body | Old and established bodies and those with regulatory functions | New and/or developing bodies |
| Why have a policy? | Means of demonstrating members are up-to-date | Means of raising status and profile of professional body |
| Type of policy | Mandatory; sanctions for non-compliance with requirements | Voluntary; incentives and rewards for participation |
| Type of measurement | Input oriented (emphasize number of hours, content and process of learning) | Output oriented (emphasize learning results from participation) |
| Monitoring of CPD | Professional body monitors compliance with requirements | Self-monitoring of learning outcomes |
| CPD activities | Updating technical knowledge and skill | Updating, broadening and deepening knowledge, skill and expertise |

*Source:* Adapted from Rapkins 1996: 217–18.
*Note:* Based on research in 1992/3 (Madden and Mitchell 1993).

Two aspects of the models are particularly notable. First, there are only two compliance policies discerned. PARN research shows that, at least a few years later, the term obligatory for a CPD compliance policy was common in the UK. Second, there is a presumption that the sanctions model is only concerned with inputs. This is still the case in many instances, but has been changing recently.

From the early years of CPD all five visions described in this chapter have been held by various players and stakeholders in and around the field. The first perspective arises out of what professionals had been doing after qualification, which had a bearing on their development and competence long before the coming of CPD. We have evidence that substantial numbers in the CPD field still see CPD this way. However, we believe that eventually few will share this vision. The second and third may be conceived in terms of two primary functions of professional bodies: providing members with useful services and regulating professional standards. We believe these perspectives will become stronger. The strength of the fourth vision of CPD, as a sham, is bound up with the seriousness with which CPD is taken by professional bodies and individual professionals. The final, supplier vision, of CPD as a form of adult education or lifelong learning, is not currently widely accepted. Nevertheless, we believe that it will inform the dispositions of many players in the CPD field in future.

# Part II

CPD has been primarily a consequence of deliberate action of professional bodies. We distinguish several types of professional bodies, but the two most common ones are our particular focus: professional associations and regulatory bodies. How is CPD governed and run by these professional bodies?

Evidence of governance and current operations of CPD is presented primarily from the UK but also from Australia, Canada and Ireland. In the four chapters in Part II we deal with compliance policies, programmes of support and ways of monitoring and regulating CPD, and finally measurement and assessment of CPD.

There is a progression in the complexity of CPD that is discernible as we move from the relatively straightforward discussion of ways of supporting CPD to ways of monitoring and regulating it, and then to how to measure and assess it. These issues require more and more appreciation of complexity between different types of professional bodies and different purposes of CPD introduced in Chapter 1. How CPD is to be measured and assessed is controversial, with strongly divided opinions. The issues involved go to the heart, not only of the complexity of CPD, but also of the reputation, sustainability and development of the whole CPD field.

# 4

# CPD GOVERNANCE

## Compliance policies

*How can a CPD compliance policy be both obligatory and not compulsory?*

## 4.1 Introduction

Different governance regimes have at their heart different compliance policies. Should CPD be up to professionals themselves to initiate, carry out and follow up or should an authority require it of them? Arguably the very phenomenon of CPD, certainly the feel of it to professionals and the view of it from other stakeholders, will vary according to the compliance policy. There is no consensus on compliance; though a long-predicted switch to compulsory policies may finally be occurring. Many have made their policies stricter, but there are instances of professional bodies moving in the opposite direction, sometimes due to resistance from practitioners.[1]

Here we explore and evaluate three governance regimes based on voluntary, compulsory (or mandatory) and obligatory compliance policies. The first of these can be understood in terms of the vision of CPD as something professionals just do. The second is more associated with regulatory bodies and the vision of CPD as supporting professional standards maintenance. The third will be curious to many, though it is the policy of many professional bodies. Evidence of the incidence of these policies in several countries is provided as well as how they have been changing.

## 4.2 Types of compliance policies

### 4.2.1 Voluntary: preserving professional autonomy and providing a service

A voluntary policy is different from no policy. A voluntary policy offers a formalization of what professionals in the past just did. Some things may count for more CPD credit than others, some may not count at all, and in many schemes something must be added to all activities to allow them to count. They must be planned, reflected upon and/or evaluated in order to be formalized as CPD. CPD provides a visible wrapper around those things a professional would in the past have just done. This wrapper, this form of labelling or certification, is regarded as a benefit to members by professional bodies with a voluntary scheme. The decision to follow the programme is entirely up to practitioners, but they are urged to participate and keep it up. Enhancing employability and career progression are emphasized.

Like any other member benefit, how vigorously professional bodies 'sell' it will differ. The professional body may charge for certain activities it provides as CPD, such as seminars run by leaders in the field. Monitoring registrations are a way of assessing the relative popularity of different activities, to decide which to provide in future. Even with no charge, such records provide the professional body with a way of assessing how well it is serving its members, which can be particularly important if they are competing for the same set of professionals. Records can be used to track whether individuals achieve the recommended level of CPD, but this information is provided to practitioners at *their* request, if they deem it useful, not as part of a regulatory regime.

## Advantages of a voluntary policy to the professional body and the profession

A voluntary policy allows for flexibility. Practitioners can do as much as they like without incurring a judgement from the professional body. A voluntary policy will not only allow for the flexibility of doing less than recommended at certain times of stress, it will also be less discouraging of those who want to do more. Many younger or more ambitious practitioners will be keen to do more. A voluntary policy is less likely to encourage formal compliance dispositions: what has become widely known in many professions as a 'tick box' attitude to CPD.

Voluntary policies are regarded by some as most consistent with the ethos of professionalism. If professional autonomy is a critical characteristic of the 'true' professional, presumably they ought to be free to choose which CPD activities they do, when and how much they should be doing.

Voluntary CPD allows the professional body to maintain a purely supportive relation with its members. Resentment against a voluntary policy is unlikely. For this reason it is often the first policy introduced, particularly by associations without statutory back up and in competition with other professional bodies.[2]

One possible objection to a voluntary policy compared with no policy, is if it is regarded as expensive, particularly if it is perceived by the membership as responsible for a rise in subscription fees. It may be regarded as a 'tax' on those who do not partake of CPD. However, voluntary policies are generally cheaper than compulsory policies and this is another reason why new and small professional bodies usually choose them.

Based on data from PARN's international benchmarking surveys of 2006 and 2009 there is a consistent correlation between smaller professional bodies and voluntary policies (Table 4.1).

## Disadvantages of a voluntary policy

If CPD is valuable for improving practice and for professional development, then this value is not being realized for the majority of practitioners in a profession with a voluntary policy. PARN estimated that 38 per cent of professionals follow CPD under a voluntary policy.[3] Therefore the clients of 62 per cent of practitioners are not gaining the benefits of being served by formally up-to-date professionals. This may not matter if those who are not participating in the formal programme do not need to do so (because they are already up-to-date having recently qualified) or if they are informally doing what is needed without registering it. However, Jones and Fear (1994: 52) contend 'it is always those who need CPD most who are least likely to do it.'

With a voluntary policy, professional bodies have less authority to promote their members as up-to-date. At least they have no comprehensive evidence to back up this claim. In the past this has not been so important as CPD has not been widespread and has not been widely understood or expected by the general public. However, those with only voluntary policies are likely to compare unfavourably in future.

**TABLE 4.1** CPD policy by size of membership: UK professional bodies in 2006 and 2009

| Policy | Year | Number of members | | |
| | | Less than 5,000 | 5,000 to 20,000 | More than 20,000 |
| --- | --- | --- | --- | --- |
| Compulsory | 2006 | 20% | 13% | 24% |
| | 2009 | 25% | 20% | 26% |
| Obligatory | 2006 | 18% | 21% | 24% |
| | 2009 | 19% | 20% | 21% |
| Voluntary | 2006 | 55% | 46% | 24% |
| | 2009 | 38% | 35% | 26% |
| Mixed | 2006 | 8% | 17% | 24% |
| | 2009 | 19% | 25% | 21% |

*Note:* Based on PARN International Benchmarking Surveys (IBS) in 2006 and 2009. 2006 sample size: 85 professional bodies. 2009 sample size: 55 professional bodies.

## 4.2.2 Compulsory: focusing on protecting and reassuring the public and raising the reputation of the profession

The terms 'compulsory' and 'mandatory' are used interchangeably, meaning a policy that must be adhered to. This will logically carry the threat of sanction for non-compliance, and can ultimately lead to expulsion from the profession, or at least the professional body. Behind this policy is the idea that the integrity of the profession and the public good depend on the participation of all in CPD.

For the threat of sanctions to be credible and seen to be fairly administered, it follows that CPD participation must be closely monitored. Otherwise it can fall into disrepute and weaken rather than strengthen the reputation of the professional body and the profession. If sanctions are not seen to follow non-compliance, the policy may come to be disrespected and disregarded. As with the general law of the land, a system of justice and punishment – carefully, fairly and visibly imposed – is required to maintain public consent.

It is worth distinguishing a compulsory policy to carry out a specified amount of CPD that leaves the content up to individual professionals, from compulsory policies which prescribe content. Friedman, Davis *et al.* (2000) cite specialists running CPD programmes who were aware of the problem of squaring compulsory CPD with the notion that members should determine their own development requirements:

> Perhaps one way of looking at this question of prescriptive CPD is that CPD is about demonstrating a commitment to oneself, one's employer, one's profession and society. When that process becomes prescriptive in terms of subject matter or content, are we not entering into the realms of a form of 'post-professional' qualification?
>
> (Friedman, Davis *et al.* 2000: 69)

In fact something like post-professional qualifications have been introduced recently by doctors and dentists in the UK under the label of revalidation (see General Medical Council[4] or Royal College of General Practitioners[5]). This is the dominant approach to licensed professions in the USA (Parboosingh 1998).

Implementing a compulsory policy has alienated some professionals from their professional body, particularly more senior professionals. Some resent the need to carry out CPD according to the rhythm set by the professional body, so many hours per year. Some may even resent the whole idea of the professional body judging their competence after they have spent many long years qualifying. From the professional body viewpoint this is a real concern, particularly if practitioners do not have to belong to the professional body in order to practise (Friedman and Phillips 2004):

> We have a voluntary CPD scheme which has been in operation since 1993. It is planned to make this compulsory. How can this best be done without

losing half the membership, bearing in mind that the Institute does not have a Charter?

(Comment made 14 December 1998 and reported in Friedman, Davis *et al.* 2000: 69)

## Arguments in favour of a compulsory policy

It certainly seems logical that activities designed to keep up-to-date and develop one's competence will improve professional practice.[6] Certain insurance companies have allowed reduced premiums on professional indemnity insurance for members of certain professions if they can show evidence of maintaining their CPD according to the programme set out by the relevant professional body.[7] These insurance companies are working on the assumption that individuals who keep up their CPD will be less at risk for claims, less likely to be credibly accused of incompetence or unethical behaviour; that is, CPD makes a difference to the quality of practice.[8]

More practitioners will undertake CPD if a compulsory policy is in place. According to Friedman and Afitska (2009), 40 professional bodies with a compulsory policy reported that an average of 99 per cent of their practitioners follow the programme compared with only 38 per cent with a voluntary policy.

It follows that clients or patients should be more likely to regard professionals as up-to-date and competent if they can be assured that all professionals in that field carry out CPD. This can be a signal obviating the need to seek particular proof from individuals. In effect, the certification of individual professionals as members in good standing of the professional body will come to be regarded as a guarantee of professional standards.

Why is this necessary? Is it not already true that the professional qualification acts as such a guarantee? The problem, as discussed in Chapter 3, is that initial professional qualifications are no longer regarded as sufficient in this world of rapidly changing technologies, legal frameworks and services available. One way of providing an accepted guarantee that obviates the problem of judging whether a professional is up-to-date is to rely on the internal processes of large and well known professional services firms. The presumption of equal competence emerging from the efforts of professional bodies, to maintain standards among professionals, is belied by vastly different prices charged for roughly similar professional services between large and small firms or single practitioners. CPD could go some way to redressing this.

Even if the individual can display a certificate from a professional body attesting to compliance, with a voluntary policy clients may find it difficult to interpret this evidence, particularly if professional bodies are issuing different certificates and on different criteria. Employers and potential employers will also be confused.

Following from these arguments, compulsory CPD has the potential to raise the *status* of the profession as a whole.[9] A further consequence would then be to encourage bright young people to choose paths that will lead to membership of that profession and to encourage existing members to stay with it. This, in turn, will contribute to raising the quality of the community of practitioners and again help raise the status of the profession. This virtuous circle is not guaranteed and may only apply some time in the future, but links making up the circle can be discerned now (Figure 4.1). The critical link needed is for CPD to become more widely appreciated among the general public.

In addition, compulsory CPD is likely to raise the status of the professional body and its members with *employers* by allowing employers to market themselves as employing the most competent individuals in their field. It allows professional bodies to brand and market themselves as guaranteeing competency with less reliance on blind trust. They can point to particular reasons why potential clients and employers should regard their members as up-to-date and competent. This can attract members to the professional body when it is not a statutory requirement to belong to it and provide income if the professional body develops a kitemark to sell to employers.

The IMI (Institute of the Motor Industry) run an accreditation scheme for vehicle technicians and their employers; Automotive Technician Accreditation (ATA). If an employer can demonstrate that their technicians meet the required standards they can display the ATA Kitemark being marketed to the public by the IMI as a marker of credibility, professionalism and skill (Exhibit 4.1). Engineers Ireland run a scheme to accredit CPD of employers (see Exhibit 10.2).

It is worth pointing out that compulsory CPD will not only raise the proportion of members carrying out CPD, it will also raise the demand for professional body services that count as CPD. Vision 2 of CPD, from the professional

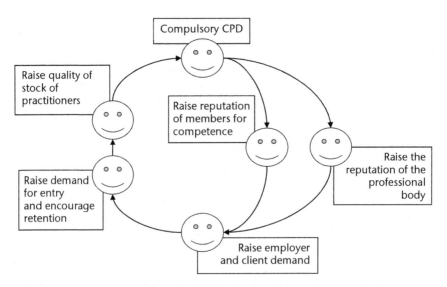

**FIGURE 4.1** The virtuous 'circle' of compulsory CPD

---

**EXHIBIT 4.1 AUTOMOTIVE TECHNICIAN ACCREDITATION – ATA KITEMARK**

All accident repair centres that wish to achieve the . . . Kitemark standard need to prove that they employ staff that is currently competent – according to the Kitemark standard this is proven by an NVQ achieved within the last three years or an industry recognised accreditation achieved within the last five years – the ATA VDA assessment meets these requirements.

(ATA 2008)

---

association's point of view can be reinforced by making CPD compulsory. For example Phillips (2010: 9–10) reports that the numbers attending sonographer conferences in Australia have roughly doubled at the same time as prices charged for attendance have increased since a compulsory CPD scheme was introduced in 2002 by the regulatory body, the Australasian Sonographer Accreditation Registry.[10]

Finally these benefits may help the profession to *retain self-regulation* by reassuring government, as well as the general public, that it is taking its own regulation seriously.

### Arguments against a compulsory policy

Many arguments can be brought against a compulsory CPD policy.

1 A common argument is that the formal wrapper CPD provides is an unnecessary layer of costly *bureaucracy*. Taking time from practice to read journals or attend events or courses is one thing, but time required to fill out forms to enable CPD to be monitored can be resented as a waste of time. Monitoring is involved with other CPD compliance policies, but far greater resources are required to monitor carefully enough to allow sanctions to be applied fairly. Even if CPD is self-assessed, these assessments need to be audited consistently. Auditors need to be trained, particularly if self-assessment includes evaluation of what is learned for practice.

2 Compulsory CPD may be viewed as a *violation of professional autonomy*. Not only is the monitoring a burden, but the policing required for a credible compulsory policy can be seen as contrary to the trust professionals believe they should command (Rockhill 1983). Many CPD specialists in professional bodies regard these as grumblings confined largely to older professionals. Logically, as one nears retirement, the practice value of CPD activities is reduced. In extreme, if you are about to retire in the next few

days, there would seem to be little scope for practice improvement from learning new techniques. The problem is to decide when Professional Development Value is too small to make the effort. Who should make this decision? One way of avoiding it is to have to carry on with CPD to the end.

3 A related argument is that compulsory CPD *violates principles of lifelong learning*; that it should be self-directed; that true learning is more likely to occur if individuals come to decide to do it for themselves (Postler-Slattery and Foley 2003; Field 2004).

4 *Fairness* can be an issue. If all members are expected to carry out compulsory CPD, it can be argued that all should have similar opportunities to do so. Practitioners in remote areas may not be able to get to events and other activities in major centres without great expense.[11]

5 Professional bodies often draw back from compulsory CPD because they believe it will stimulate *resistance* from professionals, fuelled by the previous arguments. This will rarely be in the form of overt actions such as voting to reverse the policy or modify it.[12] More commonly it generates a *compliance mentality*. People do just enough to be seen to be fulfilling their CPD. They may choose activities that are not challenging or not pay attention at these activities (Wessels 2007: 367). This is perhaps the strongest argument against compulsion. One can fill out evaluation sheets or reflection forms in a mechanistic manner, merely repeating a formula once developed even if it is not particularly appropriate for the occasion. As individuals come up to a time when CPD records must be submitted, they may rush to attend whatever activities are on offer merely to fill their record in time.

6 It has also been claimed that making CPD compulsory leads to more poor quality CPD activities being offered because of the captive audience (Perry 1995). However, evidence of *poor quality courses* available to professionals is often due to the combination of factors that include compulsory CPD, but also include monopoly of supply, and CPD requirements expressed or measured merely by evidence of attendance on courses rather than evidence of learning or practice implications.[13]

It is worth elaborating further on the possible stimulation of a compliance mentality. Worse than only doing the minimum required, some may *cheat*. Associated with the costs of administering CPD is the problem of dealing with this. People can pretend to attend events without actually doing so, by getting colleagues who do attend to sign in for them. Some might consider it scandalous even to suggest such a thing, but there is evidence for it (Chapter 7). One way of dealing with people pretending to attend, or not paying attention when they do attend, or attending activities that are not relevant to their practice, is to require more than evidence of attendance. However, people can get others to fill in reflection records and evaluation templates, or they can copy them from others. It is also possible to produce formulaic answers when asked to report on what one has learned and how it is likely to affect practice. It is even possible for individuals to collaborate and share responses. How widespread are these practices? There is little hard evidence, but certainly universities have been dealing with such practices for some time, and it is growing with model essays, and answers to possible exam questions, available on the internet.

> Plagiarism is quite distinct from theft of intellectual property, and copying from fellow students, from works which are out of copyright or open-source, or from essay banks is plagiarism, even if no-one's rights have been breached.
>
> (MacDonald Ross 2005)

Any compulsory system of regulation can lead to an unhealthy pattern of compliance scams that get discovered and dealt with only to have new scams emerge (Figure 4.2). On one side of the fence are lawyers, accountants and private consultants seeking to help clients to avoid the law, as well as less formal advisors or friends who share their tricks for avoidance (and perhaps evasion). On the other side are lawyers for the prosecution, lawmakers and other specialist administrators, reacting to breaches in the law. Each side adjusts to the other. Loopholes at any one stage are not insurmountable; however patching them up requires either more resources or a strategic redirection of resources to overcome them. Then these patches become outdated. With successive iterations, the players will come to anticipate subsequent reactions of the other side. The process itself represents wasted effort and can lead the law itself to *fall into disrepute*.

Arguably, this situation will not develop, or the pattern will be tempered and dampened by developing the disposition among professionals towards fully

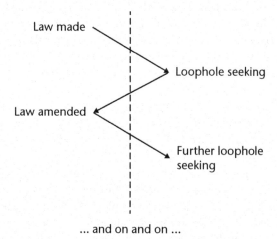

... and on and on ...

**FIGURE 4.2** The game of opening and closing loopholes in the law or any other form of compulsory regulation

participating in the CPD programme with enthusiasm founded on a visceral acceptance of Professional Development Value and values: based firmly in professional ethics. Not only will this reduce the likelihood of individuals trying to cheat, but also it should lead those who could support these behaviours to refuse to collaborate. One way of dealing with this problem is to make CPD obligatory.

### 4.2.3 Obligatory: a traditional approach

Obligatory CPD policies can be confusing. How can something be obligatory and not compulsory?[14] Surely you either have to do it or you do not! This paradox presumes the only authorities people recognize are material or physical sanctions (and incentives). It is an apparent paradox in the current era, when 'duty' is not a widely accepted or even a widely recognized concept. However, up to the early twentieth century, duty was a critical aspect of social life, particularly professional life, and it motivates many professionals today.

The principal means of maintaining authority over professionals in the past has been, on one hand, such moral suasion as congealed in ethical codes, and on the other, sanctions imposed after complaints have been made and disciplinary procedures followed; the latter being for breach of the code, rather than exclusively to one clause in the code. With this in mind, the distinction between obligatory and compulsory CPD is clear. If the commitment to CPD is an obligation, like other obligations in professional codes, the general authority of the professional body is a moral one unless there is a specific complaint raised.[15] No specific sanctions apply to non-participation in CPD as distinguished from any other breach of the code. As with dishonesty and unfairness in dealings with clients or breaches of confidentiality, there are no specific sanctions and no overt monitoring. If individuals are not caught cheating or dealing unfairly in the normal course of professional practice, they are not punished. Professional bodies do not check to see if individuals are following the code of conduct. Rather they operate on the principle that proper professionals will do their duty. They are expected to be honest and fair and are 'trusted' to be so. On the other hand, if someone is found to be in breach of CPD obligations after a complaint, they would be disciplined as with any other item in the professional code.

Tovey (1994) argued that an obligatory approach aims to preserve the notion of professional independence. The complicated nature of this can be seen from the following statement from a CPD specialist working for a professional body.

> I think the word 'encourage' is important for all grades and ages of members of all professions. I'm not against compulsory schemes, where they can be made to stick (and that is likely to be only in professions where membership of a professional body is necessary in order to practice), but even here, people will not get the most out of CPD if they are forced to comply. You can take a horse to water, et cetera . . .

(Friedman, Davis *et al.* 2000: 70)

This distinction between obligatory and the other two policies is not universally understood, even among professional bodies. There are inconsistencies. Some with obligatory policies *have* specific sanctions for non-compliance beyond sanctions for other obligations mentioned in their ethical code. They seem to be thinking of obligatory as just another way of saying compulsory (Friedman, Davis *et al.* 2000).

Again, along with different definitions of CPD, different understandings of the meaning of CPD compliance policies discourage a broad public understanding and appreciation of it.

### 4.2.4 Mixed policies: allowing flexibility

Any combination of the three policies can be pursued simultaneously by a professional body by applying different policies to different categories or grades of practitioners. Most mixed policies are a combination of compulsory and voluntary (Friedman, Davis *et al.* 2000). It is usually a higher grade for which CPD is compulsory, often carrying with it post-nominals: letters after one's name. Another way the combination comes about is when a professional body introduces compulsory CPD only for newly qualified members. This is a way of easing it in.

### Arguments in favour of a mixed policy

The compulsory element can act as a credible criterion for higher level status such as Fellows of the professional body or Chartered members of the profession.

- It can ease people into CPD on a non-confrontational basis. It is only required if you want the higher status. In a sense you get to choose if your CPD is compulsory.
- Requirements are achievable for current practitioners but act as an encouragement for former practitioners to relinquish Chartered status without actually taking it away from them (Grayston 2007).

The primary argument against mixed policies is that the added complexity may increase confusion and make it harder to compare CPD schemes among professions.

## 4.3 History of policies

### 4.3.1 Acquiring a policy

As noted in the previous chapter (Section 3.9) Welsh and Woodward (1989) found just under half of their sample had a CPD policy. We regard the late

1980s as the period of accelerated diffusion of CPD, with the late 1970s being the initiation period of slow progress. Figure 4.3 shows estimates from seven surveys of the proportion of professional bodies in the UK with a CPD policy. Figure 4.4 represents this information as a curve showing a diffusion pattern.[16] The pattern appears to represent two S-shaped curves. Each S-shape has a period of rapid growth. The first period of rapid growth occurred in the mid-1980s. A second period of rapid growth appears to have occurred in the mid-2000s.

### 4.3.2 Early mixtures of compliance policies

According to Welsh and Woodward (1989) in only 12 per cent of those with a policy was it compulsory. They only distinguished compulsory and voluntary policies. At that time either obligatory policies were not labelled as such or, more likely, the authors did not recognize the label. The presumption was that the other 88 per cent had voluntary policies. However, they reported that 60 of the 123 professional bodies they surveyed had an item in their code of conduct that referred to maintaining professional competence and presumed this to be most likely carried out via CPD.

Vaughan (1991) also did not use the term obligatory. Rather 'experimental' was a third policy asked about, along with mandatory and voluntary; this could refer to policy made available only to a subset of the membership, such as those only in London. Among the 50 who had responded to both Welsh and Woodward

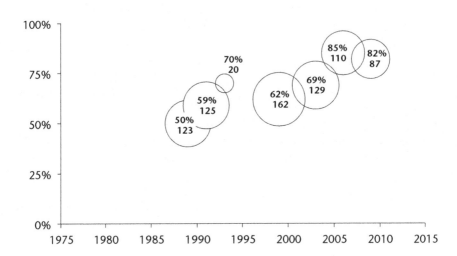

**FIGURE 4.3** Percentage of professional bodies with a CPD policy
*Note*: Bubble size indicates sample size. Based on estimates of the percentage of professional bodies with a CPD policy 1975–2009 from Welsh and Woodward (1989), Vaughan (1991), Madden and Mitchell (1993), Friedman, Davis *et al.* (2000), Friedman and Mason (2004, 2007) and Friedman and Afitska (2010).

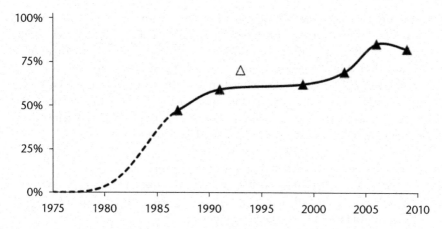

**FIGURE 4.4** S-shaped curve showing growth of penetration of CPD policies among UK professional bodies

*Note:* Based on estimates of the percentage of professional bodies with a CPD policy 1975–2009 from Welsh and Woodward (1989), Vaughan (1991), Madden and Mitchell (1993), Friedman, Davis *et al.* (2000), Friedman and Mason (2004, 2007) and Friedman and Afitska (2010).

and Vaughan surveys, the proportion with a mandatory policy rose from 10 per cent of those with a policy to 19 per cent. Those with a voluntary policy were roughly the same, falling from 71 to 69 per cent. Experimental fell from 23 to 14 per cent. It is difficult to say how many of the experimental (and voluntary and mandatory) policies reported were what are now called obligatory.

### 4.3.3 CPD in the 1990s

In 1999, 162 professional bodies responded to a survey carried out by PARN. This represented 35 per cent of all professional bodies in the UK according to the PARN database at that time. Of these 101, or 62 per cent, had a CPD policy. This was only a little higher than shown in the Vaughan survey of 1991, but it was considered to be a more thorough survey and more likely to include smaller professional bodies than the surveys of the 1980s.[17]

The estimates of types of policies for 1999 (Friedman, Davis *et al.* 2000) were:

- Voluntary     31 per cent
- Obligatory     27 per cent
- Compulsory     22 per cent
- Mixed     20 per cent

Of the mixed policies, almost all 15 per cent of those with policies, were a combination of voluntary and compulsory. For example, the Chartered Institute of Marketing (CIM) set up a voluntary CPD scheme in 1994. In 1998 a compulsory scheme was set up for members wishing to become Chartered Marketers. Only 4 per cent of the whole sample having a policy were a combination of obligatory and compulsory and only 1 per cent a combination of voluntary and obligatory (Friedman *et al.* 2000: 71). In the accounting profession formal CPD policies were introduced in the 1990s and mixed policies were recommended with voluntary or obligatory for the majority of members, and compulsory for particular specialisms. The voluntary or obligatory part can be difficult to decide. For example ACCA's CPD guidance in 1993 stated:

> All members . . . are under a longstanding obligation to ensure that the standard of their professional knowledge is maintained after qualification. Council recommended that this is conducted through the medium of Continuing Professional Development.
>
> (ACCA 1993: 1)

Was CPD obligatory or voluntary? It seems that what professionals 'just did' was obligatory, but participating in the formal CPD programme was 'recommended', presumably voluntary.

PARN found that policies implemented more recently, after 1993, were more likely to be voluntary. This suggests a time pattern for CPD policies with smaller professional bodies and more recently professionalizing bodies beginning with a voluntary policy and then moving onto more severe compliance regimes.

It is difficult to compare the policy distribution with the earlier period because of the category of obligatory being clearly there but not recognized by those surveying professional bodies up to 1991.

### 4.3.4 CPD in the 2000s

PARN carried out large-scale surveys of professional bodies in the UK and Ireland in 2003 and again in 2006 and 2009. In addition, the 2006 and 2009 surveys were carried out in Canada and Australia (see Friedman and Mason 2004; Friedman and Williams 2007; Friedman and Mason 2007; Friedman and Afitska 2010).

In the 2003 survey in the UK 69 per cent of the 129 respondents had a CPD policy. Of these there were:

- Voluntary      43 per cent
- Obligatory     27 per cent
- Compulsory     13 per cent
- Mixed          18 per cent

There was reason to believe that the sample was quite different between the 1999 and 2003 surveys, which makes comparison difficult. However, the comparison with the 2006 survey is more valid as the two surveys were mailed.

According to the 2006 survey, 85 per cent of the 110 respondents had a CPD policy. Of those there were:

- Voluntary      44 per cent
- Obligatory     21 per cent
- Compulsory     21 per cent
- Mixed          14 per cent

According to the 2009 survey, 68 per cent of the 87 respondents had a CPD policy with the following distribution by compliance policy:

- Voluntary      23 per cent
- Obligatory     15 per cent
- Compulsory     19 per cent
- Mixed          11 per cent

Table 4.2 shows the distribution of compliance policies for the UK and Irish samples in all three years.

The proportion with obligatory compliance fell substantially in both countries. There was also a consistent, but less pronounced rise in compulsory compliance regimes. This rise in compulsory compliance regimes has been long predicted (Watkins *et al*. 1996), but slow in coming; reflecting the relatively even balance of advantages and disadvantages of compliance regimes outlined above as well as the continual addition of new professional bodies.

An important contributor to the rise in the proportion with compulsory policies between 2003 and 2006 was the issue of a new International Education Standard (IES 7) by the International Federation of Accountants (IFAC) in May 2004, which came into force in January 2006. This called on all professional accountants to develop and maintain their competence. Up to then most accountancy professional bodies had voluntary policies at least for some classes of members. From then almost all accounting bodies in the world adopted

**TABLE 4.2** Professional bodies' CPD compliance policies in the UK and Ireland

|  | UK | | | Ireland | | |
| --- | --- | --- | --- | --- | --- | --- |
|  | *2003* | *2006* | *2009* | *2003* | *2006* | *2009* |
| Compulsory | 13% | 20% | 27% | 28% | 43% | 29% |
| Obligatory | 27% | 20% | 18% | 17% | 7% | 29% |
| Voluntary | 42% | 43% | 32% | 50% | 24% | 14% |
| Mixed | 17% | 14% | 22% | 6% | 22% | 29% |

*Note:* Based on PARN IBS surveys in 2003, 2006 and 2009. UK sample sizes: 2003 – 111; 2006 – 93; 2009 – 60. Irish sample sizes: 2003 – 18; 2006 – 14; 2009 – 7.

compulsory policies (Fédération des Experts Comptables Européens; FEE 2007;[18] Paisey and Paisey 2007; Wessels 2007).

## 4.4 Professional associations and regulatory bodies

Different professional bodies will assess the advantages and disadvantages of different compliance policies differently, depending particularly on their regulatory functions (Exhibit 4.2) and their size.

On one hand are professional associations which are not regulated by Statute or Charter. These tend to be smaller, representing occupations that are either new or newly professionalizing. Voluntary policies among them reflect their relative lack of authority over members and their members' desire for support rather than disciplinary governance. However, these are likely over time to move towards either mixed or obligatory CPD as they develop higher level categories of membership for which they desire criteria that are transparent and legitimate, and as they develop or revise their professional code. Leaders in the field will wish to raise the status of the profession and the professional body. They will accept the risk of the professional body losing members. Others, also thinking long term, continue to fear the professional body will lose out to other new or potential professional bodies that either have weaker CPD compliance or have a stronger reputation in the first place (because they may cross occupational boundaries from more established occupations). While there may be an overall tendency for established professional bodies to move away from voluntary CPD, the proportion of voluntary schemes stays high because new professional bodies are always forming. In addition, a few professional bodies will move from stronger to weaker compliance in the face of resistance from members, though we believe this to be relatively rare.

On the other hand, there are professional bodies with a strong regulatory public protection function, either because they have been set up as regulatory bodies or because they have long been self-regulating. With more protection from poaching of members (or registrants) because practitioners need to be members or registrants in order to practise, or in order to get business due to the reputation effects of membership, these bodies are able to override objections to compulsory CPD. It is unlikely these will change from compulsory to a less strict compliance regime except for one circumstance. This is where a formerly self-regulating professional body has been split into two: a pure professional association and a pure regulatory body. In this case the pure professional association may emerge with a voluntary policy and rely on the regulatory body to enforce compliance.

The overall proportion of professional bodies with a CPD policy is now likely to be near saturation in the UK. The small proportion without a policy is mainly those that are either too small or too new. There are always new professional bodies being established both from the splitting off of new specialisms from

## EXHIBIT 4.2 COMPULSORY CPD FOLLOWS REGULATORY CHANGES: CASE OF ACCOUNTING IN THE UK

The Insolvency Act 1986 required insolvency practitioners to be licensed before appointment and this required practitioners to comply with the requirements in relation to professional competency of a recognized professional body (RPB). These were ACCA, ICAEW and ICAS. The Companies Act 1989 required all auditors of limited companies to be registered with an RPB. In addition, RPBs could supervise their members for appointment as company auditors, but for them to become registered supervisory bodies (RSBs) they had to have rules designed to ensure auditors maintain appropriate levels of competence for carrying out company audits. Thus from the 1980s these three professional bodies had mixed CPD policies with only auditors and insolvency practitioners under compulsory CPD and the rest regarded as having an ethical responsibility to carry out CPD; that is, what we would regard as an obligatory policy.

According to Paisey *et al.* (2007: 381)

> While the regulatory changes in the 1980s did not affect all professional accountants, they did help to bring about a cultural shift whereby the professional bodies strengthened their recommendations that CPD should be undertaken by members.

This cultural shift affected CIMA as well as the other major accounting bodies. Policies initiated in the 1990s led to a widening range of professional accountants being under compulsory CPD, but with certain differences among the different professional bodies. By the time of the IFAC standard proposed in 2004 and coming into force in 2006 (IFAC 2004) the following member categories were under compulsory CPD policies (Paisey *et al.* 2007: 383):

- Insolvency practitioners (ACCA, ICAEW, ICAS)
- Working in audit (ACCA, ICAEW, ICAS)
- Applying for Fellowship status (ACCA, CIMA, ICAEW)
- Supervising training (ICAEW)
- Working in investment business (ICAEW, CIMA)
- Working in business preparing accounts (ICAS)
- Working in public interest company (ICAS)
- Working in practice (ACCA, CIMA, ICEAW, ICAS).

*For CIMA members only those in practice with fee income above £1 million.*

Following the IFAC standard all these professional bodies moved to compulsory CPD for all members.

older occupations and from the development of new occupations associated with changes in technology and new services being conceived or professionalized. Developing a CPD policy has not been the first priority for a new professional body, and if this continues to be the case we would always expect in any survey to find some that do not yet have a CPD policy.

On the other hand, a few professional bodies have no CPD policy and no intention of developing one. Some of these have ceded CPD policy to a different body.

## 4.5 International comparisons

CPD is an international phenomenon. This can be seen from the 2006 PARN survey in the four countries shown in Table 4.3. A number of features are worth noting. First, the majority of professional bodies have a CPD policy in all four countries. Second, the relative proportions of different compliance policies differ considerably.

The proportion with a voluntary policy is greatest in the UK at almost half, compared particularly with Canada and Australia where the proportion is only a quarter. This may reflect:

• Canadian and Australian samples having a higher proportion of regulatory bodies;
• the sample in the UK having a higher proportion of smaller and newer professional bodies because the database from which they have been sampled is more developed.

It is strange that none of the Canadian professional bodies indicated obligatory CPD policies. This may reflect a 'North American' attitude that emphasizes statutory regulation.[19] The proportion of Canadian regulatory bodies responding to the survey was high. This particularly reflects the provincial/federal breakdown of the responses, because regulation of the professions is a provincial matter in general in Canada, as are health and education (see Canadian Constitutional Acts 1867–1982). This factor does not seem so marked in Australia, but the sample size of state professional bodies there was very low.

The range of compulsory policies among the countries was widest, with Canadians having over half and UK professional bodies only one-fifth. However, we should add the mixed to the compulsory group as almost all the mixed will have a compulsory element. Doing this gives the range from 35 per cent and 37 per cent for the UK and Australia, through 57 per cent for Ireland to a huge 76 per cent for Canada.

Though the proportions of mixed policies are relatively small, we believe this will grow in future as it allows flexibility. With the heightened criticisms of the professions in the last 10 years, we believe this will replace voluntary and

**TABLE 4.3** Professional bodies' CPD compliance policies in four countries

|  | Australia | Canada | UK | Ireland |
|---|---|---|---|---|
| Per cent with a CPD policy | 71% | 66% | 85% | 67% |
| Sample size | 49 | 56 | 110 | 21 |
| *Compliance policy type* | | | | |
| Voluntary | 37% | 24% | 43% | 36% |
| Obligatory | 26% | 0% | 20% | 7% |
| Compulsory | 26% | 54% | 20% | 43% |
| Mixed | 11% | 22% | 14% | 14% |
| Sample size | 35 | 37 | 93 | 14 |

*Note:* Based on PARN's 2006 IBS survey; 2 per cent of the 93 bodies in the UK sample that indicated having a CPD policy did not indicate the type of compliance policy.

obligatory rather than compulsory regimes. We believe the widely predicted rise in the proportion of compulsory compliance regimes will finally occur in the near future, though largely via mixed policies. According to FEE (2007) compulsory policies apply for accountancy bodies in all but two of the 29 countries covered by the federation. However, in Norway there is a mix of policies as CPD is compulsory only for members who are responsible for audit engagements or who confirm information to public authorities (FEE 2007).[20]

# 5

# CPD GOVERNANCE

## Programme support

*Differences in definitions and compliance policies are reflected in a range of different forms of support for CPD.*

### 5.1 Introduction

A compliance policy is not sufficient for CPD governance. Together with the actual activities provided, recommended or accredited, procedures for how CPD will operate and supports for practitioners to follow these procedures are required. These amount to a CPD programme. This is unlikely to come cheap. For a credible programme practitioners will expect substantial support: resources and procedures for answering enquiries, for monitoring and recording achievements; planning and reflection guides; mentoring schemes. This will add a layer of administration leading many professional bodies to hire new staff with new skills, particularly educationalist skills.

Different governance regimes will also influence how CPD is experienced by individual professionals. CPD programmes will raise their expectations as to the quality and usefulness – the Professional Development Value – of the CPD policy. Eventually the programmes may be expected to raise the reputation of the profession and the trustworthiness of individual professionals. The likelihood of this potential being realized will depend on the vigour with which support is provided and regulatory mechanisms are pursued. It may also depend on increasing standardization of these procedures in order to raise their visibility (see Chapter 11).

In this chapter we provide a general model of CPD support. In the next we examine procedures that are part of the regulation of professionals, controlling as well as supporting them. The former are more the provenance of professional associations and the latter of regulatory bodies, but this distinction is not always clear and may change in future.

## 5.2 A model of support for and governance of the CPD process by professional bodies

Exhibit 5.1 comes from the open access part of the website of the authoritative CIPD.[1] This demonstrates a typical approach of professional associations where membership is not required to practise. Individuals should do CPD for their own benefit and employers should support employee CPD in their own interests. A subsidiary, but clear, message is that what the CIPD does for its members is important and valuable. The CIPD is worth listening to. The CIPD is worth joining. The CIPD also recognizes benefits to other employees from their members carrying out CPD.

How can a CPD programme deliver the benefits described in this exhibit? The model displayed in Figure 5.1 provides an answer. In it we specify both general programme support and support linked to particular stages of the CPD cycle.

Encouragement and guidance comes both for all phases of the cycle (such as general guidance notes on the CPD scheme and mentoring schemes) and specific to individual phases of the cycle (such as guidance questions to help structure reflection and planning templates).

## 5.3 Forms of support

CPD is still relatively new. It has developed largely from the bottom up in that individuals in professional bodies have built programmes in response to the particular circumstances of those organizations. It has not come about in response to government or initiatives of organizations that stand above professional bodies.[2] Different professional bodies have begun their journey at different points, based on:

- their regulatory role;
- their view of how important CPD will be in raising the reputation of the profession and the professional body;
- the imagination and forcefulness of individuals, who are either assigned or hired to develop CPD programmes.

Some professional bodies began with a cautious approach providing only basic guidelines under a voluntary policy. Others, generally the larger and better funded, aimed to introduce what they regarded as best practice. However, there is no consensus on what best practice is. What is included in support for CPD is affected in part by particular innovations and quirks of those developing programmes.

Beyond different starting points, a variety of programmes may be attributed to sporadic and circumscribed communication among those responsible for CPD across professions.[3] It takes time for new ideas to percolate around professional bodies and for experiences with implementation to be shared. CPD has

## EXHIBIT 5.1 BENEFITS OF CPD ACCORDING TO THE CHARTERED INSTITUTE OF PERSONNEL AND DEVELOPMENT

### How CPD benefits you

The benefits of CPD aren't just felt when you're going for promotion or upgrading to chartered membership. Many employers now value 'learning agility' as a core competency:

- Build confidence and credibility; you can see your progression by tracking your learning.
- Earn more by showcasing your achievements. A handy tool for appraisals.
- Achieve your career goals by focusing on your training and development.
- Cope positively with change by constantly updating your skill set.
- Be more productive and efficient by reflecting on your learning and highlighting gaps in your knowledge and experience.

### How CPD benefits your organization

As organizations shift the responsibility for personal development back to the individual, the ability and insight to manage your own professional growth is seen as a key strength:

- Helps maximize staff potential by linking learning to actions and theory to practice.
- Helps HR professionals to set SMART (specific, measurable, achievable, realistic and time-bound) objectives, for training activity to be more closely linked to business needs.
- Promotes staff development. This leads to better staff morale and a motivated workforce helps give a positive image/brand to organizations.
- Adds value; by reflecting it will help staff to consciously apply learning to their role and the organization's development.
- Linking to appraisals. This is a good tool to help employees focus their achievements throughout the year.

[CIPD 2010a, with the permission of the publisher, the Chartered Institute of Personnel and Development, London (www.cipd.co.uk)]

not 'settled'. Even those with the same compliance policy can have very different procedures and facilities. To give an idea of what can be provided consider the following range:

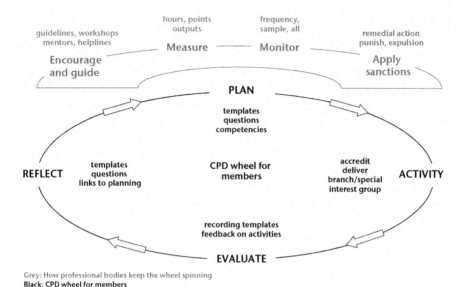

FIGURE 5.1 The CPD wheel and arch
*Source*: Adapted from Williams and Friedman (2008: 14).

1 Minimum level of support that all professional bodies with a policy provide. This includes guidance notes on what CPD is and what it is intended to achieve. Professionals are informed of the policy, what 'counts' as CPD and the number of hours per year (or per three-year period) expected. Examples of what can be considered CPD will be provided. The professional body may only list activities it provides, and leaves members to find others.
2 A step up from this minimum would be to provide a template for recording CPD activities that includes expectations of evaluation and reflection.
3 Going further, some provide a computerized recording system that allows individuals to update their CPD records online or even a system where the professional body automatically provides an online record of what an individual has done and when, and how close they are to fulfilling requirements.
4 The next step up may be to provide support for the full CPD cycle by adding planning and reflection templates. These may draw practitioners to consider future plans in terms of specific goals that could also be distinguished as short term or long term and to consider different levels of reflection, that is, on immediate and longer term value, but also reflection on practice implications beyond one's own skills, such as design of practice procedures. All of these supporting tools can contain more or less detail and guidance within them. In addition, considerable effort can be expended on providing the 'right' CPD activities. This may involve regularly surveying members and employers to understand member learning needs.

5   Moving to the other extreme, some provide a very wide range of support. The records they provide can be very elaborate, allowing the individual to reflect on and evaluate what they have done by relating them to past activities, their current and future roles, plans, personal learning styles and competency frameworks. More personalized advice and guidance delivered by CPD specialists requires considerable resources for direct provision, or for co-ordinating volunteers to give it.

The list below gives examples of the type of guidance provided by different professional bodies:

- a telephone hotline to provide individualized advice;
- frequently asked questions;
- examples of record cards and development planners;
- reading lists;
- self-analysis questionnaires to identify development needs;
- self-analysis to identify personal learning styles and a scheme for identifying which activities on offer most closely match learning outcomes to the different learning styles identified;
- reflection templates;
- competency frameworks;
- examples of effective learning methods – learning cycles;
- support groups/centres;
- examples of good practice.

Friedman, Davis and colleagues (2000) analysed guidance from 80 professional bodies. They found the most common guidance support (86 per cent of their sample) to be a record card or planning form. Record cards ranged from simple charts to log activities and hours spent, to substantial booklets comprising items such as development questionnaires, SWOT (strengths, weaknesses, opportunities and threats) analyses, planning and reviewing sections. One of their interviewees reflected that the extent of detail included in guidance and planners depended on the stage of CPD involvement of members:

There is a tremendous range of planners; some ask for date, title of activity and amount of time spent on the activity, and others are geared toward the management of your career where you can create a CV and a self-appraisal document . . . The understanding of the majority of members in CPD will probably dictate [at] which end of the scale a professional association's planner will appear. If members are running they will probably welcome the all-singing versions but if they are still in the crawling phase then a short and simple version will probably be used by more people, perhaps with the option of opting for the all-singing model as necessary.

(Friedman, Davis *et al.* 2000: 92)

This may be thought of as reflecting the early state of CPD at many professional bodies at the end of the 1990s. However, the same issue arises for professional bodies introducing CPD in the 2000s and 2010s. Because CPD is not widely understood by the general public, many of those running professional bodies rightly assume that their members need to be educated into the idea of CPD. It has to be taken slowly. Newly professionalizing occupations may contain a higher proportion of practitioners who do not just do the sorts of activities that would count as CPD. Exhibit 5.2 shows how the CIM presents CPD to its members and the general public on its website under professional development.

Guidelines can be aimed at groups beyond members or registrants of professional bodies: employers, CPD content providers and the general public, though professional bodies have been slow to address these groups. Friedman, Davis and colleagues (2000) found only 13 per cent of their sample had any reference to employers in their guidelines and only 10 per cent reference CPD content providers.

Professional bodies have always provided a wide range of learning activities for practitioners' professional development. Some activities have been designed as focused learning experiences, such as lectures on technical subjects. Some have been designed as broad enablers of learning experiences: provision of libraries, materials on professional body websites, magazines and journals. Some have not been designed with learning in mind at all, but can provide ideas for practice development as by-products: social events and regular branch or committee meetings. These activities may all be regarded as support for CPD (or the action phase of the CPD cycle shown in Figure 1.2).

---

## EXHIBIT 5.2 PROFESSIONAL DEVELOPMENT AT THE CHARTERED INSTITUTE OF MARKETING

Whatever stage you are at in your career, our continuing professional development (CPD) programme helps you get ahead – and stay ahead.

The importance of CPD in today's work environment cannot be underestimated. Put simply, it's essential to your continued effectiveness and development as a professional marketer and beyond this, to the recognition and progression of the industry as a whole.

At The Chartered Institute of Marketing, ongoing development is at the heart of everything we do. This means that all our support, training, qualifications and resources are geared towards making sure you have the right skills and knowledge to succeed.

(CIM 2009)

## 5.4 Accreditation and support for choosing activities to undertake

As noted in Section 2.4, CPD is largely controlled by professionals themselves in terms of which activities they choose to undertake. Many activities are provided by professional bodies and some provide formal courses leading to diplomas or other certificates, and thereby take on the role of an awarding body. They may also act as an accrediting body by assessing CPD activities provided by others. Recently some professional bodies have developed partnering relations with higher education institutions to provide high quality CPD activities designed for their particular profession. Accreditation may be regarded as support, by helping practitioners to decide what activities to pursue, or as a regulatory function, limiting what they can choose, if only accredited courses can count towards certain CPD requirements or provide entry to higher grades in the profession.

Accreditation literally means to give credit for something. However, it can be a confusing term because it can refer to very different degrees of rigour of process and to different objects subjected to that process.

Accreditation can refer loosely to the mere approval of something, which may simply mean it is one of many acceptable options. Even more loosely it can refer to simple recognition that an option exists, as with a listing of known training activities or courses in a relevant subject. More rigorously it can refer to the giving of a form of credit, such as credit for a certificate or degree. This will have strong consequences for the legitimacy of what is accredited. Thus we can appreciate that different professional bodies will provide different degrees of responsibility for the quality of what they bring to the attention of their practitioners. They will expend different degrees of effort to reflect their responsibility for quality. Confusingly, the term accreditation can refer to any of these degrees of responsibility and effort.

In relation to CPD courses, a professional body may simply recognize that certain activities can count towards CPD without examining them at all, or at least it may accept them as long as no complaints are received. Beyond this, with relatively low effort, approval can be given based on a course provider providing appropriate answers to a questionnaire that may be checked over by the professional body or its agent. 'Proper' accreditation will be more resource intensive and is likely to require certain standards to be maintained over time. It is likely to involve face-to-face inspection of the provider and of the courses.

Of a sample of 80 professional bodies 52 per cent stated they accredited courses (Friedman, Davis *et al.*, 2000). However, accreditation referred to any of the following:

- Members' CPD (55 per cent of sample) – usually via the awarding of a certificate of achievement, which will generally involve 'stamping' individual record cards or approving whatever output is expected. This can be a confusing use of the term, as it merely means meeting compliance criteria. This terminology was used by professional bodies with a voluntary policy. Those with a compulsory policy were more likely to use terms like compliance to indicate approval of member participation in CPD. Accreditation was often used when members upgraded their membership category based on CPD participation, to Fellow or Chartered status.

- CPD performed outside the UK (33 per cent of sample) – the professional body makes provision for members overseas to undertake CPD and recognizes their efforts. This may seem a side issue, but for many UK professional bodies, it is an extremely important activity, widening their influence, helping to raise standards internationally and providing the professional body with significant (export) income.
- The professional body's policy itself (13 per cent of sample) – via an umbrella body (primarily in the engineering sector) or via cross-policy recognition among similar professional bodies (primarily in accounting and finance).

A trend away from accrediting courses was discerned by Friedman, Davis and colleagues (2000). This was connected to initial steps towards outputs measures based on self-assessment (Chapter 8). Specifically, professional bodies were shifting the burden of responsibility towards individual participants, who were expected to decide for themselves whether a given course was useful or relevant to their own personal CPD. While promoting a certain philosophy of CPD as 'individual-centred', this was also influenced by the high cost of accreditation. The cost issue also led some to shift from accrediting courses to accrediting course providers, getting them to match their own courses to the professional body standards.

## 5.5 Mentoring and coaching

Mentoring may broadly be defined as 'a one-to-one situation, where the mentor seeks to assist the learners to reflect upon their practice and improve it' (Jarvis 1995: 121). Mentoring should be distinguished from the currently more popular activity of coaching. Mentoring is an ongoing relationship that can last a long time, while coaching is normally of a short duration. Mentoring is less structured and focuses on professional, personal and career development. Mentoring is likely to be on an ad hoc basis. Coaching is more structured, with regular meetings focusing on a specific agenda with short-term goals around specific development issues. Coaches are generally expected to be skilled at coaching, rather than needing to have direct experience of their client's formal occupational role. Mentors are more often individuals who are in a position where the mentee wishes to be eventually. Both can take place on an informal basis without money changing hands, but coaching nowadays is thought of more as a paid and a professional occupation (see Exhibit 5.3).

Mentors and coaches should be distinguished from supervisors. Participants in discussions on mentoring in relation to CPD reported that mentors should

## EXHIBIT 5.3 MENTORING AT THE INSTITUTION OF ENGINEERING AND TECHNOLOGY (IET)

The IET (2008) provides a guidance document called *We Work Better Together* (see www.theiet.org/mentoring). It also offers a one-day mentor training course. The mentor/mentee relationship is defined as follows:

> The relationship between the mentor and the person seeking guidance should be personal and confidential, quite distinct from the relationship between superior and subordinate. The mentor should challenge and support, but should neither tell the engineer what to do nor provide assessments to others. A good mentor will want to ensure that the engineer gains confidence and independence as a result of mentoring and is enabled to take full and effective responsibility for his or her own development over the next career stage. Long-term dependence on one influential person is not helpful.

Guidance is given in the IET document as to what are considered to be characteristics of successful mentors and mentees, as well as for Company Mentoring Schemes. For mentors, this includes:

*   Listening actively
*   Questioning and finding out what is important to mentees by exploring their skills, aptitudes and aspirations
*   Challenging assumptions
*   Creating an open and candid relationship and treating all that the mentee says as confidential
*   Help mentee to learn by allowing minor errors, but trying to prevent making major ones
*   Recognize when mentee should identify a need for other sources of help.

For the mentee, success of the relationship requires:

*   Understanding that the Mentor is to challenge and encourage, but not to provide answers
*   Guarding against becoming dependent on the mentor
*   Approach each meeting fully prepared.

For both participants, it is seen as vitally important that there be a recognized end for the relationship, to avoid entering into an open-ended commitment.

---

Problems with the mentoring process, for the individuals involved as well as for companies have been identified. Mentors can cause the relationship to falter by:[4]

- Lacking the time for building a trusting relationship
- Being over-protective or confining the growth of the mentee
- Being unable to give suitable advice
- Becoming emotionally involved in an inappropriate way with the mentee
- Disclosing confidential matters to third-parties
- Being involved in the line management of mentees, causing conflicts between concerns for task completion and training or development needs.

(IET 2008)

---

never impose their views, but rather 'help the mentee to address their problems themselves' (Friedman, Davis *et al.* 2000: 131) This is also true for coaches. Coaches are also critically intended to operate as facilitators rather than directors of those they coach. They enable individuals to set goals, reflect on the reality of their current situation (in terms of values, beliefs, attributes, knowledge and skills); they support the learner to identify and evaluate options available in terms of resources needed and barriers that must be overcome and they help design a strategy to decide what to do and when. That is what Whitmore (1992) labelled the GROW model:

> A mentor should be taking a long term view looking at the career as a whole, rather than the short term interventionist or boosted input of a coach or the organizational approach of a supervisor.
>
> (Whitmore 1992: 132)

Beyond 'counting' mentoring for CPD, professional bodies may run a matching service or may advertise such a service provided by employers. Credit towards CPD can accrue to mentors as well as mentees. Out of the 101 professional bodies with guidelines analysed in Friedman, Davis and Colleagues (2000), 40 mentioned mentoring. Of these only five provided a mentoring service through the professional body and six mentioned that employers provide mentoring. Exhibit 5.3 provides an insight into the approach of one professional body with a substantial mentoring programme.

Many more want to be mentors than want to be mentored. Being a mentor looks good on a curriculum vitae. Being a mentee may make one appear incompetent or in need of help. Mentoring schemes have been abandoned because of too few wanting to be mentees. Interestingly, mentoring was significantly more likely to be mentioned in guidelines of professional bodies with voluntary CPD than with obligatory or compulsory policies (Friedman, Davis *et al.* 2000).

Both mentoring and coaching have become very popular (Parsloe and Leedham 2009). The ACCA identify a coaching and mentoring 'revolution', and found that 85 per cent of their sample of 735 global ACCA members thought it would be beneficial for their organization to use coaches and 87 per cent to use mentoring techniques/mentors to develop its finance professionals (ACCA 2009).

## 5.6 Competency frameworks

A major change in support in the past decade has been the spread of competency frameworks (Exhibit 5.4). One way of defining competence is the ability to perform activities to standards required in work situations using appropriate knowledge, skill and attitude. Knowledge is not enough, you must understand how that knowledge can be applied, have skill in applying it and have an underlying professional attitude to apply it safely and appropriately, that is, in a trustworthy manner.

---

### EXHIBIT 5.4 ROYAL INSTITUTION OF CHARTERED SURVEYORS (RICS) COMPETENCY FRAMEWORK

#### Assessment of Professional Competence (APC)

Each competency is defined at three levels of attainment. You *must* reach the required level in a logical progression and in successive stages.

*Level 1* knowledge and understanding
*Level 2* application of knowledge and understanding
*Level 3* reasoned advice and depth of technical knowledge.

The competencies are in three distinct categories:

*Mandatory competencies* – personal, interpersonal, professional practice and business skills common to all pathways and compulsory for all candidates.

*Core competencies* – primary skills of your chosen APC pathway.

*Optional competencies* – selected as additional skill requirements for your APC pathway from a list of competencies relevant to that pathway. In most cases there is an element of choice.

(RICS 2008, with permission)

---

For example the CIM developed and launched a practical framework defining the competencies of marketing professionals called the Chartered Institute of Marketing Professional Marketing Standards. This was done in advance of the national marketing standards developed through the government-funded Marketing and Sales Standards Setting Body (MSSSB), at which the CIM played a lead role. Twenty-four different competencies are defined, and on each of them four levels of achievement are also defined based on four different job levels: support people, practitioners, managers and senior professionals. These are also connected with qualifications: introductory certificate for support staff; professional certificate for practitioner; diploma for manager; and postgraduate diploma for senior level professional.

## 5.7 Evaluation tools supporting self-assessment

### 5.7.1 Self-assessment

Along with the notion of obligatory CPD (and in many ways associated with professionalism itself), self-assessment of CPD accepts that not only what is done, but also the Professional Development Value of CPD activities, are best judged by professionals themselves:

> That's one thing we took from the older ideas of CPD that were based around obligation and duty we've had to say we trust people as professionals, having gone through a certain amount of torture to get their professional qualification, they have that sense of responsibility and trust.
> (Representative from CIMA, cited in Friedman and Woodhead 2008: 134)

> It is said that we are our own best judges. Certainly as a professional, if you have been trained to think in a professional way, in a methodical way, in an honest way, then you should be honest with yourself in terms of whether you can do or know X and as I say, if the specification is fairly clear, then that helps you to be more objective about measuring yourself and being honest with yourself . . . after all, professionals sign up to a Code of Conduct which has inherent implications about the currency of their competence.
> (Representative from Construction Industry Council, cited in Friedman and Woodhead 2008: 136–7)

> Self-assessment isn't the strongest mechanism in the world, but at the same time, if you put something different to what is real, then it's about the equivalent of cheating at Patience [Solitaire]. It's you that is the loser.
> [Representative from the Institute of Information Technology Training (IITT), cited in Friedman and Woodhead 2008: 154]

Primary tools to support self-assessment are templates for planning and reflection.

### 5.7.2 Planning and reflection tools

The CIPD *Raising the Standard* planning tool is shown in Exhibit 5.5.

Planning tools provide hints, reminders and questions to consider. They also give you an idea of how to think through the future as a series of steps.

## 5.8 Support personnel and the spread of techniques for supporting CPD

There have been concerns over specialist CPD staff in professional bodies looking to academics to provide CPD content. Supporting practitioners to do new

---

### EXHIBIT 5.5 PLANNING TOOL FOR CIPD MEMBERS

1   What do I want or need to learn?
2   What shall I do to achieve this?
3   What resources or support shall I need?
4   What will my success criteria be?
5   Target dates for review and completion

Be specific – clearly describe what you are planning to learn.

Check – is this realistic but challenging? Take account of your preferred learning style.

Detail the specific actions you are planning. Plan a mix of activities. Review the costs in time and money. Whose support do you need to turn this plan into a reality?

Support is often essential in making informed decisions and to motivate you to keep on target. What will you have learned (learning outcomes)?

This is the measure to show that you have achieved your objectives, the date by which you plan to review your progress or achieve this part of your development plan – be realistic.

Small successes achieved quickly will provide motivation towards longer-term goals.

(Megginson and Whitaker 2007: 65)

things is fine. Supporting practitioners to understand why they will be doing those new things through an understanding of underlying processes and the latest opinions on those processes is moving a little away from what many professionals want, but is still clearly of value, especially if it allows practitioners to see the limitations of these new things. However, providing a critical evaluation of varying opinions on the new things, particularly opinions that are no longer generally considered valid, will rightly be regarded as a diversion by many practitioners.

Other more subtle differences in the approach to CPD compared with the normal academic way of doing things have to do with who does the teaching or leading or coaching and the way practical activities are examined. Many practitioners want leading practitioners to provide content and they want the style of instruction to be more interactive. Many prefer practical examinations to be based on demonstrations of mastery of a new technique, rather than demonstrations of academic knowledge, particularly those using limited-time closed book formats. It has taken some time to learn of the particular requirements of CPD in terms of content, delivery style and assessment.

The pattern of techniques for CPD support appears to follow a double movement: widening of differences among professions as pioneers introduces new technologies and new ideas, and, at the same time, catching up and narrowing differences as the developing network among CPD specialists allows slow adapters to introduce what certain pioneers are doing. Some introducing CPD for the first time or undertaking major overhauls can leapfrog others and adopt pioneer current practice. Overall, we may expect the catching up movement to speed up as the community of CPD specialists within professional bodies becomes stronger, and develops stronger collective institutions and organizations that allow more rapid and more detailed sharing of information across different professions (see Friedman and Williams 2007: Chapter 2 on professional bodies as a sector).

# 6

# CPD GOVERNANCE

## Regulatory procedures

*If regulation of CPD is to be taken as seriously as regulation of education
standards for admission to the professions and dealing with client complaints it
will be costly. However, if done vigorously, it could raise standards of professional
practice more effectively than the other two pillars.*

## 6.1 Introduction

CPD can be regarded as a key component of professional regulation, essential
for protection of clients and the general public. It can be viewed as the third of
three 'pillars' of professional standards along with initial professional qualifications and complaints and disciplinary procedures (Friedman and Hanson 2010).
CPD can also be viewed as contributing to the sham that is touted as professionalism and what is 'really' one of many ways the professions keep themselves
exclusive, allowing them to charge exorbitant prices for their services. Which
of these opposing views of CPD and of professionalism comes to dominate
general opinion will depend critically on two of the overarching aspects of CPD
outlined in the model presented in Figure 5.1: monitoring and sanctions.

## 6.2 Evidence of Vision 4: CPD as a sham

Different but related negative views of the trappings of professionalism may
be included in the view of them as a sham. On one hand they can be viewed
as barriers; designed to keep out the many to keep up professional fees for the
few. If the requirement set for entry into the professions (and also for continued
membership) is set too high, it is likely that only people of a certain type or
class will be accepted. The notion of the professions based solely on merit and
open to all can be regarded as a sham. On the other hand if the requirements
are set too low, if it is too easy to join and continue to be a professional, professional standards can be regarded as a sham. The rigour of the professions can be
regarded as a sham.

The charge of sham elitism through unjustified entry barriers is often aimed
at the professions. In the early years of CPD, initial professional education was

widely criticized as irrelevant to practice and pitched at too high an academic level, thus posing an unjustified entry barrier (Schön 1983, 1984). The charge of sham standards was expressed in a stream of criticisms of ethical codes as mere 'window dressing' which appeared in the 1980s and 1990s (Kultgen 1982; Jamal and Bowie 1995; Brien 1998).

More recently references specifically to CPD from the entry barrier perspective have appeared. According to the UK Office of Fair Trading (OFT):

> educational and experience qualifications . . . are justified in terms of an ex ante quality control, but may act simply to deter entry to a profession . . . This category of restrictions also includes post-qualification educational or experience requirements (for example, Continuing Professional Development (CPD) requirements).
>
> (Vickers 2001: 15)

> Though CPD may form part of justifiable professional regulation as quality control or quality assurance, the OFT report suggests it could act merely as a deterrence to entry. The report concluded that the CPD requirements they investigated for solicitors and barristers 'should not appreciably restrict or distort competition.' However, this was because they 'regard the regulated minimum number of required hours as low . . . [and not] unduly onerous.'
>
> (Vickers 2001: 53, 73)

The presumption is that it could not only act as such but be designed as such.[1] Variance with the vision of CPD as an essential component of professional regulation is clear. CPD requirements are acceptable if they are low and not unduly onerous according to the OFT, but according to the vision of CPD as an essential component for ensuring professional competence they are unlikely to be effective unless the minimum requirement is high, and involves considerable effort on the part of individual professionals.

Admittedly CPD is not known well enough for the reaction to it as another sham, and an over-done barrier to entry to have stimulated much commentary. However, the second variant of the sham vision of CPD has been expressed, though not publicly. As noted in Chapter 4, it is well known within certain professions that some professionals have not been taking CPD seriously.

## 6.3 Monitoring

'There is no point in CPD if there is no monitoring. It is needed for legitimacy' (CPD specialist at professional body cited in Friedman, Davis *et al.* 2000: 111).

Professional bodies could have recorded and monitored the professional development activity of their members before the coming of CPD, but their membership database systems were unlikely to be sufficiently robust or flexible to carry out this potentially vast task before the late 1970s without enormous expense. Before the widespread availability of personal computers, such systems were the preserve of major corporations or large government agencies, particularly as database management systems were in their infancy.

Before CPD professional bodies would not have been particularly interested in recording professional development activity of individuals. If regulatory bodies recorded educational activities after qualification, it would have been to credentialize qualifications in new specialties, such as doctors qualifying to become anaesthetists. Professional bodies would have focused their monitoring resources on records focusing on their own offerings and their overall popularity, rather than the take-up of those offerings by individual practitioners. The aim of those that recorded membership activity would have been to monitor their own resource allocation and to evaluate this use of resources for the membership as a whole. How expensive was it to put out the professional journal? How widely distributed was it? How many attended branch meetings, events and workshops?[2] Not how many branch meetings, events or workshops did individual members attend or participate in. The aim would have been to produce activities that would be of use to as many practitioners as possible,[3] not either to ensure that all practitioners partook of these activities or to provide a range of opportunities with a view as to how many and which activities individual practitioners ought to partake in, in order to achieve professional development targets.

In this sense these professional development activities were not strategically supported at the level of the individual professional. This is a critical difference between the situation now and that of 30 or 40 years ago. Explicit policies on CPD reflect a new form of strategic thinking about the condition of professionals by professional bodies. Almost all professional bodies with a CPD policy sampled in 1999 (92 per cent), reported that CPD compliance of practitioners was monitored (Friedman, Davis *et al.* 2000).

Professional bodies also monitor their own policies and programmes. That survey found 50 per cent monitor their policy and 30 per cent their programme (Friedman, Davis *et al.* 2000). It is surprising that some were monitoring their policies but not their programme. At least back in 1999, some professional bodies did not have a comprehensive approach to monitoring.

Those monitoring compliance of individuals included many with voluntary or obligatory compliance policies. Why would they do this? It was to maintain the credibility of the scheme, even if no sanctions were attached to non-compliance. Monitoring not only allows professional bodies to verify that individuals are maintaining their competence by engaging in CPD, it also allows them to report on the success of the CPD programme to their members and other stakeholders.

Monitoring can be thought of as support for individuals as long as the results are fed back to them. Records can be used to build a portfolio of CPD activities to feed into plans and as evidence to employers and clients of active CPD participation. However, monitoring can also be seen as part of a control system imposing discipline on individual professionals.

At that time some were ambivalent about monitoring. 'It's their problem if they don't do it!' stated one CPD officer at a professional association (Friedman, Davis *et al*. 2000: 111). Also, a misleading use of the term monitoring in relation to CPD was revealed. While 92 per cent reported that members monitored their own CPD, only 73 per cent of professional associations monitored the CPD compliance of individuals (Friedman, Davis *et al*. 2000). Almost all practitioners filled out record cards. For those that stated practitioners monitor their own CPD and did not report that the professional body did so, monitoring meant record keeping by individuals was supported by the professional body, and did not imply surveillance of individual participation.

Almost all (86 per cent) professional bodies with a compulsory policy in 1999 monitored the CPD of their members, rather than allowing individuals to monitor themselves. In the mixed category too, nearly all (95 per cent) monitored the CPD of their members – this reflects the fact that 19 of the 20 associations with mixed policies had a compulsory element in their policy. This indicates at least two reasons for encouraging members to record their CPD: for individuals to display and legitimate their own activities and for the professional body to monitor those activities. It also implies what we may now view as an immature state of CPD monitoring in the UK at the end of the 1990s. We would expect 100 per cent of associations with a compulsory policy to monitor their members CPD. This is one of the anomalies Friedman, Davis and colleagues (2000) found when examining policies and practices in detail. While some professional bodies may have wanted to project an *image* of compulsory engagement in the practice of CPD, they did not seriously check on or follow up those who did not comply. Similarly in the next section we note inconsistencies in policies and practices regarding sanctions.

In a later survey of 54 professional bodies (Williams and Friedman 2008) those monitoring CPD were clearly correlated with degree of compulsion of compliance policy. Only 74 per cent of professional bodies with a CPD policy monitored individual CPD participation, however this was composed of:

- 100 per cent of those with a compulsory policy;
- 67 per cent with an obligatory policy; and
- 43 per cent a voluntary policy.

It is notable that almost half of those with a voluntary policy still monitored CPD. It is also interesting that the overall proportion of those monitoring CPD was lower for this more recent survey, entirely because fewer of those with obligatory and voluntary policies were monitoring CPD. The surveys are not strictly comparable, but the difference in results may reflect a real shift in approaches to monitoring CPD among professional bodies in the past decade.

CPD participation has been monitored using different techniques. During the late 2000s there has been a strong shift of emphasis from voluntary to compulsory audit for monitoring individual participation in CPD.

The 2006 PARN International Benchmarking Survey (IBS) had 64 UK professional bodies who answered the question about CPD monitoring:

- 9 per cent used survey questionnaires;
- 31 per cent used voluntary random audit;
- 25 per cent compulsory random audit; and
- 14 per cent audited all of their members on a compulsory basis;
- 'other methods' were used by 20 per cent.

(Friedman and Mason 2007: 30)

By the time of the 2009 IBS of 77 professional bodies in the UK only:

- 4 per cent reported using voluntary questionnaires; and
- 17 per cent random voluntary audit; but
- 53 per cent used compulsory random audit; though only
- 9 per cent audited all members on a compulsory basis; and
- 17 per cent used other methods.

## 6.4 Sanctions

Sanctions for non-compliance are imposed mainly by professional bodies with compulsory CPD. However, the pattern is complex. Sanctions can be anything from expulsion from the professions' register, which may mean loss of livelihood for that individual, to a simple reminder of non-compliance and perhaps a notification that the individual should become up-to-date within a certain time limit or face a disciplinary panel.

Of the 101 professional bodies in the 1999 survey with a CPD policy 44 per cent had sanctions for non-compliance. The most common sanctions were:

- removal from the register of members (13 per cent of those with a policy);
- loss of practising certificate (7 per cent);
- loss of membership (6 per cent), debarment from upgrades (4 per cent); and
- debarment from holding office in the professional body (3 per cent).

In addition, a couple used loss of Chartered title, and refusal of re-registration. An interesting sanction was that not completing CPD affected an individual's professional indemnity insurance premium. In this case the professional body negotiated a rate for its members based on the presumption that they participate in the CPD scheme. This would be forfeited if the professional body did not confirm to the insurance company that an individual was complying with the standard set out in the scheme (Friedman, Davis et al. 2000).

Some with voluntary schemes reported sanctions for non-compliance. One had a scheme of providing evidence of CPD participation to members for use with employers or potential employers. Individuals not keeping up their CPD records would lead to suspension from the scheme but not from the professional body or its register and there were no other consequences attached to this suspension:

> An individual can re-instate their participation in the scheme at any time, and can usually continue their CPD at the point where they were suspended, provided that the gap is not too long. The institute does not keep records on how many people fail to meet CPD deadlines, but their feeling is that it is 'quite low' (based on a telephone interview). The thinking behind their policy is that they wish to appear approachable and believe that members should be encouraged to participate in CPD, rather than be threatened by sanctions.
>
> (Friedman, Davis *et al.* 2000: 83–4)

Another voluntary scheme with sanctions is where 'promotion' to Fellowship or other higher grade within the profession depends on compliant CPD. One professional body excluded members from applying to be Fellows if they did not have an unbroken CPD record for three consecutive years, but once the member had become a Fellow there was no mention of changing to compulsory CPD.

Is this inconsistency? Should someone be required to have three years of unbroken CPD to be able to apply for a position and then not be required to maintain CPD after achieving it? The logic is that CPD is voluntary not only for professionally qualified individuals, but also for those who are Fellowship qualified. Three consecutive years' CPD records are evidence for qualification as a Fellow, just as an initial qualification is to enter the profession. Once either is achieved, maintaining CPD records is not required. Many professional bodies now have mixed policies, generally voluntary for ordinary members and compulsory not only to achieve higher level status but also to maintain it.

As expected almost all professional bodies with a compulsory CPD policy have sanctions, though 6 per cent of those with compulsory policies in 1999 did not mention any sanctions in their CPD literature. The presumption was that these professional bodies did not want to present CPD in a negative, confrontational light to members and that non-compliance with the policy is dealt with quietly.

Even when sanctions are applied, they are often preceded by a long period of attempts at moral suasion. For example, one respondent stated:

> When members do not complete their CPD records we will write to them on a number of occasions before taking them to a disciplinary committee . . . we want them to realise that CPD is not something that our body is enforcing on its members as means of control but that we are acknowledging the

fact that they have been learning for many years and we are showing our appreciation for that learning in accrediting it.

(Friedman, Davis *et al.* 2000: 84)

A medical college interviewed by Friedman, Davis and colleagues (2000: 86) stated that they would like to impose sanctions as CPD is seen as such an important responsibility for all medical practitioners. However, they reported that a change to the Act of 1966 that licenses these practitioners would have been required to enable the college either to make CPD compulsory or to remove individuals from the college for non-compliance. It was legally constrained. This reflected the novelty of CPD. In 1966 it did not exist. Even today there are professional bodies governed by acts that predate the 1980s. It may be that we are coming to the end of the first phase of CPD in the UK and this limitation will no longer apply.

In future there may be legal impediments to sanctions against CPD non-compliance from a different source: the Human Rights Act of 1998, which to our knowledge has not yet been tested in this area. If someone is removed from a professional register because of non-compliance with CPD policy, and if this can be shown to lead to deprivation of a livelihood for the accused, then the Act could be used to force the professional body to provide comparable support for the defence of the accused as would occur in any other trial at which a human right is at stake.

Friedman, Davis and colleagues (2000: 90) reported that most professional bodies were keen to be regarded as encouraging rather than enforcing CPD. The 'carrot' as well as the 'stick' is required: both to reassure clients, employers, insurance companies, government and the public that competence is being maintained and also to discourage a compliance or tick-box mentality towards CPD.

## 6.5 Evidence from Vision 3: CPD as a form of public protection through active regulation: a form of quality assurance

Consider first the regulation of professional standards in general.

### 6.5.1 The three pillars of professional standards

Professional standards regulation can be understood in terms of three supporting 'pillars'; two traditional ones and a new one (Friedman and Hanson 2010). The traditional pillars are:

1 Entry standards.
2 Complaints and discipline.

The traditional approach to professional regulation was to set and enforce minimum standards for entry and to ensure these standards were maintained by hearing complaints against qualified professionals, and disciplining those judged to be operating below standards required. Most of these complaints would have been made by other members of the profession. Discipline would have been either by admonition and possibly requiring remedial action such as putting the offender under supervision, or by suspension or expulsion. The underlying assumption was that professional standards would be upheld through knowledge, skills and awareness of ethical standards acquired during the entry process. After entry it was presumed that the vast majority of professionals would act responsibly and do whatever was required to keep up-to-date. Professionals themselves were assumed to be best placed to understand what was required as they operate in situations requiring highly individualized judgement and customized services. Individuals who somehow got through the first pillar without really understanding the standards required, or individual 'bad apples', or those who lapsed due, say, to adverse personal circumstances (such as alcoholism) would be dealt with through the complaints and disciplinary processes. This was 'regulation by exception'; that is, it relied on complaints coming to the attention of the regulator from the field, rather than from active monitoring and evaluation of practice.

The modern pillar is:

3   CPD and positive supports for ethical behaviour.

The first two pillars have not been replaced; rather they are increasingly regarded as needing augmentation. Changes in technology, in potential professional services offerings, and in the legal and business environment in which services are delivered, all require greater emphasis on developing competence. Ethical challenges also develop and require reacquaintance after qualification and throughout a professional's working life. Activities now labelled CPD may have been what professionals 'just did' before the 1980s, but there was no guarantee that all did it. Recently CPD is being regarded by more regulatory bodies as necessary for maintaining professional standards.

When managed by regulatory bodies CPD is almost always compulsory and monitored. The assumption that regulation can be by exception has come to be regarded as inadequate. The system breaks down if colleagues do not report problems they observe to the regulatory body, if clients and patients do not complain when they are disappointed in the service they receive or even if they consider themselves to have been abused. There are many reasons why clients or patients do not complain: fear of reprisals, distrust that they will get a fair hearing, belief that the outcome will not prevent the problem from recurring, belief that the harm done to them cannot be put right. In addition, they may not even realize that they have received a substandard service.

Another way the third pillar can be distinguished from complaints and discipline is that it is based on positive support for compliance (as described in Chapter 5) as well as disciplining, monitoring and sanctions. In this there may be overlap in programmes developed by regulatory bodies and professional associations covering the same professionals.

### 6.5.2 Third pillar: regulatory bodies and professional associations

The way Vision 3 is commonly expressed can be seen from the UK General Dental Council (GDC) website (Exhibit 6.1).

High-quality patient care is the purpose of CPD and standards for the dental profession specifically include maintaining professional knowledge and competence. For the UK Health Professions Council, the aim of CPD is to ensure that registrants 'retain their capacity to practise safely, effectively and legally within

---

### EXHIBIT 6.1  UK GDC VIEW OF CPD

'Standards for dental professionals' sets out the principles of practice in dentistry. As a dental professional, you are responsible for:

- putting patients' interests first and acting to protect them;
- respecting patients' dignity and choices;
- protecting the confidentiality of patients' information;
- co-operating with other members of the dental team and other healthcare colleagues in the interests of patients;
- maintaining your professional knowledge and competence; and
- being trustworthy.

All dental professionals should carry out CPD to support these principles. By law, dentists must take part in our compulsory CPD scheme.

#### What is CPD?

We define CPD as 'study, training, courses, seminars, reading and other activities undertaken by a dentist, which could reasonably be expected to advance his or her professional development as a dentist'.

. . . The purpose of CPD is to provide high-quality patient care. It is very important that the CPD you do takes into account the needs of your patients and is relevant to your practice.

(GDC 2009)

---

their evolving scope of practice.' CPD is therefore monitored along with the health and character of practitioners (Exhibit 6.2).

Similarly, the Ontario Regulated Health Professions Act (1991; amended 2009) in Canada regards CPD in terms of Quality Assurance. The definition of a quality assurance programme is similar to the definition of CPD as it is known in the UK: '"quality assurance program" means a programme to assure the quality of the practice of the profession and to promote continuing education, competence and improvement among the members.'

The previous examples may be considered typical ways of expressing the aims of CPD for regulatory bodies, however this is not exclusively so. The Royal Institute of British Architects (RIBA) states on its website that CPD is for consumer protection (Exhibit 6.3). RIBA is a professional association. The regulatory body for British architects is the Architects Registration Board (ARB). They have taken a stance towards CPD that is complementary to professional associations (Exhibit 6.4).

Interestingly RIBA's view of CPD goes against powerful opinions of traditional economists who argue that consumers are best protected by free markets. Certain agencies are founded on this view, such as the Consumers' Association (widely associated with the magazine *Which?*), the Consumer Protection Association[4] and the Office of Fair Trading (2001). With the recent credit crunch and the ensuing rec(depr)ession, these views are being questioned. More active

---

## EXHIBIT 6.2 UK HEALTH PROFESSIONS COUNCIL VIEW OF REQUIREMENT FOR REGISTRANTS

We define CPD as

> . . . a range of learning activities through which health professionals maintain and develop throughout their career to ensure that they retain their capacity to practice safely, effectively and legally within their evolving scope of practice.

Put simply, CPD is the way health professionals continue to learn and develop throughout their careers so they keep their skills and knowledge up to date and are able to work safely, legally and effectively.

### Fitness to practise

> If someone is fit to practise, this means that they have the health and character, as well as the necessary skills and knowledge to practise their profession safely and effectively.

(HPC 2008, with permission)

---

### EXHIBIT 6.3 CPD DEFINITION FROM RIBA

Continuing Professional Development (CPD) obligations exist to help ensure that qualified professionals maintain their competence to practise. This is true in countless professional sectors in the UK.

At its very basic level, CPD is for consumer protection. It is also a way of ensuring that architects keep up-to-date within a rapidly changing profession. CPD should also enhance an architect's current and future development (professionally, personally and for staff within a business.)

(RIBA 2009)

---

forms of regulation – such as CPD and positive supports for ethical practice – are being encouraged. 'Managers have lost legitimacy over the past decade in the face of a widespread institutional breakdown of trust and self-policing in business' (Khurana and Nohria, 2008: 70).

Clearly, bankers lost almost all credibility in the credit crunch of late 2008 which continues to make headlines over bonuses to top bankers in many countries.

It is worth mentioning that the Financial Services Authority (FSA) has been undertaking a review of investment advice designed to professionalize the sector in which CPD figures prominently.[5] According to the FSA:

> We have long stated that a one-off increase in knowledge levels (brought about by reformed qualifications) as a result of the RDR, would not on its own be a worthwhile change. We are committed to making sure that advisers maintain and update their knowledge and skills . . . We also suggested that any such activity should involve . . . an evaluation of success in meeting its objectives by way of outcome measures.
>
> (FSA 2010: 7)

However, traditional professionals are still trusted, particularly those that the general public regularly deal with, such as doctors (especially general practitioners), dentists and nurses (Ipsos MORI 2007). Though what can be labelled as 'blind trust' is disappearing (Brien 1998; O'Neill 2005).

> Those who were in the boardrooms had no clear understanding of the risks they were running. In the case of Royal Bank of Scotland, the board failed to exercise a restraining influence on such madcap schemes as the purchase for 70 billion euros of ABN Amro . . . 'Greedy bankers' is not an adequate explanation of the crisis; but 'incompetent and ignorant bankers' comes very close to it.
>
> (Kamm 2009)

---

## EXHIBIT 6.4 ARCHITECTS REGISTRATION BOARD (ARB) – GUIDANCE ON CPD

The Architects Act 1997 requires the Architects Registration Board (ARB) to issue a code . . . Standard 6 of *The Architects Code: Standards of Conduct and Practice* requires the following:

Architects should maintain their professional service and competence in areas relevant to their professional work, and discharge the requirements of any engagement with commensurate knowledge and attention.

The fact that an architect has not maintained their professional competence may count against them in the event of that competence having to be investigated.

ARB does not prescribe the number of hours of CPD you must do each year nor the topics you must cover.

Very few architects face disciplinary action from ARB's Professional Conduct Committee (PCC). However, the reasons why architects come before the PCC may give you some guidance about where your CPD should be focused . . . some architects might benefit from CPD that covers the following areas:

- financial management skills in devising and managing budgets;
- business management skills;
- project management skills;
- communication skills.

The guidance notes directs readers to their Annual Report on their website for summary of reasons why architects come before the PCC and also refer to the CPD regimes of RIBA, and other professional associations in related fields. The ARB also mentions that those it covers should 'develop a culture of lifetime learning in order to maintain competence and also to maintain employability'. It also refers to more specific uses of CPD; that evidence you have kept up to date will be needed to apply for re-instatement if an individual comes off the Register for two years or more, and that if you appear before the PCC to face a complaint 'you may benefit from being able to provide evidence that you have kept yourself up to date in the area(s) under investigation.'

(ARB 2010)

## 6.6 CPD as a disciplinary tool, as 'punishment' or remedial activity

Individual professionals may come to see CPD as stronger than a pillar of professional standards, rather as a disciplinary tool and a way of curtailing their autonomy. It can be seen as a way of forcing professionals, not merely bad apples, to do things they do not regard as valuable for their professional development; turning CPD from a positive member service to:

- a compulsory policy that is intended to support and even to 'guarantee' or at least to help legitimate the view of professionals as being trustworthy and competent; to
- a burdensome tick-box exercise to satisfy a regulator or even to satisfy the regulator of a regulator or a 'meta-regulator',[6] without much reference to whether the boxes ticked indicate genuine Professional Development Value.

This is one path of successive visions of CPD some professionals believe they have experienced. This sense of multiple vision leads to problems of focus for the CPD field.

Some professional bodies indeed use CPD in a disciplinary manner. This will appear as punishment from some professionals' point of view. If individuals are judged to be lacking in competency, they may have to undertake extra CPD such as the policy of the Institute for Archaeologists (IfA). Two of five major regulatory bodies investigated by Friedman, Hanson and Williams in 2009 used CPD in this manner, as a consequence of disciplinary proceedings.[7]

Consider the Health Professions Act of Ontario. Ontario is the most populous province in Canada (13 of the 34 million population of Canada in 2009). The Act of 1991 does not mention CPD or CPE.[8] Rather it uses the terms quality assurance and continuing competence. The essence of the approach to CPD among health sector regulatory bodies in Canada (which are at the provincial level) is as a form of sanction itself: not so much a compulsory policy with sanctions for non-compliance, but rather a sanction or punishment for a poor quality assessment. According to the Act the regulator must take three issues into account in assessments: incompetence, incapacity and misconduct. Incompetence and incapacity are closely related under the banner of lack of judgement or care. However, they are different in that incapacity concerns alcohol or other substance abuse or other kind of physical or mental incapacity, while incompetence concerns lack of knowledge or skill or the practical connection between the two, which is often called competence or competencies.

Three broad types of actions are open to the regulatory body:

1 Direct protection of the public through suspension or removal from the register or some limitation of their registration. This is the harshest punishment available beyond referring the practitioner to the criminal justice system.
2 Punishment by loss of reputation or finance. This can be as little as a reprimand and as great as removal of certain status marks such as loss of Fellowship or Chartered or other label denoting senior status. The very minimum may be even a reprimand in camera, which is intended to be a blow to the honour and self-respect of the professional. The maximum

may be removal of a hard-earned status position that provides a justification for charging higher fees and eligibility for certain kinds of work. In between are fines that may be paid to a complainant or to the professional body, and may include covering damages or expenses incurred in finding out and prosecuting the case against the practitioner or compensating a complainant.

3 Remedial action. This has been the approach traditionally taken by regulatory bodies in the past, and the attitude that had been criticized heavily in the UK, particularly against the General Medical Council in the wake of the Shipman case (Smith, J. 2004). This is where a link with CPD comes in. The punishment is to be subject to particular training and development requirements.

This is a very different approach from the CPD cycle. The focus is on continuing competence rather than continuing professional development, that is, maintaining knowledge skills and competence. The focus is not the development of the professional, but rather assessment of the practice. Competence concerns the professional's part played in the quality of the practice and the purpose of assessment is to assure quality of practice, rather than to help develop individual professionals. This is a deficiency approach. It does not begin with the professional's own assessment of their competency, their needs and how they are going to get from where they are now to where they wish to be. It begins with an outsider assessment of the quality of the practice and whether the individual is up to the standard required. If individuals are considered deficient, they must make up this deficiency satisfactorily, based on some sort of test. The quality assurance approach is not generally concerned with the process of doing CPD. In this sense the quality assurance or continuing competency approach is closer to a replication of the traditional initial qualification process. The presumption in the initial qualification process is that individuals begin from a state of deficiency; they are unqualified. The continuing competence approach is brought into force when a qualified professional is judged to be deficient through incapacity, incompetence or misconduct.

The CPD outputs approach presumes the practitioner is a qualified and trustworthy professional. Compulsory CPD is 'sold' to them as something they ought to be doing: ought to be wanting to do. The aim of measuring CPD is to assess whether the CPD they do is worthwhile in improving practice, not to assess whether practice has improved up to a required standard. It is a sufficiency model rather than a deficiency model (Exhibit 6.5).

Regulatory bodies in the United States have come to take a different approach: assessing for revalidation of professional qualifications. This approach is spreading to the UK, at least to the medical sector. Rather than emphasizing the continuous nature of CPD, this approach emphasizes competence review and tends to take place very infrequently; once every 10 years is common (Friedman and Woodhead 2008). Revalidation can be combined with regular

## EXHIBIT 6.5 CPD AND QUALITY ASSURANCE AMONG HEALTH PROFESSIONALS IN CANADA

82.

(1) Every member shall co-operate with the Quality Assurance Committee and with any assessor it appoints and in particular every member shall,

(a) permit the assessor to enter and inspect the premises where the member practises;

(b) permit the assessor to inspect the member's records of the care of patients;

(c) give the Committee or the assessor the information in respect of the care of patients or in respect of the member's records of the care of patients the Committee or assessor requests in the form the Committee or assessor specifies;

(d) confer with the Committee or the assessor if requested to do so by either of them; and

(e) participate in a program designed to evaluate the knowledge, skill and judgement of the member, if requested to do so by the Committee . . .

(5) This section applies despite any provision in any Act relating to the confidentiality of health records.

95.

(1) . . . the Council may make regulations,

(r) prescribing a quality assurance program;

(2.1) Regulations made under clause (1) (r) of subsection 1 may,

(a) authorize the Quality Assurance Committee to require individual members whose knowledge, skills and judgement have been assessed under section 82 and found to be unsatisfactory to participate in specified continuing education programmes;

(b) authorize the Quality Assurance Committee to direct the Registrar to impose terms, conditions or limitations, for a specified period not exceeding six months, on the certificate of registration of a member whose knowledge, skills and judgement have been assessed or reassessed under section 82 and found to be unsatisfactory, or who has failed to participate in specified continuing education programs as required by the Committee, or has not completed those programs successfully . . .

(Official Consolidation of the Regulated Health Professions Act 1991)

CPD if, say, one of the assessment methods once every decade is to audit annual CPD records.

Finally, CPD is implicated in certain analyses of professionalism itself as a 'disciplinary mechanism' practised by companies (in the sense of Foucault, see Burchell *et al.* 1991). According to Fournier (1999), companies are using the appeal to professionalism to align managers to company aims, particularly through appealing to individuals to take responsibility for their own personal and professional development.

Almost all professional bodies with a CPD policy exercise some functions that may be regarded as regulatory. Even professional associations that do not regulate their members[9] still regulate CPD of their members in a broad sense, at least to the extent of monitoring and maintaining records of CPD undertaken. They also maintain those records in such a way as to distinguish whether members are or are not in compliance with the policy, and whether they are fulfilling the expected programme, even if the policy is voluntary.

It is a complication of the CPD scene that the range of arrangements for the distribution of representative and regulatory functions are not strictly matched with the different CPD compliance arrangements. Many regulatory bodies do not regard the CPD policy as in their remit; they rely on the traditional two pillars. Others have recently come to see CPD as an important aspect of their public protection remit. When they do take on CPD, they govern CPD more tightly with compulsory policies. The additional resources required for these policies will generally come from the professionals themselves as registration fees, though in some cases government provides support.[10]

Sanctions can be a tricky issue for professional associations, not only for the resources required, but also for their implications for the relationship between the organization and its members. This is one of the reasons for a growing separation between professional associations and regulatory bodies. Sanctions for CPD non-compliance support the reputation of the profession as a whole, but may lead those under threat of sanctions to view their professional body as the 'enemy'.

# 7

# CPD MEASUREMENT AND THE PARADOX OF CPD

## Effective achievement of Professional Development Value?

> *Until we abandon traditional methods of assessment 'we will continue to struggle to measure the immeasurable and may end up measuring the irrelevant because it is easier.'*

(Snadden 1999: 479)

## 7.1 Introduction

Measurement and assessment of learning is inherently paradoxical and potentially contradictory.[1] Teachers and academics are well aware of the basic assessment dilemma, which is to skew learning towards passing assessments rather than understanding and appreciating the subject being taught. It is common to learn a great deal while cramming for an exam, much of which is forgotten the next day.

Measurement at minimum is intended to record accurately what is learned and at best provides an incentive to learn through providing clear targets as well as a yardstick for learners to mark their progress. But at the same time measurement always involves some disjuncture between what is measured and how it is measured. An unfortunate consequence is that assessment can encourage a compliance mentality. The measurement instrument cannot capture all the possible combinations and contexts of what is to be learned. Patterns will be noticed in the way the assessment instrument is constructed and operates. Most learners will concentrate on meeting the measurement criteria, which can lead them away from the intended knowledge teachers are aiming to measure (Shepard 2000).

Though this is a generic problem, some methods of assessment are more prey to it than others. When a small number of questions appear on an examination paper, and candidates are allowed considerable choice of which questions to answer, and the selection of topics and the way the questions are framed are repeated year after year, savvy students concentrate on developing model answers based on past exams. They will ignore some portion of the subject being taught.

Measuring CPD has been affected by this assessment paradox. In the past, the common approach to measurement has led to the whole idea being discredited in the eyes of some. The fundamental paradox of CPD is that it is at the same time both what professionals just do (and may do for strategic career reasons) and what they ought to do. It is what we think they just do, and what we expect and rely upon them to have done. Or at least it is what most professionals in the past have done, though to a greater or lesser extent, which has been invisible to clients and not clearly thought through in terms of aims and objectives by professionals themselves. Many individual professionals have not accepted that what they have to do for CPD will achieve the Professional Development Value from it as defined by their professional bodies. While we have to rely on the sense of obligation and duty as well as the character we attribute to professionals, we also want guarantees that any particular professional we see does in fact do it.

Clients need professionals to keep up their competence, but they do not really know what it is that they need professionals to do. There is no clear standard in most professions for what knowledge a mid-career professional should have, which can be certificated.[2] There is as yet no widely recognized piece of paper professionals can hang on the wall for clients to see they are up-to-date with their competence as attested by CPD. More difficult is to provide certification attesting to the other purposes of CPD described in Chapter 1: development of competencies as well as maintaining them and personal development. Do professionals have more than knowledge of well established services and techniques? Are they reflecting on those things and how they fit into the needs of the client in front of them? Are they thinking about what is on the horizon and beyond in their field and related fields? In traditional professions these characteristics are intended to be imparted during a long period of study and initial training. It had been presumed that they were then inculcated with these character traits, dispositions to follow professional norms, which would lead them to develop their competency and professionalism without need for further certification.

From the professional's own perspective CPD is at the same time three things: what they just do; what they ought to do morally as a proper professional; and what they ought to do strategically to maintain the confidence of clients/ patients, employers, government, the media and the general public. Carrying out professional development activities has always been these different things and is undertaken for these different reasons: 'automatic' or dispositional, moral and strategic. Some do it more for one or other of these motives, but most are motivated by each of these things at different times or often all at the same time.

The overall view among professionals in the UK until the coming of formal CPD schemes from the late 1970s is likely to have been towards the 'what they just do' aspect of the paradox, with professional bodies providing a range of opportunities and supports for this activity, but on an opportunistic, non-systematic basis.

Measurement of CPD throws the balance towards the 'oughts', even if it is not compulsory. Measuring CPD makes it more visible and therefore more credible and creditable. It reminds professionals of their ethical responsibility towards professional development and it encourages them to do it to fulfil expectations at least of their colleagues through their professional bodies. Measuring CPD makes its absence visible. It makes CPD a potential disciplinary tool or an engine for disciplining practitioners. It therefore provides both a carrot and a stick to encourage professionals to do CPD. In the eyes of some this reduces the autonomy of professionals. It is the thin end of the wedge towards de-professionalization. However, it can also be viewed as the tool needed to reinvigorate professionalism. How can we reconcile these two views or even choose between them?

CPD is not only a wrapper around what professionals just did anyway. It changes what is just done, particularly if CPD is measured. Measurement encourages those who find it difficult to carry out CPD, or who just do different things than expected in the CPD scheme, or who just do less than expected in the scheme, to do more than they would 'just do'. It encourages/forces many to 'get with the programme'.

It also encourages some to 'get round the programme' and induces some to resent the programme and its symbolic gatekeeper, the professional body. We believe this to be, at least in part, a relatively short-term adjustment effect of the coming of CPD. If CPD does become a widely known and appreciated phenomenon, these negative views will abate. As we will see in this chapter, much of the opposition to CPD can be dealt with by introducing outputs measures or at least supports for individuals to recognize and record outputs from their CPD.

However, there is also the criticism that in trying to measure the value of CPD we are attempting to measure the immeasurable. In Snadden's (1999: 479) judgement, at his time of writing, there were no suitable methods to assess concepts such as professional mastery, performance in practice and continuing professional development. Until such time as traditional methods of assessment are abandoned, 'we will continue to struggle to measure the immeasurable, and may end up measuring the irrelevant because it is easier.'

In this chapter we present evidence for the extent to which CPD is measured and the methods used to measure it. In particular we deal with the distinction between measuring by inputs or outputs. Outputs measures are, we believe, a sign of the maturing of CPD. They bring CPD closer to achieving its aims as expressed in most definitions of CPD: that is, they more accurately evaluate Professional Development Value or PDV. A model is presented for understanding PDV that incorporates both inputs and outputs measurement schemes.

## 7.2 Inputs versus outputs

### 7.2.1 General definitions of inputs and outputs measurement schemes

*Inputs*

Most early programmes recorded CPD participation in terms of inputs; by the number of hours of activities undertaken per year, or over a longer time period to allow for some variation per year. Some professional bodies use a points system so they can weight activities differently. Giving a paper at a conference over a period of two hours would count for more than merely attending for two hours. Points may be interpreted as an early step in thickening the institutional wrapper around CPD. With the points system, the professional body not only considers what counts as CPD, but also distinguishes activities of different value.

Friedman and Williams (2008: 36) found in their (limited sample size: 28 professional bodies) survey of CPD policies that 32 per cent of respondents had a system where certain types of CPD activity were deemed to be of a higher value than others. The common distinctions were between 'formal' and 'informal' activities, 'accredited' and 'non-accredited', 'structured' and 'unstructured' and 'examined' and 'non-examined': with formal, accredited, structured and examined activities being of higher value. In addition, 19 per cent gave 'technical/profession specific' activities a higher value than 'generic' ones.

According to the 2009 PARN IBS survey median hours per year required was 37. There can be a bewildering array of schemes for the same types of professionals if they could belong to different professional bodies. Perhaps the most striking example of this is in accounting, where in the UK at least four major professional bodies compete for membership of certain categories of practitioners.[3]

*Outputs*

There are wide differences in what are identified or measured as CPD outputs. To help pick our way through this variety we distinguish outputs from outcomes.[4]

'Outcome' is the actual effect or impact of the CPD activity – how it has affected:

- knowledge;
- attitudes, perceptions or emotions;
- behaviour;
- professional practice or organizational development.

This is only one of the phases of the CPD cycle, and therefore measurement of outcomes is only part of the output of the CPD process as a whole.

'Output' is generated at three of the four stages of the CPD cycle. Outputs can come in the form of a personal development plan at the planning stage or a reflective piece of writing at the reflection stage in addition to outcomes. We define outputs as whatever emerges from CPD activities, either individually or collectively. In this sense output is the broader umbrella term that includes outcomes.

However, there are other ways of thinking about the outcomes/outputs distinction:

1 *Direct and indirect results of CPD activities*. Outputs are direct effects or results of CPD activities. For example a plan or reflective essay or an examination grade. Most outcomes are indirect effects, requiring some intervening factor. The difference is particularly relevant for practice and organization outcomes, perhaps less relevant for learning or knowledge outcomes, though here the examination result, which demonstrates knowledge one has acquired as specifically tested by the examination and at the time of sitting, can be distinguished from the outcome of learning or new knowledge, what the professional has actually learned or knows. Intervening factors are opportunities to apply that knowledge, and time (which is likely to lead to knowledge deterioration). Outputs may be thought of as short-term impact effects and outcomes as longer-term effects, though this distinction will disappear when outputs and outcomes coincide, such as with the use of client questionnaires or peer reviews to directly judge outcomes.

2 *Intentionality*. Outputs are intended effects. They are artefacts or processes specifically required or requested by the professional body as evidence of CPD. Outcomes are both intended and unintended effects of CPD activities. What actually occurs as a result of CPD activities will depend on intervening and contingent factors, most of which are beyond the control of the individual professional, the direct supplier of CPD activities or the professional body.

Why should we be interested in measuring anything other than outcomes? The validity of measurement will depend on the objectives of CPD. If the objective is to ensure competence, then measurement of outcomes is perhaps enough. However, even here it is useful to distinguish between having a collection of competencies and having overall competence, which includes being able to judge which competencies to use and when to forbear on either technical or ethical grounds.[5] For these wider abilities that are expected of professionals it can be argued that the ability to plan and reflect on one's professional development are also needed.

To monitor the wider aims of competence development and personal and professional development of an individual, output at each stage of the CPD cycle is pertinent. Perhaps attending a CPD event had no or little impact on practice and nothing new was learned. Reflection on this event, and its lack of success, may contribute to practitioner professionalism. Most employers will be more outcome oriented, but they too are likely to be interested in more rounded appraisal.

Emphasis on outcome will depend on the regulatory function of the professional body and risks posed to clients and the general public. Where there is a life/death risk, outcome assessment is likely to be emphasized over other outputs.

To complicate the issue further we may distinguish between the quality or rigour of measuring any one of the phases of the CPD cycle, particularly of outcomes, and the extent to which the full cycle is measured. It is possible to draw a distinction between monitoring progress around the CPD cycle and measurement of the quality of the actual learning achieved or of actual changes to practice made. These different aspects of measurement of quality of CPD (or of PDV) are explicitly illustrated by the model presented in Section 7.4.

### 7.2.2 Incidence of inputs and outputs measurement schemes in different countries

The majority of professional bodies formally measure CPD in the countries PARN surveyed in 2006. As shown in Table 7.1, this varied between 59 per cent in Canada and 80 per cent in Australia. Purely inputs measures were most commonly used in Canada and least commonly used in the UK.[6]

Hours are favoured in the UK and Canada (Table 7.2). In Ireland points are more common, though the sample size was small in Ireland.

Professional bodies were asked what methods they used for gathering evidence of CPD participation. Evidence from records of activities can be regarded as either inputs or outputs measures depending on whether the records are hours/points, or evidence of planning, reflection or outcomes. Table 7.3 shows that professional bodies in the UK were more likely to gather evidence of

**TABLE 7.1** Measurement of CPD participation by professional bodies: Australia, Canada, UK, Ireland

|  | Australia | Canada | UK | Ireland |
| --- | --- | --- | --- | --- |
| Inputs | 37% | 43% | 28% | 36% |
| Outputs | 0% | 16% | 20% | 0% |
| Mixed | 43% | 0% | 17% | 43% |
| No formal | 20% | 41% | 34% | 21% |
| Sample size | 35 | 37 | 93 | 14 |

*Source:* Adapted from Friedman and Mason 2007: 33.

**TABLE 7.2** Professional bodies' basis for inputs measures of CPD participation

|              | Australia | Canada | UK  | Ireland |
|--------------|-----------|--------|-----|---------|
| Hours        | 50%       | 75%    | 60% | 36%     |
| Points       | 43%       | 25%    | 24% | 45%     |
| Other        | 4%        | 0%     | 12% | 0%      |
| No reply     | 4%        | 0%     | 5%  | 18%     |
| Sample size  | 28        | 16     | 42  | 11      |

*Source:* Adapted from Friedman and Mason 2007: 33.

**TABLE 7.3** Methods of gathering evidence of CPD participation

|                        | Australia | Canada | UK  | Ireland |
|------------------------|-----------|--------|-----|---------|
| Record of activities   | 77%       | 89%    | 88% | 86%     |
| Evidence of planning   | 17%       | 32%    | 47% | 36%     |
| Evidence of reflection | 26%       | 32%    | 39% | 29%     |
| No evidence            | 23%       | 8%     | 11% | 7%      |
| Sample size            | 35        | 37     | 93  | 14      |

*Source:* Adapted from Friedman and Mason 2007: 34.

planning and reflection compared with the other countries and Australian professional bodies less likely.

Using the whole database of 179 professional bodies across the four countries we found a positive correlation between use of outputs measures and size of professional body measured by number of individual members. Roughly only 6 per cent of those with fewer than 1,500 members used outputs measures compared with 11 per cent with 1,501–20,000 members and 28 per cent of those with more than 20,000 members.

The proportion of professional bodies using inputs versus outputs measures did not differ according to whether the professional body carried out a representative function or a regulatory function. However, of purely representative professional bodies, that is those with no regulatory function, only 8 per cent reported measuring by inputs and 27 per cent used a combination of methods. Of those with a regulatory function 32 per cent reported using inputs and 7 per cent used a combination of methods. The proportions using outputs measures were the same, 35 per cent for those with only a representative function and 36 per cent for those with a regulatory function.

According to a survey of accountancy professional bodies in 29 European countries as of the end of 2006, Bulgaria, Finland, Poland, Romania and in the UK the ACCA and Chartered Institute of Public Finance and Accountancy (CIPFA) used a combined approach; only Estonia and, in the UK, ICAS and

ICEAW, used an outputs approach. Of the accountancy bodies in the other 23 countries all used an inputs-based approach except for Greece and Portugal, which did not report having mandatory CPD. In addition, the French body reported an inputs-based approach but planned to introduce a combined approach in the next few years (FEE 2007: 17–18).

This last statistic shows a change in situation from the early 1990s, though the evidence bases are not directly compatible. According to Rapkins (Table 3.1) inputs measurement was a key characteristic of the 'sanctions model' pursued by regulatory bodies compared with outputs measurement for the 'benefits model' pursued by professional associations. Regulatory bodies favoured inputs measurement because it is easier to be clear as to what the criterion is and straightforward to identify whether it has been achieved. A decade later, though regulatory bodies are still more likely to use inputs measures, the same proportion of them used outputs measures as did professional associations. The compensating difference being that regulatory bodies were less likely to use a combination of methods, perhaps reflecting a presumption that simplicity in assessment leads to clarity and transparency.

### 7.2.3 Types of outputs measurement techniques and procedures

Friedman and Woodhead (2008: 75) identified the following techniques used in the cases of outputs measurement schemes they studied:

1 Qualitative statements/prose for explicit self-assessment
2 Questionnaires and planning templates
3 Subjective ranking of effectiveness
4 Formal examinations
5 Peer assessments/peer group discussions
6 Client/patient questionnaires
7 Practice assessment based on demographic or other expectations.

The first three are less likely to provide evidence by which outcomes can be measured. The fourth focuses primarily on knowledge outcomes. The last three techniques are more directly aimed at assessing behaviour, attitude and practice or organization outcomes.

Free-form formats for qualitative statements can be regarded as more appropriate for professionals than structured questionnaires. Designing one's own format for reflection can be regarded as evidence of professionalism. The cost is loss of rigour in making comparisons among the returns of different individuals, and identifying progress.

Some professional bodies use a system of practitioner self-rating of effectiveness on a numerical scale to weight hours of CPD. Exhibit 7.1 shows an example.

---

## EXHIBIT 7.1 EXAMPLE OF AN EFFECTIVENESS SCALE TO GUIDE SELF-ASSESSMENT OF CPD

| *Effectiveness rating* | *Criteria of effectiveness* |
|---|---|
| 0.0–0.1 | Very poor effectiveness; pretty much a waste of time and effort, or not new or not relevant knowledge |
| 0.2–0.3 | Quite modest effectiveness, but nevertheless of some benefit |
| 0.4–0.5 | An average degree of effectiveness; this should be a typical score |
| 0.6–0.7 | Highly effective in satisfying the learning need |
| 0.8–1.0 | Exceptionally effective; to be reserved for rare or profound learning experiences, or where a lot is learned in a very short time |

(Friedman and Woodhead 2008: 77)

---

Arguably, this gives a spurious sense of being more objective and more defined and rigorous than the first two techniques listed above. The professional body that used this method reported that people ranked all their CPD activities at effectiveness 0.9 or 1.0, regardless of the actual impact CPD had on them. Effectiveness is a vague term. Other professional bodies have been more explicit stating whether the weighting refers to knowledge acquired or practice implications. Also, they require practitioners to back up their judgement with specific examples. This sort of measurement may be regarded as reflecting the current early stage of outputs measurement. It may also be a contributing factor to the lack of understanding of CPD beyond the profession in question.

Peer review would seem to be the gold standard of outputs measures. Arguably only peers can truly judge whether a professional's practice is competent. This can be very expensive to administer. In addition, the validity of peer reviews is not assured. This will depend on:

- the completeness of the remit (detail of questions asked or guidance given) and the time allowed for the review;
- the proportion of direct peers consulted; and
- how honestly and carefully peers fill out whatever reporting format is required.

The Royal College of Psychiatrists (RCPsych) has developed an interesting model for peer review of CPD (Exhibit 7.2).

## EXHIBIT 7.2 PEER REVIEW GROUPS FOR CPD AT THE ROYAL COLLEGE OF PSYCHIATRISTS

The RCPsych developed its CPD peer group review system in 2001. Groups meet at least twice a year, to plan and then review the programmes for each member, but most meet more often, some as often as once a month. These groups manage themselves and are only expected to be completely objective in their plans and how they tie in with their employer appraisals (the employer being the UK National Health Service or NHS).

There can be a problem finding a relevant group, especially if you are in a rural area or are a locum. The RCPsych has a network of CPD regional co-ordinators to help people to find a relevant group, but it is still a problem in some cases.

Groups are asked to think about knowledge, skill, attitude and social skills, in relation to CPD at four levels of practice. These are issues:

1   common to all medical practitioners such as liaison with other medical specialists;
2   common to all psychiatrists such as reading articles on appraisal and supervision and monitoring their own performance with team managers;
3   common to all psychiatrists in their subspecialty (e.g. forensic psychiatrists);
4   related specifically to the member's job.

Currently they are not expected to set objectives around each of those levels every year, but the philosophy of the RCPsych is that just thinking about these levels can help members realize that they need to update their basic skills. The RCPsych does not monitor in detail whether specific activities are in fact measured. It expects the peer group to challenge an individual plan if they do not think it is possible to measure. The method by which an individual decides to measure their CPD is left largely up to them, so long as it is approved by the peer group.

The College supplies forms to help facilitate peer group discussion which are optional, but one form must be submitted by members to the college.

This is signed off by a member of the peer group and a random 5 per cent sample are chosen by computer. If selected, evidence of any external activities undertaken is requested from the individual and the member of the peer group who signed the form is asked if the development plan was drawn up satisfactorily, whether the objectives set were relevant to that person's role, and as far as they are aware, whether they attended the activities they said they did.

Measurement of CPD quality is deemed to be the responsibility of the peer Group. Currently, the RCPsych has no quality scale for assessing the forms

> received. It is either acceptable or not. Guidance material contains material on performance review, which could be seen as output measures in terms of knowledge application and impact on practice. However, performance review is undertaken by the employer, not the RCPsych.
>
> (RCPsych 2009)

There can be problems associated with what would appear to be the most direct form of outcome measure, client or patient review. Clients/patients may feel intimidated by the professional. Sometimes evidence may be officially confidential, but submitted in such a way as to allow the respondent to be identified. There is also a problem of bias in that it may be easier to get hold of clients/patients who are more likely to be positive towards the professionals. On the other hand dissatisfied individuals may be more likely to bother to fill out voluntary forms.

In addition, it is possible to develop objective baseline measures of practice based on standards of expected outcomes that can be used to judge the effect of CPD on practice. In some cases surveys and demographic evidence can be used to identify what the population of clients/patients served by a particular practice ought to be receiving in terms of service deliverables and in terms of service impact. For example, pharmacies, general practitioner practices, hospital departments and dental practices can be judged by the use of new techniques for testing or treating patients or clients and by the incidence of certain diseases. These measures can be set against demographic features of the clientele to determine expected levels of testing or treatments of disease and of rates of cure. In theory this should be achievable; however, measures used are unlikely to be perfectly accurate because the models for demographic features will be incomplete and are likely to be crude, because proxies based on readily available data will have to be used instead of direct measures. Standards of treatments and outcomes are unlikely to cover all activities carried out in the practice. The work of professionals is complex and varied. Activities that are assessed will be affected by other demands on the practice. In addition, there are possible negative consequences of using what must be non-comprehensive characteristics of practices in assessments. They are likely to be particularly vulnerable to the assessment paradox and skew effort toward assessed activities to the overall detriment of the practice.

There are also fundamental problems of assessing the link between CPD participation and practice:

- Changes in practice may have occurred for other reasons.
- Changes in practice often occur in a social or collective context with individuals learning, coming to an understanding of what they have learned,

and changing their behaviour and the practice delivered all in co-operation (or in struggle) with colleagues (Gold *et al.* 2007).

• New understandings emanating from participation in CPD may have no immediate effect on practice. CPD outcomes may be a long time in coming since certain CPD activities are intended to be preventative, or relate to dealing with situations that may arise infrequently.

## Outputs measurement techniques and procedures – supplementary information gathering or audit and other forms of quality control

Assessment of outputs can generate a compliance mentality, just as inputs assessments have in some cases. CPD specialists in some professional bodies using outputs measures report that some people 'try to see what they can get away with', referring to written statements of reflection. This may involve recording what they regard as the minimum level of detail. Friedman and Woodhead report the case of one professional body finding when they provided examples of what reflections members could include in their self-assessments 'some members actually copied the content of the examples, trying to pass it off as their own work' (2008: 76). A further and perhaps more worrying problem with self-assessment to measure outputs is a tendency to overestimate competence. This has been found to be the case among health-care providers who have performed particularly badly on external assessments such as peer observation, chart audits and cognitive tests (Davis *et al.* 2006; Sargeant 2008).

Self-assessment to measure output has been justified on grounds of preserving autonomy and trust in professionals to assess their own competence.

Many representatives of professional bodies expressed the view that only the practitioners themselves know exactly what is effective CPD for them. Many allow individuals to make their own assessment, but support or reinforce their judgements. This is commonly done in two ways:

1  More guidance can be provided through competency frameworks; that is, expected benchmarks in terms of particular competencies, knowledge and techniques or procedures. These can also have attached to them expected levels of competence as well as areas of competence or competencies; that is, level of mastery as well as content to be mastered.

2  More robustly, self-assessment can be supplemented by audit. 'A CPD audit seeks to provide "reasonable" assurance that the record is free from material error' (Friedman and Woodhead 2008: 81). Audit concerns verification of measurement rather than measurement itself. Some professional bodies only provide audit on request from members; some audit a random sample of submissions; some only audit records of members or registrants who carry a high risk in their practice, such as those directly dealing with the

general public; some audit all members over a certain period of time (see Section 6.3).

### Fineness of measurement

Outputs measurement schemes may merely identify specific outputs of CPD activities such as a reflection form. In this, as with inputs schemes, there is something specific expected that must be judged as either adequate or not. Many schemes go further, finding some way of judging the quality of these forms, but are still concerned only with whether the forms pass a standard of adequacy. For example whether practitioners reflect not merely on the quality of the CPD activity as a valuable experience, but why this might be so, referring to specific knowledge, competency or practice expectations.

Outputs-based schemes may specify ordinal measures, judging quality in a broad sense of different levels: as with university grading schemes that identify pass or distinction levels, or the more elaborate first, upper and lower second or third class degrees. Or they may use a cardinal scale specifying not only whether one score is better than another, but also by how much, say by giving specific test scores or providing scores in terms of standard deviations.

The effectiveness scale set out in Exhibit 7.1 appears to be precise, but it may be thought of as an ordinal judgement made into a cardinal measure by fiat. Very poor, modest, average degree, highly, exceptionally effective are terms that relate to each other ordinally. All we can say is that one level is higher than another. Is the difference between very poor effectiveness and modest effectiveness the same as the difference between average degree of effectiveness and highly effective?

### 7.2.4 Comparing inputs and outputs schemes

Table 7.4 compares inputs and outputs measurement schemes distinguishing initial from long-term effects.

We believe many professional bodies overestimate how difficult an outputs-based approach will be. They do not realize that elements of output orientation can easily be introduced. One reason for this is that when they think of an outputs-based system they are thinking primarily of an outcome system.

### 7.2.5 Evaluation of inputs approaches

Because the inputs approach is easy to implement, simple and easily understood by practitioners, it is relatively easy to monitor and control compliance. The easily quantifiable record of CPD participation can justify sanctions where necessary. However, costs to ensure measurement accuracy and comprehensiveness have grown to counter abuse. Lack of rigorous monitoring by some professional bodies in the early years has led to the whole idea of CPD being discredited in

**TABLE 7.4** Advantages and disadvantages of inputs and outputs approaches to CPD measurement

*Initial advantages*

| *Inputs* | *Outputs* |
|---|---|
| Simple; easily understood by members | Allow practitioners to monitor progress towards CPD goals and set intermediate goals for themselves beyond accumulation of attendance records |
| Easy to implement | Provide evidence for what CPD is intended to achieve to professional bodies and other stakeholders |
| Compliance simplicity and relatively easy to use CPD records as benchmarks for higher level roles within the profession, such as Fellow status | Give greater credibility to use of CPD by professional bodies as benchmarks for higher level roles within the profession, such as Fellow status |

*Long-term advantages*

| *Inputs* | *Outputs* |
|---|---|
| | Encourage members to value their professional body for its contribution to professional aspirations, as well as and rather than exclusively giving value for money |
| | May stave off demands for greater accountability and challenges to professional integrity and competence in the face of high-profile failings within the profession and in related professions |
| | Raise the profile of the profession and the professional body in the eyes of various stakeholders, including demonstrating the public service purpose of the body |
| | Technology of outputs measures is improving. Credible and comprehensive links between CPD participation and outcomes are yet to be made but are likely to be in future |

*Initial disadvantages*

| *Inputs* | *Outputs* |
|---|---|
| Lack of direct connection to aims of CPD leading to mechanical compliance and/or abuse by individuals | Concern and resentment by some practitioners at being 'tested' |

**TABLE 7.4** *(continued)*

| *Initial disadvantages (continued)* | |
|---|---|
| *Inputs* | *Outputs* |
| | Availability of a range of outputs measures can lead to confusion and a view of most measures as inadequate because they do not go 'all the way' |
| | Initial implementation may not involve credible verification and evaluation procedures. Many professional bodies report low levels of CPD record returns where they are not mandatory |
| | Use of reflection may lead some to consider a bias in favour of those who can 'tell a good story' without independent verification that may be introduced at a later stage |
| | Many systems cannot guarantee that competencies maintained or developed explicitly within a CPD framework will be satisfactorily executed in practice; i.e. link outputs to outcomes |

| *Long-term disadvantages* | |
|---|---|
| *Inputs* | *Outputs* |
| Visibility of mechanical or perfunctory compliance can encourage a climate and community of such attitudes to CPD | Outputs measures promise much. It may be a very long time before they can deliver reasonably accurate and robust measures of achievement of the aims of CPD |
| Visibility of abuse can encourage a climate and community of abusers and compliance complexity | CPD cannot guarantee up-to-date professionals |
| Both of the above can encourage cynicism towards CPD | Outputs measures can also be abused, though perhaps less easily than inputs measures |
| Network drag for umbrella bodies as some jurisdictions find it difficult to switch from inputs measurement systems | |

the eyes of some. Abuses are relatively transparent. Getting a friend to sign in for oneself or falling asleep at a lecture is a public act and can rapidly become widely known among a community of practitioners. It leads to an impression that others are not taking CPD seriously, though outputs systems can also be abused.

The more fundamental criticism of inputs measures is that they do not directly indicate whether any learning, change in behaviour or impact on the organization or on clients/patients has occurred. Measuring only by inputs implies that all CPD activities allowed under the scheme will be of sufficient quality to lead to professional development and that individual participants will be sufficiently attentive and receptive to reap that development.

There are subtle difficulties with what activities practitioners carry out for their CPD credits that will not be picked up by inputs measures. Not only may practitioners pick activities that are convenient (by time or location) rather than beneficial, but they may also choose topics that they are familiar with or that they find particularly interesting, but which will not lead to improvements for the client or patient (Revel and Yussuf 2003).

### 7.2.6 Evaluating outputs-based approaches: the value of Professional Development Value measurement

Outputs measures directly attempt to provide evidence of what CPD is intended to achieve: that is, PDV. This can be of value to professionals, to professional bodies and to other stakeholders in the CPD field (particularly clients and employers as well as the general public).

Measuring PDV from CPD is of value to individual practitioners because it can provide a way of:

1  organizing their CPD that allows for a sense of progression;
2  setting and achieving targets that may act as a motivator to keep on with CPD;
3  displaying achievements to employers and future employers to support career development;
4  displaying achievements to clients/patients and thereby raising the profile of their competence and professionalism.

Measuring PDV is of value to professional bodies because it can provide a way of:

1  being of use to members thereby binding members to the professional body;
2  raising the reputation of that profession and encouraging more to try to enter it, thereby raising the quality of the pool of new entrants;
3  raising the profile of the profession with government and thereby both reducing the chances of more heavy-handed regulation and increasing the likelihood of that profession being granted certain market privileges (such as requiring practitioners in new areas to have the qualifications of that professional body or to be licensed by that body).

The cost of outputs-based CPD measurement systems based on self-assessment and without substantial audit are low, though such systems can suffer from a lack of credibility. For audit to be credible substantial investment is required. Even if most of the substantial time required for audit is borne by volunteers, the cost of co-ordinating CPD auditors and of training them can be considerable (Friedman and Woodhead 2008).

Professional bodies that have attempted to measure outcomes, particularly effects on practice or organization, have experienced high costs and some dissatisfaction among individual members. There is a danger that outputs measures will turn members off CPD. According to a representative from the UK CIC:

> You start to move into the whole business of license to practice . . . unless you are formally seen to be competent in a particular area, should you be given license to practice? I think that probably, as the institutions stand at the moment, [that is] a bridge too far. At the end of the day, all those institutions are in the numbers game and if you make the rules too hard then you don't get as many members joining or . . . [staying] on as members.
>
> (Friedman and Woodhead 2008: 137)

PDV measurement serves the public interest in three different ways:

1  Most directly, measuring output will presumably encourage more CPD that has higher outputs or higher PDV. This will presumably lead to improved quality, reduced cost and more rapid introduction of new professional services.
2  Less directly, improved professional services will benefit entire economies and societies due to more ethically and technically competent services improving general quality of life and increasing a sense of security or trust in professional services available.
3  Indirectly, it may encourage more individuals in society to take a more professional approach to their work, more occupations to adopt CPD schemes that will raise productivity and effectiveness, thereby leading to improved economic and social benefits.

However, these latter benefits may be a long way off. As we have noted, CPD and ways of measuring PDV from CPD are not well understood.

Outputs measures are likely to improve in future due to improvements in online technology, establishment of standards in auditing and off-the-shelf training of auditors. This may be cumulative. Improvements in the supply of outputs-based measurement techniques stimulate growth in demand for such systems, as pressure on professional bodies to provide systems that generate evidence of continuing competence and professionalism in their fields grows, and as what can be achieved improves and becomes more widely known.

Overall, experiences of professional bodies that have switched to outputs-based systems have been positive. A number of individuals within those professional bodies who had been sceptical of the change have become 'converts' (Friedman and Woodhead 2008: 89).

## 7.3 Measuring Professional Development Value (PDV)

In Section 1.4 we introduced the concept of Professional Development Value to indicate the aims of CPD as set out in either a statement of aims, or embedded in the definition of CPD used by the professional body. Measuring PDV is to judge the impact of CPD on the professional development of all the individuals meant to be participating in it. PDV varies by professional body. Some emphasize development of professionalism, accentuating reflection, ethics and continuity of development activities. Others concentrate more narrowly on closely defined competencies to be acquired or to be kept up-to-date. For others a wider and more roughly defined notion of long-term competence development is emphasized. To identify and measure the contribution of a scheme to PDV that would apply to all different schemes, a complex and comprehensive model is required. This is the aim of the model presented below.

The PDV of a CPD scheme can only be judged, in our opinion, by examining its contribution through a complete progression around the CPD cycle, and may require several circuits of the cycle. If a single circuit has a large impact on the individual's professionalism, the CPD scheme can be said to have a high PDV.

Ideally, a measurement technique will be capable of detecting the correct PDV of a CPD circuit and of particular phases of the CPD cycle. Outputs measures have the capability of identifying PDV, and the model illustrates the extent to which various types of outputs measurement fulfil this capability: that is, according to their ability to reliably and accurately detect and measure the achievement of aims (or purposes) of CPD in the broadest sense.

It is possible for a practitioner to achieve high Professional Development Value (achieve the purposes of CPD to a high degree) from their participation in CPD without it being detected by an outputs measurement system. A high PDV may be achieved without following any formal CPD programme at all, by doing what professionals 'just do'. They may attend events and reflect on their experiences, implement new ideas in their practice after attending lectures without filling out reflection forms and without submitting evidence of practice changes for peer reviews or practice assessments, without even producing evidence that they attended.

## 7.4 A model of CPD measurement and PDV

The model shown in Figure 7.1 is adapted from Friedman and Woodhead (2008). At its heart is the CPD cycle (Exhibit 1.2). The model includes a scale

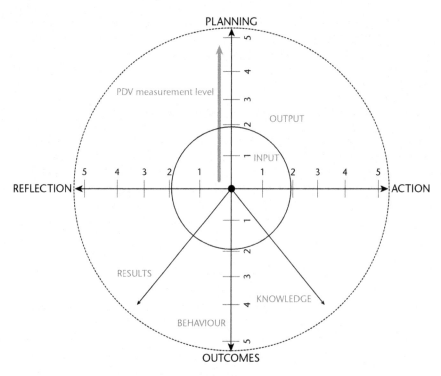

**FIGURE 7.1** Model of CPD measurement evaluation
*Source*: Adapted from Friedman and Woodhead (2008: 15).

at each phase of the cycle. Friedman and Woodhead (2008: 11) refer to the position of the technique on the scale as the 'PDV measurement level', that is, the level of accuracy with which the technique can detect or measure PDV. This is composed of:

- The accuracy with which the measurement scheme can distinguish between different PDVs. Low accuracy indicates a system that could only identify whether or not any PDV had been achieved. Greater accuracy could identify the attainment of low, medium or high PDV. A highly accurate measurement system would discern even more levels between 'medium' and 'high', or could distinguish the distance between these categories (a cardinal measure).
- The highest PDV the measurement scheme is capable of detecting. For example, inputs measures can only (at best) demonstrate that something was done, without detecting the value or impact of that activity. There is a range of maximum levels of PDV outputs measures can achieve. A low maximum PDV at the outcomes stage of the CPD cycle is self-assessment as to whether learning objectives have been met. Such a scheme does not

detect whether the learning objectives are high or low, or how well CPD has improved practice. CPD may have led to huge PDV for a particular individual, but this outputs scheme could not detect the magnitude of this value with any accuracy beyond the subjective opinion of the practitioner.

PDV measurement as depicted in the Friedman and Woodhead model was based only on evident or surface accuracy of detection as defined above. They did not consider reliability of measurement techniques used. This would require substantial research among many practitioners and over a considerable period of time. This work is yet to be done.

The outcomes phase of the CPD cycle has been split into three rays. They may seem to form a natural sequence. First, new knowledge is gained. Second, that knowledge is applied, leading to changes in behaviour and possibly changes in attitudes towards that knowledge and expertise as well as towards the achievement of improved practice and organization outcomes. The highest level of result and the one closest to the overall aims of CPD is for changes in knowledge, behaviour and attitudes to lead to effects on those receiving and otherwise influenced by the outcomes of CPD: that is, to make demonstrable differences to client wellbeing and/or to organizational goals.[7]

While each ray is a separate scale that represents measurement techniques applied to that phase of the CPD cycle, by itself it would not accurately indicate the PDV an individual has achieved. PDV measurement must be based on the combined level achieved over all phases of the cycle. Each ray contributes to overall PDV, but not necessarily in an additive or consistent manner. As Friedman and Woodhead note (2008: 14):

> Higher levels on reflection may contribute more to overall macro-measurement of PDV when they are combined with higher levels on planning, than when they are combined with lower levels on planning.[8]

Friedman and Woodhead specified five main PDV levels on each ray, marking significant points in the progressive accuracy of the measurement system based on the cases they studied. These levels have different significance for each phase. The inner circle on the model shows the boundary between inputs and outputs measures. The outer circle represents the 'frontier' of CPD measurement: the most sophisticated outputs measurement system that can currently be envisaged. This is likely to 'expand' over time as new techniques and new schemes are introduced.

This model does not depict an individual's CPD output or their PDV, nor does it show the value of a professional body's actual CPD scheme as a whole. Rather it is a way of judging the value of a CPD measurement scheme. Table 7.5 shows the criteria for judging measures of contribution to PDV for each ray as developed by Friedman and Woodhead.

**TABLE 7.5** Criteria for judging each dimension of the PDV model

| Value | Planning | Activity | Outcomes | Reflection |
|---|---|---|---|---|
| 0-1 | | Note of activities | | |
| 1 | | Record of hours | | |
| 1+ | | Record of hours plus evidence of attendance<br>---<br>Points system<br>---<br>Evidence of participation | | |
| 2 | Goals set<br>---<br>Assess needs<br>---<br>Planned activities/ timescale | | Use/impact of learning alluded to<br>----<br>Questions to aid self-assessment<br>---<br>Assess against learning objectives yes/no | Open-ended |
| 3 | Structured review of role plus expectations<br>---<br>Loose competency framework | | More structure to self-assessment<br>---<br>Criteria for different levels for self-assessment<br>---<br>Audit of self-assessment | Structured review of role/ situation<br>---<br>Group reflection |
| 4 | | | Objective scoring in combination with self-assessment | Question templates<br>---<br>Questions linked to competencies<br>---<br>Audit of reflection records |

**TABLE 7.5** Criteria for judging each dimension of the PDV model (continued)

| Value | Planning | Activity | Outcomes | Reflection |
|---|---|---|---|---|
| 4+ | Detailed competency framework | | Objective assessment methods | |
| | --- | | --- | |
| | Online planner | | Peer/client appraisal | |
| | --- | | --- | |
| | Link point allocation to different competencies | | Objective statistical benchmarking | |
| | | | --- | |
| | --- | | Mixed assessment for different aspects | |
| | Prioritization | | of CPD | |
| | --- | | | |
| | Individualization | | | |

The general guide for the specification of level on each ray was as follows:

1 Inputs.
2 Inputs/outputs frontiers.
3 Outputs measurement of relatively low sophistication and accuracy.
4 Outputs measure of medium to high sophistication and accuracy.
5 Outputs measure at the limit of available sophistication and accuracy, pioneer techniques in use.

Friedman and Woodhead only felt confident enough in their observations (based on 15 case studies) to award a level of 4+ rather than 5. In addition, they cautioned:

> what is indicated on the scales are not stable points, in the sense that the building of one step on earlier ones need follow the same order for all professional bodies. Some professional bodies may begin the planning support with a simple tool that asks individuals to review their role. Others may begin straightaway with a detailed competency framework for the profession.

(2008: 16)

Achieved PDV measurement levels will depend on how techniques are applied. For some techniques, PDV measurement achieved will depend on which other techniques they are combined with. For example, online planners in the planning scale, by themselves, will not provide much of an indicator of a high level of PDV in planning, unless they rest on a detailed competency framework.

The action phase scale only stretches from 0 to 2. Measurement of action or activities is by definition measurement of inputs, though outputs can be inferred from inputs. If the range of activities allowed is limited to accredited activities, higher levels of PDV are more likely to result. In the table a distinction is made between merely recording activities or hours and a points system. We regard a points system as more likely to indicate PDV. More than distinguishing what is allowed from what is not, a points system allows one to judge by how much activities should count.

The outcomes scale has no values between 0 and 2. Level 0 can indicate no outcomes are measured, but if any outcomes are registered this must be at level 2 or above and not within the inputs circle on the model.

It is possible to discern tentative principles from Friedman and Woodhead's work based on confidence in the ability of the measurement system to identify both fine gradations of PDV and higher levels of it. These would be:

• Use of self-assessment.
• Use of audit to supplement self-assessment.
• Use of external assessors, i.e. examiners or peers or clients.

These are stages in the achievement of objectivity in the measurement and contribute to confidence in the accuracy of the measuring instrument. This may be controversial. The presumption is that professionals cannot be completely trusted to produce accurate records of the PDV of their CPD. This presumption is made not only on the basis that they may make mistakes, or even cheat, but also on the presumption that they may not know what high PDV is. They may be unaware of by how much CPD can contribute to personal and practice outcomes. This may require a knowledgeable and sensitive outside observer. Though some may say use of external assessors could reduce PDV by encouraging a compliance mentality.

Confidence in the accuracy of the measuring instrument is not the same as the fineness of the measure itself. For this to be judged it is necessary to develop other criteria. This is being encouraged through competency frameworks. Competency frameworks vary enormously. The following levels may correlate with increasing accuracy of the measurement of PDV based on them.

• Use of loose competency framework with few broad competencies specified.
• Use of detailed framework in terms of many different competencies specified.
• Use of detailed framework with specification of mixes of competencies required for certain roles, both specified horizontally and vertically and/or use of judgement on extent of achievement of different competencies based on clear criteria with examples. What is one able to do, or what equipment

can one use to achieve particular results that would be matched to particular roles, including a hierarchy of roles.

While this progression describes finer calibrations of PDV, how these competencies are formulated will be important. Higher PDV will be associated with competencies to produce particular outcomes for clients or organizations.

The history of CPD measurement can be sketched on the model presented in this section. First there was movement along the activity ray representing inputs (from merely collecting incidents of participation, to requiring hours and then to requiring points). Then there was outward movement along the other rays, perhaps first only for knowledge outcomes as well as simple plans and free-form reflection statements, and later measures of behaviour and practice outcomes resulting from participation in CPD activities through self-assessment forms. These movements continue outwards as stages of the CPD cycle are measured more strictly and more objectively (audit and peer or client review). In effect this would be a change from measuring what and how much professional development activities are undertaken, towards identifying and then measuring their Professional Development Value.

Using the model to trace the history of CPD measurement is only crudely accurate. There is a trend towards outputs measures and towards more effort and objectivity in the nature of the measures: from stand alone self-assessment, to audited self-assessment[9] and then to assessment by others. However, some professional bodies collected outputs information near the beginning of the CPD field (Rapkins 1996) using planning and reflection forms based on self-assessment. In addition, from the outset, some formal CPD activities carried with them measures of knowledge outcomes. Courses as part of Master's degrees and diplomas awarded by higher and further education institutions would have provided those enrolled with certificates indicating performance on examinations and project assessments carried out by independent academics.

## 7.5 Applying the model to particular professional bodies

Figures 7.2 and 7.3 show how the model was used in Friedman and Woodhead (2008). The model provides a map onto which the positions of a professional body on each scale are plotted to create a star or radar diagram. Figure 7.2 shows the CPD measurement map of the Chartered Institute of Management Accountants (CIMA). Note how extended the planning and reflection points of their 'star' diagram are. CIMA has a particularly strong planning side to its CPD programme. The single planning phase of a typical four-phase CPD cycle is elaborated into three phases in the CIMA six-phase cycle (Define, Assess, Design, Act, Reflect, Evaluate). Members must define their role and break it down into key responsibilities and then assess their position in terms of that role. They must also explicitly consider whether they are meeting the needs of

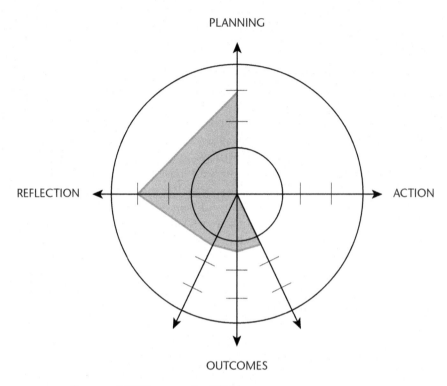

PLANNING

REFLECTION

ACTION

OUTCOMES

**FIGURE 7.2** Suggested PDV pattern for CIMA
*Source*: Adapted from Friedman and Woodhead (2008: 27).

various stakeholders. An online planner with an attached 'competency land-scape' is provided for members to identify competence gaps and work out how best to address them; that is, to design their own set of CPD activities. At the reflection stage there is a set of questions intended to guide not only individual reflection, but also one-to-one peer dialogue and group reflection in workshops.

This is a clear example of CPD focused on personal and professional development. Monitoring concerns the way practitioners plan their CPD and reflect on it, rather than on measuring outcomes. In fact CIMA's CPD programme used to be called CPPD, Continuing Personal and Professional Development. CIMA note that for them CPD compliance is based on trust: 'it is the responsibility of members to assess their development goals and needs, select the most appropriate activities, and design their CPD programmes accordingly' (CIMA 2010).

A quite different outputs measurement scheme was that of the Institute of Auditors in Germany [Institut der Wirtschaftsprüfer in Deutschland E.V., in Friedman and Woodhead (2008: 45)] as shown in Figure 7.3.

This looks like an inputs-based system in that hours are recorded: an average of 40 per year. However, the Institute carries out practice audits to check that the content of CPD requirements have been incorporated; that is, to check that

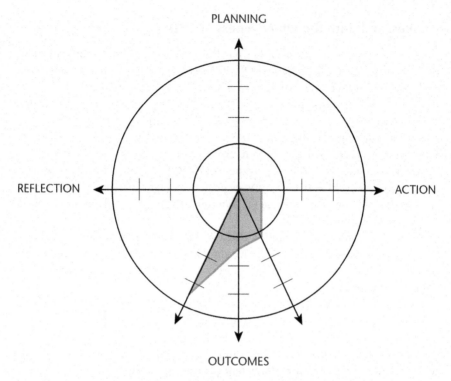

**FIGURE 7.3** Suggested PDV pattern for Institute of Auditors in Germany
*Source*: Adapted from Friedman and Woodhead (2008: 45).

the practice is using up-to-date methods. Therefore rather than auditing CPD records, the quality of the practice work itself is audited. This is a peer review: different firms visit one another, monitored by an independent oversight board. If deficiencies are found, a further investigation is undertaken in which practitioners are interviewed, and invoices and CPD attendance sheets are examined. This is to ensure the firm has both carried out audits properly and maintained a system to monitor CPD. Compulsory audits are carried out every three years for large firms and every six years for smaller ones. No record of learning or reflection is required, though larger firms use such a system for annual performance reviews of employees. The Institute is more concerned with monitoring companies than individuals and it is only the auditing skills of the auditors that are of concern, rather than their wider role as an accountant:

> literature in any form does not count at all, because you can always say that you've read so many articles, but you can never really prove that. So we've taken out all the soft skills and the leadership skills people tend to go there and then just assume that they are going to be granted CPD credits, which is of course wrong.
>
> (Friedman and Woodhead 2008: 156)

## 7.6 Research into the effectiveness of CPD

Interestingly, the little research that has been carried out on the effectiveness of CPD at achieving Professional Development Value has primarily been carried out on CPD schemes where the policy of the professional bodies has been to measure it by inputs. Wessels (2007), examined effectiveness of mandatory Continuing Professional Education (CPE) requirement of the 40 hours of courses a year required of accountants in North Carolina, USA since 1985.[10] In effect, this was the study of outputs from an inputs-based system. The CPAs were asked to self-assess the effectiveness of the CPE courses they had taken in the previous year. Effectiveness was evaluated by eight questions ranked on a five-point scale (strongly agree, agree, neutral, disagree, strongly disagree). The results are shown in Table 7.6.

A problem with this research is that it is based on self-assessment without audit or other triangulation or objective support, and assessment long after some of the events as well.[11] These very supports are what professional bodies provide with outputs measures.

Nevertheless, Wessel's data indicate that a substantial majority of CPAs believed that CPE helps improve the image of their profession and that it increases their knowledge base, the latter being a key outcome in the model presented below. On whether CPE courses contribute to competency and help to protect the public from incompetent professionals, assessments were positive, with 60 per cent and 48 per cent respectively agreeing, but with 16 per cent and 28 per cent disagreeing. It is also worth noting that the more personal and material self-interest motivations are not supported. CPE is regarded as effective for increasing employability by only 31 per cent (roughly similar to the 23 per cent who disagreed). A far larger percentage disagreed than agreed that CPE enhances or increases income or earnings.

The question of whether CPD is effective will be answered somewhat differently depending on the perspective of those who ask the question. Wessels' questions reflect concerns of the professionals themselves. In this, professional associations will be interested in very similar things, though perhaps they will be more concerned with a more detailed calculation that distinguishes between the PDV from different suppliers and of different types of activities; that is, their evaluations will be more concerned with operational issues such as which suppliers to accredit and for which subjects should supply be encouraged. In this the professional association will be interested in inputs measures as well as outputs measures.

On the other hand, regulatory bodies and professional associations with regulatory functions will be more interested in outcomes and particularly client/patient or consumer outcomes. Other stakeholders will be almost exclusively interested in what may be regarded as the set of ultimate outcomes, improvement of the condition of those who receive professional services that have been affected by CPD. There has been work on these issues, particularly on the

**TABLE 7.6** Self-assessed effectiveness of CPE by accountants in the USA

| Effectiveness statement | Strongly agree or agree | Strongly disagree or disagree |
|---|---|---|
| When CPAs are required to take CPE courses, it helps improve the image of the profession | 85.2% | 4.4% |
| CPE courses generally enhance or increase my current knowledge base | 85.5% | 3.5% |
| CPE courses generally provide valuable contact with experts in the field | 58.7% | 10.3% |
| When CPAs are required to take CPE courses, it makes it more likely that CPAs are competent | 60.3% | 15.9% |
| CPE courses generally provide useful networking opportunities with peers | 48.7% | 13.0% |
| When CPAs are required to take CPE courses, it helps protect the public from incompetent professionals | 48.0% | 27.5% |
| CPE courses generally enhance or increase my employability | 31.2% | 22.5% |
| CPE courses generally enhance or increase my income/earnings | 15.9% | 38.1% |

*Source:* Adapted from Wessels, S.B. (2007) 'Accountants' perceptions of the effectiveness of mandatory Continuing Professional Education', *Accounting Education*, 16(4): 365–78. Reprinted by permission of the publisher, Taylor & Francis Ltd, http://www.informaworld.com.

effectiveness of training and learning and development programmes organized by employers. This is not the same as CPD, but the techniques for measuring effectiveness and the vast number of serious problems facing those who attempt to measure effectiveness are similar. These studies will be discussed in Section 9.7.

## 7.7 Conclusions

The expected positive effects of measurement are that it:

1 Provides targets and progress reports to help practitioners benchmark themselves against a standard.
2 Provides incentives and sanctions to encourage compliance and discourage non-compliance of practitioners.
3 Provides more appropriate evidence that practitioners and professional bodies can use to demonstrate PDV achievements.
4 Encourages trust by clients and employers in the professionalism of practitioners.
5 Encourages trust and raises the reputation of the professional body and the profession as a whole.

6 Raises the reputation or reduces the challenges to the reputation of all professionals and of professionalism itself as not being worth the status and economic benefits they enjoy.

These are, by and large, the same benefits of CPD itself. Arguably, outputs measures, and particularly outcomes measures, if they are validated, enhance the value of CPD on items 4–6 above and add the special contribution of items 1–3.

There are reasons why measurement of CPD may not be a good idea. Professional Development Value of CPD can exist without being measured. For some, it is enhanced without being measured or even formally organized. According to the traditional view, professionals should be trusted to know what is needed to maintain and develop themselves and to do what is required to achieve what is needed. Once qualified, not only do professionals have the expertise to begin to practise in a competent and trustworthy manner, but also they can be relied upon to continue to do so throughout their professional career.

Measurement may be regarded as at the heart of the fundamental paradox of CPD. The argument against measurement is reminiscent of the popular view of the Heisenberg Uncertainty Principle:[12] that measuring something alters it in unpredictable ways. In physics the uncertainty principle only applies to atomic and sub-atomic level particles. However, in social science or popular science this is sometimes called the observer effect (also known as reactivity).[13] People change their behaviour when they perceive they are being watched. Of course measurement and monitoring is intended to have an effect. Beyond merely recording what professionals just do, it can encourage them to act so they will be measured favourably or at least so that they will achieve the standard required: a strategic measurement effect. Some will be motivated to do more, others will use their understanding of the measurement system to do less than they might have done or will waste their time trying to do less. There will be a focus on what is measured and what can be displayed, rather than what is actually achieved. While it is relatively easy to measure knowledge it is harder to measure the ability to use knowledge appropriately or competently. While it is relatively easy to measure competencies, it is harder to measure competence. Changes in behaviour are observable, but changes in attitudes are much harder to discern, never mind measure. Changes in practice and particularly in quality of services delivered to employers and clients/patients are also very difficult to measure, especially as deterioration or improvements may only occur over a long period.

This leads to the problem that Snadden (1999) pointed out in relation to the use of portfolios of certificates of CPD participation cited at the beginning of this chapter. Outputs measurements represent a move towards measuring the relevant, but if it is not straightforward and can be expensive, so CPD may continue to be measuring the less relevant.

One reason for the lack of public appreciation of CPD is the plethora of systems different professional bodies use to measure it. It will be difficult to inform clients/patients and employers, much less the general public, of what CPD is and what it can contribute to professional competence and trustworthiness if the extent and quality of CPD carried out by individuals cannot be communicated in a manner allowing comparisons across the professions. The model outlined in this chapter offers a way for professional bodies to view their CPD measurement systems as a whole, and to allow them to benchmark their systems against others more easily. This can be a step towards developing a system whereby the public will be able to recognize and appreciate how CPD can contribute to their confidence in professionals.

# Part III

In Part III we draw together our view of the fundamental mystery of CPD noted in the Introduction. Why is it that something that is potentially so important and significant for the economic and social wellbeing of all society is not widely recognized as such?

We return to themes discussed in Part I: complexity, different visions of CPD, different ways of interpreting how CPD is changing and is likely to change in future, and the implications of this for the stakeholders or players in and around the CPD field as well as for professionalism itself.

We begin with a statement linking the complexity of CPD with what we term the fundamental 'paradox' of CPD, and these are used to help understand the fundamental mystery of CPD. Why has CPD had little impact on government policy and general discourse through the mass media?

We then address other broad questions posed in the Introduction. What does the coming of CPD imply for society and the economy as a whole? What does it imply for the way in which people interact and for their economic prospects? Is the potential for CPD's influence likely to be realized in the foreseeable future?

We can only speculate on these issues. They are tackled from three perspectives. First, the internal logic of CPD or rather various visions of CPD are extrapolated. Second, the likely effects of changes in the environment of the field on it in future are explored. Third, the changes that CPD is likely to stimulate in the environment of the field that are likely to cause long-term changes to the field.

We conclude with a number of issues that will impact on these speculations about the future of CPD. Issues that are likely to tip the balance of forces and visions in the field in different directions: whether professional bodies are able to act in concert to raise the profile and the quality of CPD, and whether CPD will remain under the governance of professional bodies, or migrate to the provenance of employers or governments.

# 8

# COMPLEXITY, PARADOX AND MYSTERY

## Potential of CPD yet to be realized

*Trust and autonomy. Proof of competence and personal development. Can these pairings be (made) compatible? Have perceived incompatibilities held back recognition of CPD?*

## 8.1 Introduction

CPD is complex, paradoxical and something of a mystery. Complex in that it attempts to achieve multiple aims, some of which are incompatible or lead to policies and procedures that are incompatible. CPD is paradoxical in that it attempts to reveal, and in many cases to structure and control, an essentially private context-initiated collection of actions and morally driven habits. The mystery is that CPD barely registers with the general public, it is rarely the subject of government policy and is only recently attracting academic research in spite of it being a widespread practice for the past 30 years. Here we argue that the complexity and paradox help explain the mystery.

## 8.2 Complexity: multiple aims

Definitions cited in Chapter 1 show that CPD is intended within the professional bodies sector to be all of the following:

- a way of ensuring that professionals are up to date and competent, aimed primarily at reassuring clients, employers, government agencies or the general public;
- a way of supporting professionals' personal and professional development, by both:
  - allowing them to take control of their competence and their careers in an era when professional careers need tending, by operating a framework that encourages planning, reflection and evaluation of training and education activities they undertake and consider undertaking; and
  - strengthening their own internalized ethic of professional integrity.

These aims need not be incompatible, but the ways they are pursued can easily be, and the different policies and procedures appropriate to each are likely to diverge more and more as the aims are closer to being achieved. Proof of competence at its heart requires objective independent assessment. Personal and professional development is unlikely to: rather self-assessment is critical. Proof of competence suggests a need for summative assessment, while for personal and professional development formative assessment is more appropriate, to the extent that assessment is required at all.[1]

Personal and professional development is at its heart, internally driven and idiosyncratic. A critical aspect of professional working is a substantial degree of individual autonomy.[2] Professionals need an orbit of freedom to decide what services to provide, guided by what the client (or employer) requests and what they know or can find out. Similarly, they need considerable latitude to decide what they need to find out to support their decisions and service provided. Much of what they do to keep up their competence, and to develop themselves in the longer term, will depend on personal and context-specific factors. It will depend on their curiosity and their moral commitment to reading and seeking out other learning opportunities. It will depend on challenges and conundrums thrown up by day-to-day practice. It will depend on chance conversations with colleagues, sometimes at seminars and conferences. Often even at those times, conversations that do not directly follow the official programme of topics, and take place at breaks or on the way home can be relevant. To be effective it is important that professionals put themselves into situations that will allow them to receive such information and to discuss issues with members of their professional community, without having to anticipate exactly what they will learn. This cannot easily be tested with traditional examination methods. Informal knowledge and the recognition of patterns of problem presentation, which require apprentice-like guidance from mentors and colleagues, have been widely recognized by analysts of professional working (Schön 1983; Eraut 2000).

On the other hand, proof of competence must be standardized in some way, if it is to be read by others as proof, if it is to be transparent and credible. A common language of competency needs to be created. Competency frameworks are being developed in many professions and within many large organizations employing professionals. These may be regarded as early versions of such a language. Currently these frameworks are largely profession-specific. They all have design features that defy easy translation across professions. How many levels of achievement are identified and how are they distinguished? Is there merely a rise in the standard of competency for each level, such as distinguishing apprentice, journeyman and master – or novice, practitioner and expert – or is there a new quality introduced at higher levels, such as for the RICS (2008), with reasoned advice being added at the top level as well as depth of technical knowledge. In effect hundreds of 'sub-languages' are being created with reference to individual professions and different specialities within them. These can be 'read' by others in the profession or specialty, but do not provide what proof of competence is intended to convey – reassurance to non-professionals, to employers and/ or clients/patients that the individual professional can be trusted to provide a service up to the expected standard. Proof of competence requires a compulsory policy, strict monitoring and a measurement system that allows this proof to be conveyed easily to stakeholders.

## 8.3 Complexity: multiple visions associated with alternative and overlapping concepts

A second aspect of the complexity of CPD is that it overlaps to differing degrees with many other concepts. At the time of the coming of CPD these potentially overlapping concepts were held by different groups that have become players and stakeholders in the CPD field. As the new field emerged, these more established concepts have affected the way different players view CPD. They have become the basis for different visions of CPD. Some of these pre-existing views have not been affected by CPD, though it would seem logical that they would be. Arguably some of these views have retarded the development of CPD. Their strength has in effect crowded CPD out of the vision of certain stakeholders, or rather CPD has not developed sufficiently to impact on the visions of these stakeholders.

### 8.3.1 Largely compatible concepts and visions: Visions 1 and 2

The following are initial views of activities that have become CPD in the eyes of individual professionals in particular:

- Social and educational activities professionals just did as part of the community of practice.
- Individualized or private things professionals just did to maintain their competence such as reading, seeking advice from colleagues.
- Career development activities such as taking courses.

These we have grouped together as Vision 1. Professionals would have been most likely to hold this vision and act toward CPD with dispositions or habitus shaped by these concepts. This is a positive vision of CPD but perhaps frustrating for some. It would encourage professionals to undertake CPD as a formalization of what they would have done anyway and it can support career development. However, it can also stimulate resentment of CPD as an unnecessary burden, a waste of time given that it requires recording what individuals had been doing anyway informally.

Those running professional associations would have viewed CPD through the lens of Vision 2 and seen it in terms of the following concepts:

- A way of increasing participation in professional body activities.
- A member service in itself that professional associations can offer.
- A source of income.[3]

Concepts behind Vision 2 are clearly compatible with the coming of CPD. Education was already a concern of professional associations in designing syllabuses and accrediting providers of initial professional qualifications. Some may have been concerned that some of their former functions in this regard were being taken over by universities and further education institutions. In this they are likely to have embraced investment in post-qualification education. Concerns of professional associations to provide services valued by members and to raise revenues have become more acute, with criticisms of the professions of the early 1970s and the general decline in membership of voluntary associations from the 1970s referred to in Chapter 3 (Putnam 2000).

Concepts behind Visions 1 and 2 can be regarded as mutually compatible and potentially self-reinforcing. Professional associations reinforce and in some instances create communities of practice through their branch, special interest and sectional networks. By credentializing informal and formal activities undertaken by professionals individually, as well as their community activities, they can contribute to career development of their members. This draws members closer to the association as they can (try to) use their CPD records to support annual appraisals, promotions and job applications. They can reduce professional indemnity insurance premiums and gain senior professional appellations such as Fellow and Chartered, which can help in marketing their professional services. In addition, they will be more willing to pay for activities provided by their professional association than if the incentive was purely inherent interest in the activity. This in turn can raise the reputation of the profession as well as encouraging more to join the profession and the professional association. This was the reason we described CPD as a potential 'killer application' for professional associations (Section 3.3).

### 8.3.2 Paradox and potentially confusing concepts associated with Vision 3

The situation becomes much more complicated when we consider another set of concepts that encourages another vision of CPD. In Vision 3, CPD is viewed as the third pillar of professional regulation and guided by the following concepts:

- Professional standards and competence.
- Consumer/client/patient protection.
- Public interest protection.
- Disciplinary mechanisms regulatory bodies can apply.

Ultimately, this vision associates CPD with a far more significant role in social life. If CPD can be linked to protection of clients and the general public through improvement of professional practice, it is likely to become as important for professionalism as implied in the Introduction. It may then be thought just a matter of time before CPD would be attended to by the media and government policy makers. It is logical that something like CPD should be devised in answer to the kind of criticism expressed by Milton Friedman (Section 3.5) that we have little reason to expect a physician (or any other professional) to be competent, based on qualifications earned decades earlier.

However, for CPD to take on these functions, it must to some extent clash with the positive feedback loop described above. If CPD is what professionals are expected to do by some authority, even if closely linked to their peers (if it is what professionals *must* do), then it can be regarded as more of a bureaucratic burden, particularly if the content of CPD activities is specified.

The paradox of CPD is that it supports, structures and formalizes a continuing lifelong process that cannot be clearly or completely pre-specified and must rely on the enthusiasm and sense of ethical obligation of individual professionals. It is an attempt to record and often to monitor a process that hitherto professionals have been trusted to do. It must do this without destroying professional autonomy, curbing their enthusiasm and sense of calling, or dulling their embrace of ethical obligations. CPD must rely on characteristics of professionals that arise from their autonomy and commitment to maintaining expected standards of service, while at the same time submitting professionals to scrutiny and assessment. They are autonomous, but are assessed as to whether they have been using their autonomy in appropriate ways. While the aim of CPD is to encourage trust that professionals are competent, it may be regarded as a sign that they are not trusted.[4]

In the past initial qualifications were accepted as certifying the assurance of a professional standard quality service. It has been in the nature of tasks that professions carry out, the occupations that are amenable to professionalization, for which the public have had to trust them to do whatever is needed to develop themselves and keep themselves up-to-date, without requiring them to prove this by more than displaying their initial qualifications and perhaps their membership in a professional body.

The nature of professional work, particularly for those who deal directly with clients, means precisely that what is required is not easily anticipated. It is almost impossible in advance to test a professional on all the techniques and resources required to deliver all the services they may be asked to provide in the future, even if that future is only the next year. Professionals themselves must seek out educational opportunities that suit the direction in which their particular practice is leading. Opportunities are presented to professionals in the form of journals and magazines sent to them by their professional body; the list of activities, events and courses organized or accredited by their professional body; and other sources of knowledge such as suppliers of equipment or materials used in practice or different kinds of education providers. Professionals must expend effort to take up these opportunities.

Most of these educational opportunities do not involve formal activities. It would be difficult to assess this activity or to specify in advance how much time they require. Many will involve searching until some required piece of information is found. For example browsing journals in adjacent fields, searching the internet, setting up and reading RSS feeds or Delicious accounts, wikis or blogs, conversations with colleagues either at the workplace or at events (which may be social rather than educational events) or through a social networking community such as LinkedIn or Facebook.

Ultimately CPD cannot act as a guarantee of competence. It can be a contributor and it can be assessed and so act as a measure of likely competence, much like initial qualifications. One way of doing this is to set CPD up in terms of revalidation or reassessment on a periodic basis. This can be used when one changes jurisdiction and when one changes career direction within a profession. In some fields, primarily medical ones, it is becoming the norm.

### 8.3.3 Competing concepts that could be associated with the CPD field: Visions 4 and 5

The following concepts that have fed into different visions (and potential visions) of CPD are currently held primarily by those we have called passive stakeholders: those affected by the field, but not affecting it at present.

Vision 4, held by commentators on the professions and some members of the public, refers to negative concepts that have been applied to professionals for centuries and could be applied to CPD:

- Conspiracy against the laity.
- A bastion of privilege with arcane symbols of privilege.
- Barrier to competition.
- Sham or merely aspirational window dressing.

Concepts associated with Vision 4 have had little play with CPD so far. In a sense these negative views of professionalism discourage close attention to aspects of professional behaviour that do not visibly affect the laity. For example, CPD is not directly referred to by professionals to justify raising professional fees. To the extent that CPD is thought about by those holding this vision of the professions, it is likely to be seen as symbolic of professional privilege. Along with grand offices in the heart of expensive London, the regalia and the honorific titles and post-nominals, CPD may be regarded as fancy conferences held at high-class venues, obscure-sounding journals and weighty lectures. If anything this view discourages looking closely at what CPD is intended to achieve. Rather this may be regarded as contributing to a latent view of CPD, one that may appear in future.

Arguably for this vision to become widespread and elaborated it requires CPD to have been taken seriously by many, or at least to appear to have been. However, this vision may work against those outside the core of players taking CPD seriously. It may come to influence policy makers against CPD and so needs to be addressed, particularly the concept of it being yet another sham or purely aspirational aspect of professionalism. This vision may have contributed to complications regarding the next vision of CPD.

Vision 5 refers to concepts held by educationalists and some government policy makers before and since the coming of CPD:

- Lifelong learning.
- Adult education.
- Recurrent education
- Continuing education.

These concepts might be expected to have encouraged CPD, particularly its provision by government-funded organizations. On the surface, and logically, CPD is a primary example of all these concepts. CPD is the lifelong learning of millions (Friedman and Afitska 2009). However, these concepts (at least the first two) have not been applied to CPD, nor have they encouraged CPD as much as one might expect. Though the concept of CPD was at first proposed and 'nursed' at university departments of adult education and continuing education, these institutions have not become the core of the CPD field. Rather the core has been primarily composed of professional bodies.

In part this has occurred because these departments have themselves been peripheral to the primary aims of universities. In part it is because these concepts have been interpreted as applying to remedial education and in policy terms, meant to encourage those who had missed out on education when young. We will speculate on whether this will change in the future in Chapter 11.

There is a link between Vision 4 and the meagre application of Vision 5 to CPD. The line of reasoning runs as follows. Professionals are seen as unjustified bastions of privilege. CPD is regarded as privileged activities of the professional 'class'. Lifelong learning is seen as remedial education for the less privileged in society who missed out on education when young. CPD is therefore not seen as lifelong learning. Certainly CPD is not seen as something that should be supported by government resources, even to the extent of encouraging research into it.

Employers of professionals are another set of stakeholders who might have been at the core of the CPD field and key players in it. Here we introduce a further vision. We argue that it was not particularly important at the beginning of CPD, but has grown as the CPD field has developed and arguably has had a negative effect on the CPD field.

## 8.4 Vision 6: CPD as training for professional employees

Some concepts have developed around the same time as the emergence of CPD, in part stimulated by the same conditions. Investment in company training for higher-level staff, particularly for managers, emerged in the late 1970s and early 1980s. The following concepts can be associated with CPD as a form of employer training.

- Company training for higher level staff.
- Development of shared organizational values connected to skills and competencies.
- Organizational learning (and development).
- Personal development plans and planning.
- The Learning Organization.
- Performance appraisal criteria.

These concepts may be regarded as competitors to CPD, though they need not be. CPD can be used for performance appraisal and it could be an important ingredient in company training and organization learning. However, the origins and early development of the CPD field, which could have been based in large employing organizations, particularly professional services firms, emerged elsewhere. CPD could have developed as an extension to apprentice-like arrangements offered by employers in co-operation with professional bodies (and sometimes higher education institutions) to cover post academic, pre-qualification activities. It is possible to imagine apprentice-like instruction organized for novices to be given to qualified professionals as their careers progress, in the same way that outcomes can be portable between companies for these apprentice-like pre-qualification periods of study such as law-firm training contracts and housemanship for doctors. However, there are barriers to portability of this way of proceeding among competing organizations.

First, there is a standard argument against spending on training by organizations; that the return to the investment in training will be lost to the company when trained individuals leave. If every company trains equally, this should not be a problem as incoming recruits will bring returns on training investments by other companies. However, there is a temptation to 'free ride' on training by others. These companies will have a competitive advantage due to lower costs and this will discourage others from training. Ultimately, very few companies will spend more than the minimum on training. Where there is substantial training, governments have had to provide subsidies, such as in Germany.[5]

Second, the dominant view of training in the management literature has emphasized the importance of linking it to the internal organization culture in order to strengthen shared commitment to the company.

Exhibit 8.1 shows how Peter Drucker, arguably the most influential 'management guru' and the father of modern management thinking, envisioned professionalism and professional learning within corporations.

Drucker's position is clear. Professionalization of management is to be resisted.[6] It leads managers away from involvement in the large corporation; away from the art of general management towards narrow specialisms and towards uniformity of thought (or rather unifying thought centred on fields other than the organization). Large corporations must provide opportunities for individuals to grow: to provide training and to protect this investment by promoting individuals within the corporation.

---

## EXHIBIT 8.1 DRUCKER ON PROFESSIONALISM AND MANAGEMENT

In every large-scale organization there is a natural tendency to discourage initiative and to put a premium on conformity. The large corporation often does not have the means to stop or even to discover the bureaucratic dry rot after it has set in. The premium on expert knowledge contributes substantially to this danger because it puts emphasis on the 'professional view' as does the isolated life which the average managerial employee of the large corporation often leads.

(Drucker 1993: 38)

. . . we certainly suffer from a tremendous overvaluation of the formal education offered today and of the diploma as a proof of attainment or ability. [There is a] failure of the corporation to provide opportunities in which a man can show his latent abilities. This is partly the result of the tendency towards excessive specialization which would be counteracted by the training of generally educated men.

(Drucker 1993: 143)

No greater damage could be done to our economy or to our society than to attempt to 'professionalize' management by 'licensing' managers, for instance, or by limiting access to management to people with a special academic degree . . . any serious attempt to make management 'scientific' or a 'profession' is bound to lead to the attempt to eliminate those 'disturbing nuisances', the unpredictabilities of business life – its risks, its ups and downs, its 'wasteful competition', the 'irrational choices' of the consumer – and, in the process, the economy's freedom and its ability to grow.

(Drucker 1989: 9–10)

This emphasis on company training as a contributor to company culture and shared values was given a strong stimulus in the West, influenced by the Japanese style of management that became of consummate interest with the Japanese competitive challenge in the 1970s, and was widely publicized in books appearing in the early 1980s (Baranson 1981; Ouchi 1981; Pascale and Athos 1981). A key aspect of the large Japanese company approach to employee relations has been to develop a long programme of induction training into the company on entry and to follow this up with internal study circles focusing on improving performance of groups.

The trend has continued with what has been the most popular management book of all time, *In Search of Excellence* by Peters and Waterman (1982). Peters worked at the very influential McKinsey management consultants where the 7S model of large company management was developed. The model places shared values at its heart, surrounded and interlinked with the other six 'S's: strategy, structure, systems, style, staff and skills. Exhibit 8.2 shows how Peters and Waterman envisioned learning as part of excellence and the importance they placed on values of the company.

Other management theorists recognize norms and policies that involve the role of framing and learning systems within the organization. Argyris and Schön (1978) regard the challenging of the organization's underlying norms, policies and objectives, or what they call the governing variables, to be the hallmark of a learning organization. There is a presumption here that the 'organizational skin'

---

**EXHIBIT 8.2 EXCELLENT COMPANIES ACCORDING TO PETERS AND WATERMAN**

1   A bias for action, active decision making – 'getting on with it'.
2   Close to the customer – *learning* from the people served by the business.
3   Autonomy and entrepreneurship – fostering innovation and nurturing 'champions'.
4   Productivity through people – treating rank and file employees as a source of quality.
5   Hands-on, *value-driven* – management philosophy that guides everyday practice – management showing its commitment.
6   Stick to the knitting – stay with the business that you know.
7   Simple form, lean staff – some of the best companies have *minimal HQ staff*.
8   Simultaneous loose–tight properties – autonomy in shop-floor activities plus *centralized values*.

> (Peters and Waterman 1982: note the terms emphasized in italics)

should be strong. Outside advice from 'experts' is to be subjected to critical review.

This way of thinking could be regarded as compatible with CPD if the organization is able to form a good relation with professional bodies in order to keep up the challenge to its governing variables, but it can also be regarded as largely anathema to CPD, if CPD is recognized to be a form of development for professionals organized according to the norms of their sector-specific professions, and largely by their professional bodies and anathema to organization-specific norms. Exhibit 8.3 demonstrates what Peter Senge (1990), the main popularizer, regarded as an ideal type or idealization of this line of thinking: the Learning Organization.

This ideal picture shows how organizations 'should' operate, rather than their actual practice, though Senge claims that some organizations approach this ideal and that his disciplines can be followed by others.

This is a particularly sophisticated picture and complex in relation to CPD. Senge recognizes the danger of very strong internalized cultures. With something like lifelong employment and strong pressures against staff leaving the company, they develop a mindset that is impervious to outside ideas. The 'not invented here' syndrome that can arise from this management strategy can render a company vulnerable to major shifts in technology and its general competitive environment. CPD has the potential to counter this problem, particularly by encouraging personal mastery, but it can also weaken the internal culture of the company.

## 8.5 Confusion among players and stakeholders

Complexity contributes to confusion about CPD in that many will hold more than one of these visions, not merely because there are different aims of CPD, or because they align with the interests of different categories of players or stakeholders, but also because CPD can be valued and 'used' in many different ways. CPD can be viewed as both a member service and a form of lifelong learning to people working in professional associations. Sometimes this can hamper CPD. Those in regulatory bodies may regard it as a form of public protection, but may also consider it to be relatively weak compared with other forms of professional regulation and may therefore also regard it as something of an aspirational policy. Some employers will associate their own training programmes with CPD, but others will see CPD as anathema to their attempts to create a strong organization culture. However, even the latter may use evidence of CPD when they have to hire experienced professionals.

These differences are changing too. Professional associations are also coming to see the maintenance of competence as part of how they can raise the reputation of their profession thereby protecting the public, and regulatory bodies are coming to develop or accredit courses and activities that support CPD rather than merely monitoring what is carried out and applying sanctions.

## EXHIBIT 8.3 LEARNING ORGANIZATIONS ACCORDING TO PETER SENGE

> . . . organizations where people continually expand their capacity to create the results they truly desire, where new and expansive patterns of thinking are nurtured, where collective aspiration is set free, and where people are continually learning to see the whole together.
>
> (Senge 1990: 3)

Learning Organizations use five component technologies or 'disciplines', each of which involves practices, principles and an essential state of being of those who have mastered them:

1 Personal mastery – individuals must develop a vision and recognize their ignorance and incompetence in relation to this vision as well as their growth areas. They are confident in their vision and their progress towards it. It involves a spiritual level beyond expertise, a commitment to truth and a commitment to the vision as a calling. This clearly is connected to the vision of a professional.

2 Mental models – 'deeply ingrained assumptions, generalizations, or even pictures and images that influence how we understand the world and how we take action . . . [this discipline] starts with turning the mirror inward; learning to unearth our internal pictures of the world, to bring them to the surface and hold them rigorously to scrutiny. It also includes the ability to carry on "learningful" conversations that balance inquiry and advocacy, where people expose their own thinking effectively and make that thinking open to the influence of others' (Senge 1990: 8–9). Senge is influenced by Schön's (1983) notion of the repertoire of models professionals use for reflection. However, this is only one of the five disciplines and by itself can become entrenched and thwart needed changes.

3 Building shared vision – genuine commitment rather than simple compliance is encouraged by revealing shared 'pictures of the future'. For leaders to merely dictate their own vision without clarifying, sharing and engaging others in it will be counter-productive.

4 Team learning – 'the discipline of team learning starts with 'dialogue', the capacity of members of a team to suspend assumptions and enter into a genuine 'thinking together'. To the Greeks dia-logos meant a free-flowing of meaning, through a group, allowing the group to discover insights not attainable individually' (Senge 1990: 10). 'The process of aligning and developing the capacities of a team to create the results its members truly desire' (Senge 1990: 236).

5    Systems thinking – this involves appreciating certain concepts such as that actions have consequences that may be delayed and depend on feedback loops. More broadly it concerns 'a shift of mind from seeing parts to seeing wholes, from seeing people as helpless reactors to seeing them as active participants in shaping their reality, from reacting to the present to creating the future' (Senge 1990: 69).

Systems thinking, the fifth discipline, integrates the others. All the disciplines are important. Leaders must design the learning processes whereby people throughout the organization 'develop their mastery in the learning disciplines' (Senge 1990: 345). They must also be stewards of the vision and teachers of it. The vision is not theirs alone. They serve and share the vision.

Some employers are committed to serious training of higher level staff and to an ideal of the Learning Organization. Top management and HR management in these organizations may interpret CPD as something completely defined and developed by the company, without reference to CPD policies and programmes of professional bodies (for example KPMG in business services or Reed in the recruitment sector).

Others without such a well developed and well resourced strategic approach to company training may find it convenient to use CPD activities organized by professional bodies as a resource for their staff. They would accept the definition of CPD of the professional bodies their staff belong to. Still others may develop partnerships with professional bodies to more clearly link professional body monitoring and assessment of CPD with their own employee appraisal systems. These are more likely to be professional services firms with a high concentration of professionals connected to a particular professional body.

Suppliers of training for professionals may connect with professional bodies, employers of professionals or the individual professionals directly. This will affect the way they market their products and the way they define CPD. The recent training gateway – a portal brokering post-qualification courses and modules between UK universities and primarily employers (though it is open to all) – does not use the label CPD (see www.thetraininggateway.com). Rather it uses work-based learning or training because it was decided that the term CPD would be too confusing to employers.[7]

By and large higher education suppliers see CPD as a collection of training activities or encounters that may add up to a qualification. Recognized degrees and diplomas are their comparative advantage in the marketplace.

It is open to all CPD suppliers to provide support for the whole of the CPD cycle. There is no reason why they should not provide planning, evaluation and reflection tools that slot in with what professional bodies produce. Some providers are doing this, particularly ones that provide online courses.[8] However, this does require a change of vision of CPD from the supply of training to support for continuing aspects of the CPD cycle.

## 8.6 Paradox and complexity contributing to mystery

The breadth of CPD practice among millions, its potential consequences for the economy and arguably the general welfare of the public, would lead us to expect CPD to be the subject of vigorous research effort, media attention, public debate and policy initiatives. Currently CPD hardly registers in the mind of the general public. It is practically absent from general media reporting in the UK. It is not the subject of explicit government policy and, with a few notable exceptions, is hardly the subject of academic research.

According to Rothwell and Arnold (2005: 18) '. . . there has been little empirical investigation of what kinds of CPD professionals engage in and why.' This view repeated a similar one expressed by Sadler-Smith and Badger (1998: 74) referring to the CPD research agenda as 'impoverished'. Paisey and Paisey (2004) concluded that CPD was an under-researched area in spite of considerable research attention given to professional accounting education.[9] This was echoed by Rothwell and Herbert (2007), Paisey and colleagues (2007) and Wessels (2007).

This is a mystery. How is it that something so important for society and for our economic wellbeing is hardly recognized?

One explanation is that CPD is new, but this hardly explains the extent of the gap between its size or significance (at least potential significance) on one hand and the public attention it receives on the other.

A second explanation is that CPD is not a uniform phenomenon across the professions. CPD recognition is hampered by the complexity of CPD and confusion among players and stakeholders as described above.

A deeper explanation is the fundamental paradox of CPD; that CPD is at the same time both what professionals just do and what they ought to do (and may be required to do). Professionals are both trusted and not trusted to keep themselves up-to-date.

There are many professionals who do not think they need CPD or ought to be forced to do it even if it is designed sensitively. Consider the following statements by professionals:

> I think that certainly when you reach, when you're in a profession, I think it's something that you yourself should expect of yourself anyway to keep yourself continually up to date.
>
> (Friedman, Davis *et al.* 2001: 108)

> I think I was annoyed when I got the [CPD] stuff where they said they expect me to write a sort of professional development plan every year, I

think well what the hell, you know that's entirely up to me, I'm a professional person, I don't have to jump through hoops to do this . . .

(Friedman, Davis et al. 2001: 109)

Some professionals see CPD as something apart from what they would normally do. They see it as something imposed by their professional bodies. We
therefore have the odd situation of professional bodies trying to convince their
members that CPD is very broad and includes what they would have been just
doing before.

> We want them [the members] to understand that CPD is a generic term
> for anything you can learn from, provided that it relates to [our subject] or
> running their business . . . so we are trying to get them around the idea that
> so many things can count, from the very little, going up to the advanced
> degree and everything in between.

(Friedman and Williams 2008: 36)

Compare this with the quotes above and the practitioner quoted at the beginning of Section 3.2, who criticized CPD with the claim that it is just what s/he as
a professional did anyway. Here is a representative of a professional body's CPD
scheme saying just that, but saying it as though the professional body has to be
'trying to get them [the practitioners] around' to this 'idea' that what counts as
CPD is close to everything the practitioners might just do to keep maintaining
and developing themselves as professionals.

The paradox of CPD is an aspect of the general paradox of professionalism:
that the nature of the tasks performed by professionals both encourages us to
seek assurance of quality, but at the same time requires us to rely on the professionals themselves. Another way of looking at this paradox in relation to CPD is
that we want to monitor and evaluate or measure what professionals are doing
to keep up, but at the same time have to accept that some of the things they do
cannot be measured accurately or easily. We both must trust that they will keep
up their technical and ethical competence, and at the same time want evidence
that they are keeping up their CPD (even if the evidence will always be flawed).

# 9

# DYNAMICS

## CPD today and tomorrow

*CPD is complex and dynamic. Painting a picture of CPD today requires an act of imagination and analysis, pointing out how CPD is changing today and therefore how it is likely to look tomorrow.*

### 9.1 Introduction

There are many ways we can describe CPD today. Here we focus on the core players in the CPD field: professionals, professional bodies and CPD specialists. Here we pull together themes pursued in earlier chapters to show not only how CPD has changed since the 1980s, but also how it is likely to change over the next three to five years. We specifically deal with:

- a trend towards more CPD; that is, growth in the CPD field with more professions taking it up and it occupying more of their time as well as more resources of professional bodies;
- more compulsion;
- increasing involvement of regulatory bodies;
- greater use of technical support and delivery of CPD through newer software packages, the internet and Web 2.0 technologies;
- outputs measures associated with more structured CPD, more monitoring and recording and more specific support for CPD through forms and templates to help encourage and guide planning, reflection and evaluation of CPD activities;
- more evidence that CPD produces value not only in terms of professional development but also in terms of practice improvements and positive client/patient/consumer/employer outcomes; and
- professionalization of the CPD field supporting professionalism in general.

## 9.2 Growth in the CPD field: more today and most likely more tomorrow

Judging in terms of its incidence, CPD has been a spectacular success, either according to numbers covered by a formal policy, or by the numbers actually participating in a scheme. Formal CPD has spread to being almost the norm for professional bodies in the UK, with 85 per cent having a policy.[1] PARN estimates that 3.4 million professionals in the UK actually participate in a CPD programme as defined by a professional body (Friedman and Afitska 2009).

We predict this will continue for the following reasons:

1  The numbers of professionals in occupations already considered to be professions are generally growing and more new services are emerging apace, particularly in developed countries as manufacturing and the product element of services move to developing countries.

Medical advances encourage demand for more medical procedures requiring more medical professionals. This applies also to complementary and supplementary health services. Added to this has been the huge growth in expectations of public services. The welfare state grew particularly in the 1960s and 1970s, and although the ideology of governments has turned away from a pure welfare approach, social expectations are such that the proportion of people employed as professionals providing education, social services and local government services has grown. The growth of financial services, particularly in the UK[2] has also meant a huge rise in the number of professional advisors and analysts. The increasing complexity of social relations (as traditional mores and constraints, particularly from religious sources, have declined) has led to a more litigious society.

Professionalization of more occupations may be expected as there is a clear trend in developed countries towards new service sector occupations. As incomes grow, more personalized or customized goods and services are demanded. As people become more time-conscious, more things they would do for themselves or have done for them informally by friends and relations are carried out by specialists. The tendency towards adults living alone and two-parent families with two earners will contribute to this demand. These new service-sector occupations are becoming professionalized.[3] In addition, there has been a huge rise in managers and new management specialisms that have recently been professionalizing.

2  Though the proportion of professions with a CPD policy is high, it is likely to rise even higher as knowledge of the importance of CPD for the very definition of professionalism grows.

As CPD becomes a clearly established essential part of a professionalization project, professionals in other countries are likely to take up CPD, either due to further internationalization of UK professional bodies, or as professional bodies in other countries develop strategies to meet the challenge coming from the UK.

3 The proportion of professionals under a CPD policy who follow the programme will rise as more professional bodies introduce more compulsion.

The proportion of professionals with a policy who are following the programme varies with the compliance policy. The trend towards compulsory CPD will raise this proportion. This will be accelerated as more regulatory bodies develop CPD policies as they favour compulsory policies.

4 CPD becomes an early step towards professionalization among newly professionalizing occupations.

New occupations go through a process of professionalization that involves setting up a CPD policy and programme at some stage. How quickly CPD emerges depends in part on whether the new profession has emerged out of an older one with a CPD tradition, or if it is a new occupation entirely, the latter being slower to come to CPD. PARN has been asked by numerous small occupation groupings to help with setting up professional bodies, and by newly formed professional bodies to help set up CPD schemes. A consequence of this trend is that CPD is coming to be regarded as an essential part of the process of professionalization itself. CPD is becoming one of the earliest steps in that process.

5 The expected amount of CPD activities and associated aspects of the CPD cycle – as effort put into planning and reflection and assessment of outcomes – may be expected to grow.

The CPD 'bar' is expected to rise as different professions come to compare what they do with others. In effect, the institutional wrapper that is CPD will become more elaborated around the actual learning activities.

We therefore predict that CPD will become more widespread, involving more individual professionals.[4]

In Chapter 2 we cited the estimate of 26 per cent of professionals to have been undertaking CPD in the UK in 2009, representing 12 per cent of the labour force (Friedman and Afitska 2009). We believe this will rise to more like 60–70 per cent of professionals and roughly one-third of the labour force within the next 5 to 10 years.[5]

## 9.3 More compulsion and clearer sanctions for non-compliance

Compulsory compliance policies for CPD have been long predicted (Watkins *et al.* 1996). We provided evidence for some rise in such policies during the 2000s in Chapter 4. Nevertheless the proportion has remained at only around one-quarter of those with a policy. We believe this slow trend towards a rising proportion with compulsory policies will continue over the next decade.

Pressure to demonstrate that professionals are doing CPD has grown since formal CPD policies first emerged. CPD is increasingly associated with assuring clients and/or employers of continuing competence and fitness to practise. The pattern discerned in Chapter 4 was that as professional bodies grow, they tend to move from obligatory or voluntary policies to mandatory ones as shown in matched sample changes between 2003 and 2006.

There appear to be both demand (or pull) and supply (or push) reasons for moving towards compulsory CPD. Demand reasons relate to the need not only to assure clients or employers, but also to dampen government enthusiasm for regulation, which has waxed and waned and waxed again, affected by general ideology and occasional public failures among individual or groups of professionals. On the supply side there is the greater ease with which complete monitoring can be achieved with developments in IT, particularly the availability of integrated database systems that allow general member records to be combined with CPD records.

Compulsory CPD policies are a wrapper around professional development activities that change what is being wrapped. Rather than merely being encouraged to read journals and attend events, the discipline of following a procedure is introduced in relation to these activities. Activities do not stand alone and are not to be regarded as an independent collection. Rather they are part of a programme, planned for and reflected upon according to guidelines and templates provided by the professional body (and some employers). Widespread compulsory CPD would make it into a programme as intimately associated with professionalism as initial qualifications. Arguably, this is needed for CPD to fulfil its potential.

The picture is complicated because the pressures towards compulsory CPD are different for professional bodies of different types and in different environments. The choice of policy is still largely one affected by the legal position of the profession and the relation between practitioners and their professional bodies. At one end are professions without statutory status and where several professional associations compete for members. Each individual professional association will be concerned to persuade members of the value of CPD, but will not be keen to alienate members and potential members and so will opt for voluntary or obligatory policies. At the other extreme are licensed professions with separate regulatory bodies. Fewer regulatory bodies have CPD policies compared with professional associations, but those that do tend to have compulsory policies, and their numbers are growing.

## 9.4 Regulatory bodies and the third pillar of professional standards regulation

As noted in Section 6.5.1, Friedman and Hanson (2010) suggested that CPD is coming to be seen by regulatory bodies as a core of a third pillar of professional standards regulation to complement initial qualifications and complaints/disciplinary procedures. Most of the expected changes reported by the 13 regulatory bodies they studied were within this third pillar (CPD and Positive Supports for Ethical Behaviour).

Just as one now sees a professional's qualification certificates proudly displayed in public places, we might expect CPD certification to occupy similar pride of place. This has not yet occurred, but we think it will in future, particularly as more regulatory bodies take on CPD, and as they come to benchmark themselves against each other.

## 9.5 IT-based support for CPD recording and assessment, online delivery and social networking

The availability of more useful and less expensive IT support, particularly through the internet, favours the development of the CPD field, in terms of widening access both to CPD activities and to more sophisticated outputs from planning and reflection.

### 9.5.1 Recording and integrated systems

Arguably, in the early years, CPD was itself encouraged by the availability of cheaper and more robust IT systems with more features to support management of CPD records. Recording an individual's professional development activities may be regarded as the basic wrapping around what professionals previously just did. Recording via IT-based systems can enhance recording by allowing practitioners to update their own records online and at the same time automatically have them fed into plans for further activities. Some allow suppliers of CPD activities to automatically update records of attendees and their examination results. Newer systems also allow for these records to be integrated with records of membership status.

Up to the late 1990s IT systems that could perform the database requirements of professional bodies, whether or not they could integrate CPD records, were disappointing. An investigation into online and IT support for CPD undertaken by PARN for the DfEE[6] in 2001 (Friedman, Davis and Phillips 2001) found many professional bodies with 'horror stories' of IT suppliers promising systems that were inadequate and/or were delivered late, ran over-budget and crashed after operating a short time.[7] Since then systems have become more robust and affordable. More recent research found much higher satisfaction among professional bodies with online recording systems for CPD (Williams and Friedman 2008).

### 9.5.2 Delivery via the internet

For many years there has been great interest in online CPD courses, particularly among professional bodies with far flung membership and especially those with substantial membership in different countries. Until recently such courses have suffered from inadequate flexibility and interactivity. Instead, most professionals use the internet to access learning material informally. For example a survey carried out in 2001 for the UK IPG (Friedman and Senior 2001) revealed the most common ways of using the internet were browsing websites and downloading reference materials, used by 51–55 per cent, while only 9 per cent reported using the internet for formal e-learning activities.[8] In a more recent survey carried out in 2008, 4,335 professionals reported that they had participated in CPD delivered in the following ways during the past 12 months (PARN 2008a: 13):

- Informal, self-directed (e.g. reading, research)   89 per cent
- Work-based, experience on the job   74 per cent
- Face-to-face delivery   72 per cent
- Online   53 per cent
- Text-based distance learning   33 per cent
- Use of corporate intranet for learning   31 per cent

Several very active suppliers have emerged in the past few years, including organizations that have developed three-way partnerships with both academic producers of materials and professional bodies who accredit or sponsor courses. Course suites with connections to competency frameworks and learning-style assessments as well as templates for reflection and evaluation have emerged. In some areas different professional bodies are vying for the attentions of the same professionals in the same subjects, such as various management specialties, teamwork and basic IT skills. This is driving up quality.

### 9.5.3 Web 2.0 and social networking

New tools for interacting electronically have emerged in the last few years under the label of Web 2.0 (such as blogs, tweets, wikis): indicating a shift from broadcasting one-way communication from organizations to their customers/publics/members, to collaborative user-generated content. Social networking refers to web services or environments that allow people to make connections with and link to others and share information about themselves. They enable communication among people who share interests. This not only includes people who may be friends, acquaintances or colleagues in other environments – local neighbourhood, school, university, working environment – but also links people from different cultures, countries and backgrounds who may share interests, lifestyles or professions (Ellis and Williams 2010). Facebook is the most popular of these sites but there are many others, such as Linkedin, MySpace and Bebo.

Use of Web 2.0 by professional bodies is in its infancy, though a substantial number of professionals are using wikis. According to a survey carried out by PARN covering 7,338 professionals in 2009 (Ellis and Williams 2010), 60 per cent reported using Wikipedia and 29 per cent using other wikis to support their work, while none of the other Web 2.0 technologies were used by more than 20 per cent other than national media blogs (23 per cent) and individual blogs (22 per cent). Only 14 per cent reported using Facebook and 17 per cent YouTube. It is interesting that Wikipedia was also by far the most common use of Web 2.0 technologies for leisure among these professionals (73 per cent) and a high proportion used other wikis (35 per cent) compared with those using YouTube and Facebook for leisure purposes (61 per cent and 47 per cent respectively).

These tools may be considered as alternative ways of carrying out networking activities such as branch meetings and events at HQ, but they are potentially CPD activities. More directly online delivery of CPD activities may be facilitated through Web 2.0 technologies, both for delivery of certain aspects of those activities (RSS feeds or wikis) or entirely delivered through social networking technology (Second Life or Facebook). We believe this will continue to encourage CPD participation.

## 9.6 Outputs measures: more directly measuring Professional Development Value

In the past decade more professional bodies have been switching to outputs measures and more have been moving towards higher PDV outputs measurement systems as described in Section 7.4. Those with some element of outputs measurement rose from 31 per cent to 47 per cent for a sample of 64 professional bodies responding to both the 2003 and 2006 PARN IBS (International Benchmarking Survey) of professional bodies. The proportion rose from 47 per cent to 56 per cent for the 46 who responded to both the 2006 and 2009 IBS surveys.[9] We expect this to continue.[10]

Judging CPD systematically by some output measure can invest it with validity beyond merely tracking and recording what professionals just do. Outputs measures provide something new: a systematic consideration of the value of what professionals do, co-ordinated by, and accredited by, a professional body. This is particularly so of outputs measures on the outcomes axis of Figure 7.1; that is including assessment of the outcomes of learning activities on professionals' own knowledge, behaviour and practice and even more important, the effects of CPD on clients or employers. Beyond taking courses or reading out of interest, pleasure or even to keep up-to-date, this is carrying out these activities in a professional manner – in a reflective, a planned or a strategic manner – clearly circumscribed by standard procedures.

## 9.7 Progress on measuring the immeasurable: evidence for positive outcomes from CPD for clients and other stakeholders

The Holy Grail of CPD analysis is to ascertain and evaluate positive outcomes for consumers/clients/patients or for employers that may be clearly attributable to CPD. Ideally these studies should report on their validity (the degree to which measures truly assess what they intend to measure) and reliability (consistency or reproducibility of measurements). Learning outcomes can easily be assessed and routinely are assessed for formal CPD activities, but improvements in practice are much more difficult, particularly assessing the contribution of informal CPD.

It is much easier to identify CPD activity that can be linked to client or employer outcomes if the CPD activity is a formal, well-defined event that is clearly intended to influence professionals towards a new technique or procedure, which is claimed to improve practice in a specific manner and thereby to improve client or employer outcomes in an identifiable way; for example, a workshop explaining how to use a new piece of medical equipment or a new diagnostic procedure linked to use of the equipment and then linked to the effect of the change in practice on patient outcomes.

Most studies that successfully connect CPD to practice outcomes assess formal rather than informal CPD, and these studies are usually undertaken by or funded by those who are trying to influence professionals towards adoption of new techniques or procedures. Reasons for this bias towards the formal and the directed are fairly obvious. Formal CPD will normally, particularly in recent years, have attached to it specific objectives (though usually confined to learning objectives). Pre-specification of intended outcomes allows their assessment to be more clearly defined and independently judged.

Professionals may know that CPD has been effective in improving client outcomes, and the aim of the evaluation stage of the CPD cycle is to get them to assess their CPD in terms of outcomes. Getting professionals to evaluate their reading or other informal activity is difficult because the positive outcomes that can occur may not be the clear objectives of the CPD activity, and in addition it may be impossible to identify the influence of the CPD activity on outcomes independently from other contributing factors. For example, say a professional learns that a new technology is available at a social event or by the mention of it from a mentor. Then they search the internet for more information on this technique, find a useful article and then decide it is worth trying out the technique. It may be that in order to do so further research is needed to find support for actual implementation. Let us say that this leads to better client outcomes. How much of this improvement can be attributed to the professional's attendance at the social event or from the mentor conversation? How much to their informal internet search or reading the article?

A particular problem with measuring the influence of any aspect of professional regulation on professional practice is that the effects are likely to take a long time to become manifest.

Few studies have been undertaken. They are almost exclusively concerned with measuring the outcomes of CPD for a single profession: they rarely refer to work carried out in other professions. For some professions there is a tradition of publishing this work in widely accessible academic journals: medicine and education primarily. In most other fields the studies are part of a *grey literature*, reports undertaken by professional bodies or commissioned by them from private research or consultancy organizations. These reports are regarded as of limited interest; limited to the membership of the professional body or even just to those running it and its CPD programme; limited also in time because they have been specifically undertaken for a time-limited reason – to support a recent or upcoming costly change of CPD policy or to provide material to address a new government initiative or negative media attention.[11]

This literature may appear on professional body websites, though usually in places not easy to access and possibly in members-only sections. After what would appear to academics as an unseemly short period of time (perhaps a few years), the report would be drawn even deeper into the website, archived somewhere, or even deleted altogether.

In the medical field there is a strong tradition of CME and most studies in the medical literature assess the effectiveness of this rather than CPD. Generally, CPD is presumed to be wider than CME and encompassing it: CME is education and training; CPD also includes informal development activities and more self-directed activities.[12]

Marinopoulos and colleagues (2007) carried out a systematic review of literature on the effectiveness of CME. They concluded that the overall quality of the 136 articles they found to be relevant was low,[13] and therefore they could only derive tentative conclusions from it. Nevertheless, they concluded that the literature overall supported CME being effective. Most consistent positive achievement and maintenance of objectives (what we call PDV) were found for knowledge, attitude or skills outcomes (22 of 28; 22 of 26 and 12 of 15 studies respectively). On balance, studies were less likely to report positive outcomes for practice behaviour (61 of 105 studies) and even less for clinical practice outcomes (14 of 33). Broadly, they concluded that 'live media [conducted in person] was more effective than print, multimedia more effective than single media interventions and multiple exposures more effective than a single exposure' (2007: v).

Brown and colleagues (2004) examine the effectiveness of CPE training for asthma treatment. Doctors were allocated to an experimental group that received extra training or to a control group receiving no extra training. Number of hospitalizations and visits to the doctor by patients of the two groups of doctors were studied over a two-year period. A primary difficulty in demonstrating CPD effectiveness is that benefits can take a long time to accrue, implying that a longitudinal approach should be incorporated into research design (Guskey 2000). This is one of the major strengths of the study. Because of the longitudinal approach, as well as the use of a control group, the random allocation of doctors, and because the study controlled for intervening variables associated with the condition of the patients, it provides a valuable model for linking undertaking CPD and positive outcomes, not only for patients but also for cost effectiveness of the professional service studied.

In the education field there are also serious studies attempting to assess the effects of CPD on pupil or student outcomes. Penuel and colleagues (2007: 922) note that there has been an 'increasing concern' to describe the link between 'design and conduct of professional development and subsequent improvements to both teacher practice and student learning outcomes'. This is identified as a major shift in emphasis from previous decades when research attention was mainly focused on 'evaluations of teacher satisfaction with professional development experiences' (2007: 923).

Penuel and colleagues acknowledge that they have only provided limited evidence for part of the chain of influences that are needed to make the case for participation in professional development activities, designed with particular objectives, causing improved client (in this case student) outcomes. They note that policy makers 'argue that such studies are needed' but they admit:

> relating a chain of evidence that links student learning to teacher learning, professional development, and policy is remarkably challenging; and so far, most studies, including this one, have elected to look at components of this chain.
>
> (2007: 953)

There are problems, associated particularly with assessing large-scale programmes for teacher professional development, which are delivered by different suppliers to teachers in many different circumstances.[14] Specific information is needed about different suppliers and their approaches to the design of professional development activities and information about different teachers and their teaching contexts. Ideally, as is very well recognized in the medical field, one should compare experiences of those participating in programmes with control groups; however, there are few studies in the education field that take this approach.

Friedman and Hanson (2010) provide an overview of studies of the effectiveness of professional standards regulation in general, covering all three pillars. They emphasize the difficulty of moving from examining the opinions of professionals on the value of CPD for their practice towards practical measures of client/patient outcomes. We predict that the problems will be overcome with serious effort and resources applied to this issue in future as more come to recognize how widespread CPD will have become and as the claims for it from professional bodies come to be recognized and challenged in academic circles.

## 9.8 Professionalization of CPD contributing to raising professionalism in general

Following from the trends described above we detect a rise in the knowledge expected of CPD specialists in professional bodies and in the degree to which CPD policies and programmes are becoming the subject of greater reflection and concern for ethical as well as technical issues.

The knowledge expected of CPD specialists has grown in consequence of the growth of the field. There are more professions with a CPD policy to benchmark against. As CPD is coming to be recognized as more central to the financial viability of professional associations, to the mission of professional standards regulation among regulatory bodies and generally for the reputation of each profession, there is more pressure to find out what others are doing and to reflect on one's own policies and programmes. The computerization of records and more recently the development of online courses, and the growing importance of social networking and other Web 2.0 technologies, is also adding to the spread of expertise required within the CPD function of professional bodies. The rise in knowledge required is also associated with outputs measures as they require an understanding of Professional Development Value of different CPD activities as well as encouraging more and more substantial supports for CPD planning, reflection and evaluation.

Compulsion makes the consequences of how the CPD policy is administered more serious as it involves sanctions against individual professionals and in turn this raises pressure on those running the policy in professional bodies to reflect upon how they justify not only their actions in relation to an individual who is non-compliant, but also to justify the compliance policy itself and supports provided for those individual practitioners to comply. The ethical basis of CPD becomes an issue. This also leads to increasing demand for evidence that CPD produces value not only in terms of professional development but also in terms of practice improvements and positive client/patient/consumer/employer outcomes.

Professionalization of CPD will involve:

1  A more self-conscious, considered or reflective attitude towards professional development.
2  A specific linking of professional development activities to the aims of CPD as per its definition; that is, to PDV, involving the commissioning of studies into effectiveness of CPD and awareness of those studies, even if they research practice in very different professions.
3  A greater degree of accountability and transparency of CPD not only to professionals but also to employers, clients/patients and the general public.

A consequence of the above will mean CPD is:

4  More likely to become a legitimizing force for continued status and trust-worthiness of professionals, for rising professionalism in general.

We regard (1) and (2) as leading to internalizing CPD by professionals. It is a critical element in the development of the field: the deepening of the field. The wider meaning of outputs measures relates to (3) and (4); that outputs measures provide evidence that practitioners are behaving in a professional manner; that they are reflective practitioners, not only contemplating how they can improve their practice, but also linking learning and thinking with doing. We believe this aspect of CPD measurement has the potential to raise CPD towards a lifelong credentializing process for professionals and widening the field of CPD beyond the professionals who carry out CPD activities. A new era of CPD and professionalism may emerge, whereby the whole idea of being a professional will be bound up with continuous credentialism as well as, and perhaps even instead of, initial qualifications. It will not be about meeting professional practice standards as a student and a trainee in early years, but rather a continuous process of skill, knowledge and competence development, maintenance and redevelopment as ever-changing techniques and awareness of environmental conditions are adjusted to.

This is not yet achieved. The credentializing potential of CPD is not easily realized because the way CPD is presented is diverse and not easily understood by employers, clients and practitioners in other professions. Outputs measures that seem to be measuring the same thing are incompatible across professions. Professions differ in the templates they provide for reflection or planning. They differ in the degree of reflection that would be considered the minimum acceptable to get through an audit. They differ in the level of detail and the complexity of their competency frameworks, at least for those who have a framework. This makes it unlikely that the current rise in outputs measures and compulsion will achieve the full potential for raising the status of CPD, and for raising the status of professionalism itself until something else occurs: what is needed is for these measures to become more comparable.

One way this could happen is for standardization to be imposed 'from above' (national government, or the EU, or an international standard-setting body such as how IFAC operates for the accounting profession worldwide). This could be envisioned as a strict limitation of what counts as CPD; only activities for which positive output and practice outcomes can be demonstrated. It is likely to require a set of reviewers and accreditors, possibly peers, but perhaps a new form of CPD specialist.

This will have consequences. More and more specialized resources will be required to run CPD programmes with greater effort from the practitioners. There is a danger that the 'strength of weak ties' (Granovetter 1973), or productivity arising from light-touch regulation, will be lost. This could mean that more and more professionals, especially younger ones who are currently enthusiastic about CPD, will come to resent it as a burden and worse as a challenge to their autonomous professional judgement. This would lead not only to widespread avoidance and evasion, but also to the possibility of a change in the nature of professionalism itself: a reduction or deprofessionalization. Whether this develops will depend on who controls or institutionalizes CPD and on how detailed the standards are. The greatest danger will be that the standards are not flexible enough to take into account special circumstances, not only of different professions and of professions in different countries, but also of different situations of individual professionals. In effect, the essential difference between CPD and CPE could be eroded or lost. CPD could become less about development and informal activities because they are harder to standardize and verify. However, this would mean reversing developments that have been building for several years in the CPD field.

Rather than a standard being imposed on the professions, we suggest there is already a 'bottom-up' process occurring whereby a 'language' of CPD measurement is developing and spreading, thereby allowing different measurement systems to be compared and spreading understanding and appreciation of CPD as effective in achieving PDV. This path towards standardization will involve more sharing of practice among professional bodies.

We return to the issue of standardization of CPD in Section 11.3.

# 10

## CPD FIELD BEYOND TOMORROW

## Affecting players and passive stakeholders

*CPD has breathed new life into professional bodies. Will it grow? Will it last?*

### 10.1 Introduction

In Chapter 9 we examined how the CPD field is developing based on surveys and case studies. That development trajectory is not uniform or simple or steady, but we are confident that the trends identified provide a good picture of the field in the next few years. Here we speculate on this trajectory continuing in the longer term, say the next 5 to 15 years. We explore implications of this speculation, first considering the field as a whole, and then examining the types of players and stakeholders introduced in Chapter 2; not merely in their relation to the field, but also in terms of consequences of the field's development on their own social and economic positions.

The trends we have identified amount to the emergence of the CPD field as a major feature of the fabric of society. It may be thought of in its dynamism as a vortex attracting not only more and more people into its compass as players, but also more resources: more economic, social and cultural capital. As the field becomes more populated and richer it will change its players, and deepen their dispositions towards the field. It will also shake the paths of stakeholders who are currently only loosely connected or hardly aware of the CPD field. Ultimately, we predict the end of the CPD mystery.

This is conjecture. In the next chapter we consider possible derailments from this path, as well as certain dilemmas that players and stakeholders are likely to face.

## 10.2 Coalescence of positive visions of CPD based around professional bodies

### 10.2.1 More players and more resources in the field

The first trend we identified in the previous chapter was towards more CPD. New players are being drawn into the CPD field: new professional bodies adopt CPD policies and also because more adopt compulsory policies, more come to follow a CPD programme. This requires more CPD specialists to administer programmes, particularly as more adopt outputs measures and as outputs measures are able to identify higher levels of PDV (Section 7.4). In addition, numbers of CPD specialists grow in other institutions. New suppliers are formed and existing educational suppliers develop offerings to serve the growing CPD market. Universities come to regard CPD as an important market and not only are there more specialists supplying courses and other learning opportunities, but also CPD becomes a hot topic for academic research. New developments in CPD will be interrogated in academic journals and the wider media to assess their effectiveness for raising the standards of professional services, under the new expectation that they would normally do so (and the greater disappointment if it is found that they do not). Certain academics and journalists will regard CPD as their specialist areas for research, reporting and comment. Increasing use of IT and Web 1.0 and Web 2.0 (and Web 3.0, etc.) also draws in new players: technology providers on the supply side and intermediaries providing advice on CPD technology come to consider themselves as CPD specialists.

There two others ways of interpreting 'more' CPD.

First, the size of the CPD field as a resource base for players and stakeholders will grow. Not only more jobs, but a growing proportion of better jobs become available as CPD specialists come to manage others, rather than being managed by non-specialists, as in most professional bodies in the past. Also the general status of those working in the field will grow. For example those concerned with CPD are likely to be treated less as second-class citizens at universities.

Second, CPD will become a given for professionals, rather than a set of decisions (whether or not to participate at all, how little can one get away with). It will enter more deeply into the psyche of professionals and become more clearly dispositional. Defining stakeholders as individuals and groups who are affected by the CPD field leaves open how much or how deeply they are affected. Not only will more stakeholders come to recognize they are affected by the CPD field (more employers, clients/patients as well as politicians and non-specialist journalists), but also they will come to regard CPD as more and more newsworthy and worth paying attention to, more important for their lives. How CPD is carried out may be an issue, not whether to participate. As such it will no longer be regarded as a challenge to the autonomy of a 'true' professional (much as the 'imposition' of a written professional code of conduct is no longer thought of as a challenge to the essence of the professional as a gentleman). Memory of the decision to make CPD compulsory in almost all professions will fade; it will be regarded as the norm. There will, of course, still be individuals who evade their CPD requirements, but this will come to be regarded as a poor reflection on those individuals, rather than as an indication of a problem with the idea of CPD or of compulsory CPD policies.

## 10.2.2 Convergence and divergence

Other characteristics of the field will change. As more opportunities develop for CPD specialists in different professional bodies to interact, knowledge of good and interesting practice will spread. This will encourage a narrowing of the range of CPD practice among professional bodies. The trend towards common approaches will be further augmented by pressures to standardization to meet expectations of other stakeholders, namely clients (or client pressure groups) and government. This does not mean that CPD will become static or completely uniform. There will always be new developments: new content, new delivery mechanisms, new support methods, new measurement and recording techniques. However, the lag between introduction by pioneers and take up by the majority of professions will diminish.

The balance of aims of CPD, or rather what counts as PDV, may alter. With more regulatory bodies taking on CPD, the balance is likely to turn towards CPD becoming aimed more at competence than at personal development. However, it is notable that in the American medical field there are currently calls to incorporate personal development and personal responsibilities into what has been called Continuing Medical Education. There is a growing view that attending courses, especially those specified by authorities and sponsored by commercial interests, are simply not working and do not lead to patient benefits (Campbell and Rosenthal 2009).

## 10.2.3 Recognition of CPD among stakeholders

In these circumstances CPD will come to be regarded as the most substantial portion of the lifelong learning that occurs in society. Lifelong learning will no longer be limited to what it in effect implies to many today – remedial adult education, education in later life for those who missed out on secondary, further or higher education when young.[1] It will be viewed as an education arena and a market on a par with the importance of the education of young people. It will be recognized as a critical factor in economic competitiveness, viewed as critical for not only the quality of the huge range of professional services delivered, but also for the general level of trust in the society. As such it will be viewed as worthy of considerable government policy, media attention and general public awareness.

How will the different players and stakeholders come to change in relation to the much greater and more significant field that CPD may become?

## 10.3 Significance for professional bodies

CPD will be regarded as having been a shot in the arm for professional bodies, particularly those in professions where there is no licensure and no requirement for individual practitioners to belong to any particular professional body.

### 10.3.1 Raising membership, participation and reversing decline in social capital

A perceived general decline in voluntary effort and particularly increased employer reluctance to support employee 'volunteer' activities for their respective professional bodies during office hours have led to a concern for declining member support for professional body activities and ultimately a decline in membership. Coleman (1988) and Putnam (1995, 2000) documented a general decline in traditional forms of social activity in the United States since the 1950s. Putnam provided evidence of decline in membership of professional associations as one form of the general decline in social capital, though not until the late 1970s (Putnam 2000). This has worried observers in the USA, where decline in social capital is regarded as a decline in the social cohesion that keeps society together (Putnam 1995, 2000; Paxton 1999).[2]

However, PARN has found that membership of most professional bodies has been rising in the past decade (Friedman with Afitska 2007). It may be that making CPD a cornerstone activity of the professional body and convincing members that carrying out CPD is essential for the maintenance of their professionalism is giving professional bodies a new way of supporting the 'value proposition': a new way of justifying cost of membership subscriptions in terms of the value of membership to practitioners.[3] This would be expected to continue if the CPD field develops as we have predicted in this chapter.

### 10.3.2 Member services to CPD: organizing, assessing and accrediting

When professional associations develop a branch network, a programme of activities and publications, they are acting consciously and strategically to support existing communities of practice, to extend them and to develop new ones among their members. The strategy is to make available opportunities for networking, to pull individuals into the orbit of those networks, by the quality and convenience of their activities, or by general exhortations on the membership to attend. Individual members are not forced to participate. Participation of individuals is not monitored, except for subscription payments and the actions of senior volunteers sitting on governing bodies or committees. Non-payment of dues by the general membership, and non-attendance of those on committees and councils, would be noted, apologies accepted up to a point, but then negative consequences or sanctions may apply for persistent non-payment or non-attendance.

Those running associations would reckon their programmes a success if a substantial proportion of the membership attended. The quality of activities would entice attendance, presuming practitioners wished to develop themselves. This expectation was not made explicit by specific policies, not until the 1980s. The presumption that practitioners would be maintaining and developing their competence and undertaking personal and professional development were so infused in the minds of those leading the profession that it was not, generally, even noted in ethical codes. Concerning expertise, the only obligation expressed was not to claim more expertise than one possessed. Only after the development of explicit policies on CPD did obligations to keep up competence or expertise began to appear in professional codes, and more recently explicit references to CPD have been added. It is likely that CPD will explicitly be written into most professional codes in future and there will be an elaboration of related obligations, such as to support the CPD of others.

With the coming of CPD a seismic shift of understanding has been occurring. From merely one among many activities professional bodies provide, CPD has generated a transformation in the way almost all activities of professional bodies are perceived. Rather than merely services provided by the professional body to members, they become either CPD-accredited activities or not. 'Should they count?' think CPD specialists and those running professional bodies. 'Do they count?' think individual professionals. These questions need to be asked of most activities if the professional body uses inputs measures. If outputs measures are used, the questions are different, but still they are asked of almost all activities. 'How can or should activities be linked to knowledge, attitudes and behaviours expected of the members, and how can they be linked to outcomes for clients/patients or employers?' think CPD specialists. 'How can I formulate how the activity relates to my development plan and how may it be evaluated in terms of my knowledge, my practice and outcomes for those I am providing services?' think individual professionals. These questions are entirely new for input regimes. What is new in the output regime is that these calculations are more consciously and formally being made, more comprehensively being made. Such explicit calculations will lead the activities provided to change, with an incentive to offer more activities that could count as CPD, and count for higher value, more PDV, being offered than in the past. Using outputs measures makes the calculation even more important and more complicated. Now the issue of standards of CPD (third pillar) can become comparable to the issue of standards of initial professional qualifications (first pillar).

### 10.3.3 Shifting from first to third pillars of professional standards regulation

We can see now (with the perspective of understanding the importance of CPD) that professional bodies have taken a hard view of entry requirements and a relaxed view of what professionals do once over the hurdle, unless they do something unacceptable and are complained about or caught at it. Now with CPD as a third pillar of professional standards, it is possible that professions will become more relaxed about initial requirements, or that initial requirements will be framed in a manner more consistent with CPD (less academic, more practice oriented).

### 10.3.4 More networked and more public organizations

If professional bodies are to succeed in maintaining their control over CPD, they have to engage both with suppliers of CPD activities and with those who use the results of CPD beyond the professionals themselves. There have been particularly successful incidents of partnerships between professional bodies and universities on one hand (Friedman and Williams 2008)[4] and with employers on the other (see Exhibit 10.2). However, these are isolated cases. They may be expected to increase in future, leading professional bodies to become more like networking organizations. In effect this extends a long-term trend for many professional bodies to form relations with education institutions and employers in relation to initial qualifications. Generally, relations with higher education institutions are department specific – Institute of Archaeology with archaeology departments, Institute of Chartered Accountants with accounting departments – but with so high a proportion of CPD being generic, relations with other departments and with centres of enterprise or community relations within universities that deal with CPD and therefore with other aspects of the hierarchy in universities are being formed. Recognition of professional qualifications by employers in their recruitment requires a far less intimate connection with professional bodies than recognition of CPD as part of regular employee appraisal.

Rather than the mysterious and enclosed organizations presented to the public until the 1970s, professional bodies have gradually been opening to public scrutiny. In part, the forces that encouraged the emergence of the CPD field, discussed in Chapter 3, also have been encouraging professional bodies to become more transparent to the wider public. This will continue and intensify. The need to reassure potential clients and employers that professionals remain competent long after initial qualifications, which has been encouraging outputs measures, will also encourage a more public approach to information about CPD programmes. Details of these programmes are still often hidden in members-only sections of professional body websites. This must change, and we predict that it will change, especially as the language of CPD and its measurement becomes more settled.

One way of professional bodies becoming more public with their CPD would be for a clear kitemark to emerge that becomes widely recognized as associated with genuinely high PDV. This would raise the profile of CPD beyond the individual professions. It would help employers to judge the value of CPD evidence provided by potential recruits and clients to recognize more trustworthy professionals. The CPD measurement model outlined in Section 7.4 is intended to facilitate such comparability, and could underpin such a kitemark.

## 10.4 Significance for professionals

CPD will no longer be seen as a new label for what professionals just did before CPD came along. Rather CPD will be seen as what professionals just do. This institutional wrapper will become an expression of what professionals just do, rather than a separate thing from it.[5] Professionals will come to see CPD as an essential part of being a professional in the same way as the idea that professionalism means being qualified.[6]

Initial qualifications will come to be seen as only a first step in being qualified to practice as a professional. One consequence will be that initial qualifications become less important. Letting someone loose on the general public by stamping the imprint of qualification at the moment of graduation or certification will only mark a beginning point in the process of continuing professional competence. If CPD included preceptorships as the Nursing and Midwifery Council are introducing or other forms of supervision and mentoring from the moment of qualification, it would become less important that those individuals are fit for purpose even if they are fit to practise.[7] It may be that this will lead to shorter initial qualifications or that it will encourage alternative routes to qualification.

It also may mean that individual professionals become less secure in their positions or at least less autonomous. To be a professional will not mean that one is simply presumed to keep up-to-date, but rather that one needs to demonstrate this through CPD. However, it may help to preserve professional autonomy within the bounds of maintaining a commitment to lifelong learning and demonstrating it. While professionals lose some degree of autonomy concerning their professional development, they may raise how well they are trusted by employers and clients to provide up-to-date services with less direct control over their working procedures.

## 10.5 Significance for CPD specialists

As the number of CPD specialists grows, and as the expertise required of them expands with new techniques for measuring and supporting PDV being developed, they are likely to become a recognized profession with their own representative and regulatory bodies. Growth of the knowledge base will encourage more academics to become part of the CPD field, leading to what is likely to become an independent learned society. This will be encouraged by research that systematically addresses links between CPD provisions and PDV.

Which CPD activities provide appropriate learning and practice experiences? Is there an advantage to simulation exercises or group learning or other new forms of CPD provision? How else can the effectiveness of those experiences be enhanced in terms of knowledge acquired, appropriate attitudes and behaviours and ultimately in terms of practice improvements and positive outcomes for clients/patients and employers? Do CPD offerings need to be tailored for certain types of professionals, based, say, on their learning styles or their levels of experience?

We may expect the introduction of an initial qualification for CPD specialists which requires familiarity with this information as well as knowledge of the different methods for supporting and regulating CPD. A CPD policy and programme for CPD specialists will be developed. These may be administered through the learned society, professional association or regulatory body, but it is likely that all three would participate in the area.

## 10.6 CPD and mass media

We would expect a new type of CPD specialist to emerge: the CPD journalist. As the incidence of CPD grows, and with rising expectations among employers, clients and patients for evidence of CPD, the market for news about CPD will grow. At some point new magazines will emerge with titles like *CPD Today*, or *CPD World*. Eventually the general news media will take up the subject. Education sections of *The Guardian* and *The Independent* will carry items about CPD. *The Times*, *The Telegraph* and *The Financial Times* will carry inserts on the professions with items on CPD, as well as supplements on specific industries or technologies. These newspapers will also carry inserts exclusively devoted to CPD across professions as well as regular features and editorials about aspects of CPD. Special features on CPD may appear on television and websites which provide comparable information about CPD programmes. One could imagine a series on the origins and development of CPD. Journalists writing for these media will become 'experts' on CPD. Thus the mass media will come to depend on specialist spokespeople from the CPD field.

## 10.7 Significance for suppliers of CPD: Vision 7 – CPD as a lucrative market based on a valuable commodity to be purchased and sold

One effect of the flourishing of CPD is that it both encourages the growth of existing suppliers and encourages new ones. It also encourages a change in orientation of suppliers of training more broadly to rebadge what they do as CPD. This may require more than merely a labelling exercise. It can involve having to match the way training is connected to behaviour and practice outcomes along lines developed in CPD programmes. This clearly will become more important as output requirements move up the PDV scales. Some will do this readily, some reluctantly. As the CPD field grows this is likely to become more important in the balance of education and training supplied within society as a whole.

The notion of tertiary education as a distinct and final phase of individuals' experiences of education may be diminished and come to be viewed as second-ary education is today: a phase framed by primary and tertiary education. So perhaps tertiary education will come to be framed by secondary education and something else, maybe quartenary education, or a return to the label of adult education, or perhaps a new interpretation of lifelong learning will emerge.

We must consider not only suppliers of CPD activities such as training or events or reading material. There are also suppliers of total solution CPD, that is, systems of CPD courses delivered online or through the internet and social networking systems, which also provide materials related to different phases of the CPD cycle. It is uncertain how many of these systems approaches will survive if CPD becomes more standardized with convergence of CPD among professional bodies. Many of them serve niche markets and can be distinguish-able in a highly fragmented market. For example, not only are medical CPD providers providing training in medical procedures, some provide generic man-agement and team-working training, which may overlap both with provisions from other professional specialists such as legal or engineering specialists, but also obviously by management and organizational development specialists.

Longer-term effects of this change would be, first, concentration in the specialist CPD supply 'industry' to where the big money is: employers. Many small-scale suppliers of specialist CPD training that may have been aimed at professional body accreditation will market these offerings to employers rather than relying only on their links with professional bodies. This will contribute to a trend just now beginning, of employers taking on the label of CPD to rebadge their training and employee development programmes for higher level internal staff. It may even lead them to do this for all internal staff if the CPD label becomes strong enough, encouraged by suppliers.

In effect, we may consider a new vision of CPD to develop: that of a valuable market which attracts more and more varied suppliers.

## 10.8 CPD and higher education institutions

### 10.8.1 The changing place and status of CPD in higher education institutions

Currently we seem to be at the beginning of what is likely to be a rush among universities and other higher education institutions to get 'into CPD'. As noted in Section 2.9, apparently universities in the UK currently (2009) account for only 8 per cent of the CPD market. It is interesting that most universities in the past had shown a commitment to adult education as a service to the local community (Section 3.8) but just as the CPD bandwagon was beginning to roll in the 1980s and early 1990s, several universities dismantled these structures or downgraded them as pressures to show excellence in research and teaching on degree programmes was intensified in the UK (and elsewhere).[8]

Universities aspire to become high-quality research and teaching institutions, taking in the best qualified students possible. With the gradual, but steady, reduction in the proportion of university running costs coming from the UK government based on student numbers since the 1970s, and the rise of funding connected to research assessment ratings in the 1990s and 2000s, those universities who could, have oriented themselves more and more towards research. In addition, universities have been expected to raise more income from fees and other sources (such as enterprise development). One way around this problem has been to take in non-EU students for postgraduate degrees, where fees are not controlled by the government. UK universities particularly gained from stricter American entry requirements applied to foreign students after 11 September 2001. However, in the last few years this bonanza has fallen off as Asian countries have been building their own higher education capacity. Teaching directed towards mature students, particularly employees and for CPD, seems a natural alternative.

One consequence is a rise in the proportion of students who are less likely to be funded by their parents and are therefore more demanding, less willing to put up with what they receive. In addition, the student body of the university is becoming more loosely attached to the institution. Universities no longer hold students full time for three or four years, or more if they go straight on to Master's or PhD degrees. They are becoming more 'porous' communities with more part-time students and students studying for shorter periods.[9]

CPD provision by universities is part of a broader change, in the UK in particular, away from the traditional model of subject- or discipline-based departments filled with academics whose incentives are primarily to publish research in high status journals or publish books that are well reviewed and often quoted. Those academics have always taught, and teaching quality has been a factor in promotion processes, but far less measured and individually assessed. Generally, teaching success has concerned whole departments and much of the assessment of departments has had to do with the rigour of student records.[10] The gradual reduction in public funding has led universities to enter markets for education, research and by-products of these activities including CPD. Generating revenue from market-oriented activities requires more complex and more mission-critical university administration. More administrative support is given to winning research grants and research contracts. Courses, particularly those charging full cost-covering fees, require marketing. In addition, the relatively new activity, or rather newly encouraged activity, of spinning out new enterprises based on university research requires business start up and business development expertise.

Considerable CPD activity still takes place in traditional academic departments and this may be expected to continue. This is often a rather informal arrangement, relying on a particular individual academic with links to a professional body. Often this activity has remained beneath the radar of central university administration in its strategic purview of activities. Therefore it is often not properly rewarded and sometimes accounted for in odd ways in formal university budgetary processes as it does not fit with the traditional model of teaching and research through subject-based departments.

Most CPD teaching has come to be separated from traditional departmental activity. Teaching methods rely less on traditional academic expertise of theoretical and literature awareness and more on relevance to practice. Such courses are often taught by individuals who are only loosely connected to the university, part timers and those on fixed employment contracts and fixed service contracts; not, by and large, active researchers. The stronger the research tradition of the university and the more income from successive research assessment exercises, the greater the separation both hierarchically and horizontally between providers of CPD and 'proper' academics. Special units to provide CPD have been springing up all over the university sector. They often do not stand alone, but are joined with other 'off-line' units under the label of Enterprise or Innovation, charged with transforming university research activity into patents and setting up companies based on such patents or other new technologies, products or services. A different approach taken by some universities is to set up units to liaise with local business and multinational business with a connection to the area in which the university is located. Often this work has been supported by government through Regional Development Agencies. Certain CPD opportunities arise directly from this activity.[11]

In future we expect these units will grow and become a more important part of university life. CPD and enterprise development can overlap in that through organizing the teaching of CPD these university units gain important contacts with both professional bodies and employers of professionals, which can be used to develop new products and especially new services through expertise at universities or connected to it. In addition, we expect these units will become more connected to traditional university life, perhaps even completely integrated. This change will take place in two very different ways.

First, earning critical revenue streams, these units are likely to extend their influence into other parts of the university. Heads of departments will be expected to encourage students and staff to develop enterprise-potential activities. Academics will be encouraged to make available teaching designed originally for traditional undergraduates and postgraduates to others. The modularization of university courses, originally designed to encourage undergraduates to move among universities, will be further developed into smaller and smaller units to accommodate individuals only able to come for very short courses as part of their CPD. In addition, individuals from CPD and enterprise units will work with traditional academics to find ways of melding the two activities. Such an approach is already being marketed on a national scale as the Training Gateway (Exhibit 10.1).

Another form of integration will be for academic studies on CPD to find their way into more and more respectable journals, thereby legitimating the research done in this area in the eyes of other academics. This will require more

---

### EXHIBIT 10.1 TRAINING GATEWAY

The Training Gateway is the free 'one-stop shop' from which to source corporate, vocational and executive training from the UK Training Providers. It was established in 2008 with a grant from HEFCE (Higher Education Funding Council for England).

The Training Gateway allows easy and direct access to over 2,600 named training providers, it offers the most comprehensive access to high level corporate, vocational and specialist training in the UK for middle and senior managers and technical specialists. Initially developed to support UK universities and colleges, and representing every UK university and over 70 further education colleges, the Training Gateway is now working with UK-based private training providers and consultants.

The Training Gateway can provide access to:

- Over 100,000 courses
- World-class skills and knowledge
- Accreditation of in-house programmes
- Custom designed courses
- Work-based learning
- Online and e-learning programmes
- In-house delivery
- Educational partnerships with universities and colleges across the world.
                              (The Training Gateway 2010, with permission)

---

providing CPD to see it as part of broader educational and sociological ideas, as well as in terms of its role as enterprise easily studied by academics. Early philosophical underpinnings of lifelong learning, such as from Dewey (Section 3.8) will come to be recognized and combined with what must be regarded as the fundamental research programme for CPD academics, to link CPD to client, patient, employer and other stakeholder outcomes. New specifically labelled CPD departments will emerge and be accepted into the community of other subject-based academic departments. On the other hand, and at the same time, traditional subject-based departments may embrace CPD as part of their teaching remit and accept those who specialize in this area as proper academics based on their research output. It may turn out that the joining of CPD with enterprise units will be a temporary phenomenon in some universities.

### 10.8.2 CPD and the place of academic knowledge

CPD may contribute to a more profound change in universities and their place in society through a change in the relative value placed on practical as opposed to academic or theoretical knowledge. This has been suggested by some theorists on professionals, as well as management theorists and organization analysts for some time.

> Let us search, instead, for an epistemology of practice implicit in the artistic, intuitive processes that some practitioners do bring to situations of uncertainty, instability, uniqueness and value conflict.
>
> (Schön 1983:49)

Arguably universities began with an emphasis on more philosophical knowledge derived from religious doctrine and debate.[12] They developed a more practical bent in the Victorian era. During the expansion of the 1950s and 1960s universities became a hotbed of more critical and philosophical thinking.[13] While in the USA they were accused of links with the military and many at that time expressed the view that universities should be a secure and protected place of learning, not strictly to provide knowledge or people for industry or the military. This attitude was particularly strong in the late 1960s and early 1970s with the wave of radicalism connected to the war in Vietnam.

Arguably, these views encouraged a focus in universities on more theoretical and academic knowledge. However, the tide may be turning and CPD may play a part in rolling back this emphasis on abstract academic knowledge.

By the 1990s government policy in the UK came to be aimed at orienting higher education institutions and further education institutions to be sensitive to employer needs. This has encouraged more emphasis on transferable skills or competencies. This turn towards the practical, while not directly attributable to CPD, can be expected to be promoted by the growth of CPD. CPD encourages more practical teaching, stimulating universities to hire staff with direct experience of, and continuing connection to, real life professional work. The effect of hiring such people will also rebound on CPD, improving the standing of CPD courses, linking them to university quality control and to degree and diploma credentials.

Thus universities will have not only a more loosely connected student body, but also a more loosely connected staff. This change in the nature of students and staff may have profound implications for academia itself.

## 10.9 CPD and employers (and recruitment agencies)

Employers are likely to play a pivotal role in the long-term future of the CPD field. For the future of the field as we have described here to be realized, many employers will have to be drawn into CPD. For this to happen stronger connections are required between professional bodies and employers, particularly employers that specialize in providing professional services in one or a limited range of professions. Outputs measures for CPD organized by professional bodies will have to emphasize evaluation of CPD in terms of outcomes of value to employers.

A second issue to address is the difficulty for employers of many different professionals to recognize different and incompatible CPD systems from different professional bodies. This problem for large companies was noted by several representatives of large corporations in early 2009.[14] This Tower of Babel aspect of CPD will have to change for more large employers to become positively involved. Exhibit 10.2 shows the scheme for employer CPD accreditation run by Engineers Ireland. At the time of writing we would regard this as a very forward-looking programme. It was sponsored by the Irish government and has been running since 1999. Since 2004 Engineers Ireland have been running an annual CPD Company of the Year awards programme. There are also several articles on the website dealing with the issue of effectiveness of CPD among participants in the scheme. More programmes of this sort would be expected.

To link CPD to employee appraisal systems a common language of CPD is needed, which will allow different CPD measurement and recording systems to be translated. All CPD programmes need not be the same, but the way individuals are assessed and achievements recorded requires a system that allows different policies to be calibrated on a measurement yardstick, which allows differences of quality to be distinguished from differences of quantity.

This will not be an easy task.

One way this can occur is for groupings of companies or professional bodies to devolve responsibility to agencies for comparing CPD among different professionals. These would in effect be recruitment agencies, though they may also act as human resources consultants. More and more large organizations are turning to recruitment agencies to limit the number of inappropriate initial enquiries for key positions as more and more people acquire access to job vacancies through internet sites and apply using standard letters and forms.

Recruitment agencies can afford the specialized resources required to assess CPD of applicants as well as other qualifications. However, they will realize the need to develop systems that allow their applicants' CPD accomplishments to be assessed by potential employers and will begin to develop systems themselves for translating different professions' CPD recording systems into a language that employers can accept.

## 10.10 CPD, Professional Development Value, clients and the general public

Achieving and improving Professional Development Value benefits society by improving professional services to clients. There is still little hard evidence of the extent to which this is achieved because outputs measures of CPD are in their infancy and because it is difficult to isolate the effects of CPD from other factors affecting the quality of practice. It is logical to assume that CPD does add to PDV and ultimately to improved client service, though some have doubts. One must remember that what CPD must be judged against is not that professionals do nothing once qualified. Rather it is against what professionals

# EXHIBIT 10.2 ENGINEERS IRELAND'S ACCREDITATION OF CPD SCHEME FOR EMPLOYERS

Funding for the Engineers Ireland CPD Accreditation Scheme was achieved in partnership with the Irish Department of Education and Skills. CPD Accredited Employer standard marks an organization with good systems and practices that allow its engineering staff to grow, learn and develop throughout their career.

Engineers Ireland assist employers to facilitate engineering staff to become and remain:

- Technically up to date
- Professionally well-rounded
- Capable of handling responsibility and taking initiative
- Competitive in the international arena

## Mandatory criteria for accreditation

To be considered for CPD Accredited Employer status, your organization should provide evidence of the following mandatory good CPD systems and practices:

1 Internal CPD Committee
2 CPD Policy
3 Performance management and development system
4 Formal CPD – minimum five days average per annum recorded
5 Mentoring for professional development
6 Linkages with professional institutions/learned bodies
7 Knowledge sharing activities
8 Evaluation of CPD impact

## Advisory good practices

Employers of more than 100 engineers and technicians will be asked to address:

9 Postgraduate educational activity
10 Competency frameworks/talent management

Only larger organizations with complex operations and rapid rate of change will be audited against the full 12 criteria.

11 Advanced knowledge management practices
12 Fostering of creativity and innovation.

(Engineers Ireland 2010, with permission)

'just did' in the past, though clearly some professionals just did much less than others. CPD is a way of establishing a floor or standard below which those with professional qualifications and an active professional body cannot go, as long as the policy is complied with.

If CPD is effective at delivering PDV society will benefit from improvements in quality of services, reduced costs to services and new services for clients/patients. CPD may also less directly reduce negative consequences of untreated problems. This may lead to public benefits by, for example: reducing the number of days off work due to improved health services; reducing fraud and raising transparency and accountability due to improved financial services; less accidents and health and safety problems due to improved engineering and safety professional services. Arguably, also professional services firms in countries with highly developed and highly linked CPD programmes to PDV will be more attractive to potential recruits. This will allow such firms to recruit from a wider pool and thereby make them likely to recruit better candidates. Again it is both a reason for individuals with good potential to be attracted to countries with a reputation for high-quality CPD and professional services firms that actively support CPD. This in turn is likely to yield substantial, but diffuse economic benefits.

In these senses the coming of CPD and the continuing development of the CPD field may be regarded in the same way as a broad technological change within a particular industry or market. Early adopters will gain. This may mean that professional services sectors in countries that lead in CPD will be more effective than those in other countries. This may then mean an improvement in competitiveness where CPD is well developed. In some professions, professional bodies are international already, but in others the coming of CPD may make it easier for them to internationalize.

## 10.11 CPD and government

Governments of different political hues may be expected to be sympathetic to different visions of CPD though we must emphasize that the next two paragraphs are broad generalizations.

Social democratic and socialist regimes tend to prize lifelong learning, and connect it to providing equal access to education as a way to provide remedial education for those not able to avail themselves of the standard level education in their youth. It is connected with adult education and generally concerned with lower level education such as basic numeracy and literacy as well as offering the opportunity to take up skilled work. Skill tends to be the focus of their programmes.

Conservative regimes are less concerned with equal access and more with quality of service. There are two approaches conservative regimes take. One is to emphasize the importance of character and the ethical element of the professions and consequently of CPD. The other is the more neo-liberal approach, which Mrs Thatcher eventually took, emphasizing the importance of competition for achieving quality of service. This approach was anathema to the professions, regarding them and presumably CPD, as barriers to competition (that is, Vision 4).

It will be interesting to see how the Coalition Government views the professions and the CPD field. Perhaps it will display a blend of approaches. However, if CPD becomes widely recognized as important for social and economic well-being, it is likely that the government will take a more active stance towards it.

## 10.12 Shifting situation of the players and stakeholders

We perceive the 'map' of the players and stakeholders in the CPD field (as shown in Figures 2.3 and 2.4) to be changing and predict it will continue to change as shown in Figure 10.1. Overall the arrows are primarily pointed to the right with more players becoming more involved and more dependent on the field. We are confidently predicting this for the current core players: individual professionals, professional bodies and CPD specialists. In addition, we are fairly confident in our prediction that HEIs and FECs will become more dependent on CPD (this is shown by solid bold arrows). We are less confidently predicting

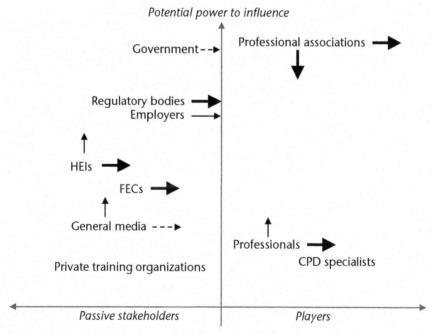

**FIGURE 10.1** Map of players and stakeholders in the CPD field showing shifts in positions on an optimistic view of its future

this for employers and even less so for government (shown by solid but unbold or dotted arrows). It is only if the former players shift significantly as shown that employers, government and the media will become more involved (shown by dotted arrows).

Greater involvement does not translate directly into more influence for all players. If anything we predict that professional bodies will have less influence in the field if employers, education institutions, the media and government become more involved, even based on the future predicted in this chapter in which they remain at the core. For the field to flourish, even if it is still dominated by the vision of CPD of professional bodies, these latter groups will have to have greater influence. Professional bodies will have to be more sensitive to the needs of employers and client/patients by making their CPD schemes more legible and transparent to these groups.

# 11

# VISIONS AND FULFILMENT

## Will the *real* CPD please stand?

### 11.1 Introduction

In Chapters 9 and 10 we examined the sweep of CPD development in a rather linear fashion, examining evident trends that may be expected to continue and then thinking through their likely long-term consequences. We examined what may be regarded as the inner logic of the CPD field as it has been developing up to now and produced a 'best guess' future scenario.

Here we tackle the more complex, emergent and potentially contested nature of CPD as illustrated by the many different visions discerned in previous chapters. We attempt to anticipate not merely the extension of current trends, but also likely critical turning points. These may be anticipated if the balance of support for different visions of CPD changes, leading to different ways individuals will operate within and in relation to the field. Our purpose here is to stimulate conversations about CPD informed by a wider view of what may be at stake.

The most common definition of stakeholders of an organization is that they are agents or groups of agents that affect and are affected by that organization's decisions and actions (Freeman 1984). Throughout this book we have referred to stakeholders of the CPD field as though the field is a phenomenon of comparable (but not equal) substance as an organization. We have distinguished players as stakeholders who are not only affected by the field but also affect it through strategic actions they take. In Chapter 10 we examined how various stakeholders have been affected and may be expected to affect the CPD field in future. Here we consider, first, that stakeholders may not play the permissive role towards the gathering CPD field predicted in the previous chapter, and second, the possibility that certain stakeholder groups may turn the field towards a very different future.

We also consider rebound effects: consequences for the shape and structure of the CPD field from changes in stakeholders, which were themselves stimulated by the development of the field. These secondary and tertiary effects are of course complex and contingent on other social and economic changes that are hard to anticipate. We also recognize that different rebound effects will happen at different times.[1]

## 11.2 Realizing the visions: a virtuous circle

Let us review arguments already made. CPD is a new phenomenon, but it 'wraps up' activities and attitudes that have long characterized what professionals 'just did', or at least an idealization of what most professionals just did. CPD is an institutionalization of these activities, but that institutionalization is as yet 'light'; a thin wrapper of procedures and rules around professional development activities. CPD is also more than mere wrapping; it can change the nature of professional development activities. In transforming activities most professionals just did into the activities phase of a CPD cycle, CPD becomes both more visible and more effective (more likely to achieve high PDV) by making those activities more consistently subject to planning, reflection and evaluation.

Enhancing the visibility, consistency and effectiveness of professional development activities can transform CPD into an important support for professional career enhancement as well as into a significant pillar of professional standards. It can then support employee appraisals and recruitment decisions. It can bolster confidence in professional competence and general reliability. It can contribute to professions regaining trust.

For this grand vision to be realized, CPD policies must become more widely appreciated by stakeholders. Employers will need to see CPD as valuable. They will need to recognize links between doing CPD and effectiveness of their professional employees. It will also be important for clients, patients, governments and the general public to see that CPD is being taken seriously by regulators. Sanctions for non-compliance need to be seen to be applied. CPD as the third pillar of professional standards needs to be more widely appreciated.

Other stakeholders will have to make more substantial adjustments towards CPD in both thought and action: education and training suppliers, commentators on education and government departments concerned with education. A rather different way of regarding CPD is as part of the supply and demand for education and a critical component of lifelong learning. Visions of CPD as the lifelong learning of millions and as an integral part of the huge education and training market add a further component of a grand vision of CPD for the future.

The market for formal courses, comprising certain forms of professional development, long predates CPD, particularly postgraduate courses leading to specialization within a profession. With the coming of CPD a wide range of shorter and less formal activities become certifiable, even if not credit-bearing (though this latter development too is coming). Activities that are now regarded by many professions as CPD are becoming accredited (through accreditation of prior experiential learning, or APEL, schemes – for an example see the developed programme at Middlesex University 2009) and can then be 'added up' with current formal education earned credentials such as university diplomas and degrees. The more this occurs, the more we expect CPD will be regarded as a lucrative opportunity by suppliers and potential suppliers. More will be invested in those activities. Much of the investment will have to be oriented towards making CPD offerings compatible with the way CPD is institutionalized by professional bodies. For example, more educational activities will have to relate not only to professional practice per se, but also to the CPD cycle. Links between educational activities and planning and reflection in the formats expected by professional bodies will be required. Links to competency frameworks will be required.

CPD may then come to be regarded as a primary component of education. At the same time lifelong learning will itself be transformed in the minds of policy makers and the general public from its current position as remedial learning for those who missed out as children and young adults, to something that is carried out by most adults, at least almost all professionals. The vision of CPD as the exemplar of lifelong learning and the critical component of the learning society may then prevail.

What these visions have in common is their mutual compatibility; moreover, they are mutually reinforcing. There are many ways we can see this virtuous circle operating. For example, if CPD is regarded as important for professional careers and worthy of the attention of regulators, on one hand, and if it is regarded as a critical component of lifelong learning and the subject of a large market in education and training products and services, it is likely that it will attract much more academic interest. The resources required to carry out substantial studies of the effectiveness of CPD in achieving PDV and particularly its effectiveness at stimulating positive outcomes for clients and employers (and preventing negative outcomes) will be forthcoming. It is likely that these academic studies will convince players and stakeholders that CPD is at least, in part, effective. If effective it will lead both to better professional services and thereby to client/patient and public benefit. This would presumably lead to greater public awareness of CPD and to greater trust in professionals.

Another example of the virtuous circle operating would be that if CPD is regarded as effective at improving client and employer outcomes, evidence for it will be increasingly demanded in the market for professional labour and professional services. This in turn will raise the demand for CPD and for CPD of higher and higher quality. This will lead to competition among suppliers and also will help spread better techniques for CPD design, content and delivery. Again this competition in CPD supply will not only drive up quality but presumably raise the likelihood of strong evidence of effectiveness of CPD being discovered by academics. This will lead to greater government support for CPD and in turn even greater public awareness of CPD.

What could go wrong with this picture?

## 11.3 Withering of the CPD field? Missing/breaking links

One reason why the prediction may not occur is because important connections in the virtuous circle of development break or are not made or are resisted. Five types of links are critical for the virtuous circle:

- Links to achieve effective CPD; that is, links between doing CPD and positive outcomes for clients/patients and other consumers of professional services.
- Linking achieving effective CPD to demonstrating that CPD is effective.
- Links that cross traditional boundaries among professions: consistency and a common language.
- Links to stakeholder groups.
- Links that cross traditional boundaries within each of the stakeholder groups, and among them.

### 11.3.1 Linking doing CPD with outputs and outcomes

The link between CPD and practice outcomes may not be made. There are a number of separate links this covers.

Logically first is the link between a professional body's CPD policy and individual members following that policy in the expected manner. Policies may be avoided all together or, more likely, may only be carried out in a perfunctory manner rather than joining in the spirit of what is expected. Though particularly a danger with inputs measurement methods, even with outputs measures some may only do the minimum, or worse, they find ways of not doing what is expected but make it look like they have. A climate of behaving in this way develops as old hands teach the newly qualified these tricks. If professional bodies are slow to recognize and respond to these abuses, the whole idea of CPD falls into disrepute.

Second, links must be made in the long chain between doing CPD and achieving beneficial outcomes, that is between:

- doing and learning;
- gaining knowledge and changing attitudes;
- changing attitudes and changing behaviour;
- changing behaviour and changing practice and finally;
- changing practice and better outcomes both for the professionals themselves (career), for those that receive their services (clients, patients, employers) and finally those that are affected by their services, but not via a direct service or employment contract (the general public).

As we have noted, it is possible for practitioners to attend CPD activities and come away with no new knowledge (still less changes in attitudes, behaviour or practice) and still have this count towards their annual CPD requirement if measured purely by attendance, by inputs. Even if learning has occurred and that learning is recorded, further steps are required before we can be assured that clients or patients will benefit.

For example, it is one thing for a structural engineer to learn that a certain new material for bridge building is available and its advantages and disadvantages. It is another thing for them to think about using this material for a particular project. It is another thing to actually use the material. It is another thing for the material in actual practice to lead to lower costs or a higher quality bridge (that is, in the circumstances that the bridge must endure, which may not quite match the circumstances envisioned by those selling the new material). It is another thing for this to be observable as of benefit to the client or employer and finally another thing for the general public to observe the higher quality of the bridge (say that it is closed less often in high winds or for essential maintenance, which may not be observable in the short run). The effectiveness of the CPD will be lost if any of these links are seriously broken.[2]

### 11.3.2 Slow progress with 'proving' PDV arising from CPD, especially practice outcomes

It may be that although CPD is effective – doing CPD leads to better outcomes for users of professional services – few are persuaded this is true. To convince the academic educationalist community will require large-scale, long-term and expensive research. There have been some studies as discussed in Sections 7.6 and 9.7, but these often appear in the grey literature, published by professional bodies or agencies providing the CPD activities, and these are not subject to peer review. The few articles that have appeared in peer-reviewed journals have been narrowly focused on a particular set of professionals in a single profession. Even with a plethora of such studies, convincing clients and the general public that CPD leads to better and more secure standards of professional competency will be difficult. It will be particularly difficult to produce research results to convincingly demonstrate that the many different forms of CPD and the many different types of professionals are more effective as a result of CPD.

Even more difficult will be convincing clients and the general public that CPD reduces the likelihood of professional incompetence. CPD may reduce the number of such cases, but could never eliminate them all together. Convincing the public of the effectiveness of CPD will require a huge investment in producing comparable statistics thus providing a comparable baseline in different professions that would allow the effects of CPD to be observable. The effectiveness of such statistics to influence public perceptions can be easily undermined when spectacular individual cases of incompetence or misconduct come to the public's attention.

### 11.3.3 Linking CPD across traditional professional boundaries

There are two types of problems here. One is the technical difficulty of creating a common language or set of practices that most professional bodies might adopt, which would allow cross-professional comparisons to be understood. A second is a strategic issue: will professional bodies want comparisons to be made?

#### The technical problem

Arguably, CPD is not well understood even by practitioners under CPD policies because of conflicting ideas of what CPD is and what it is for. This leads to different views of how it should be monitored and measured, how it should be controlled and by whom. In part because of these confusing issues CPD is relatively unknown and largely absent from discourse in both academia and mass media. One reason for this situation is that CPD is subsumed by many professional bodies as part of their internal working practices.

CPD had developed within individual professional bodies often either in isolation from the others or only in concert with others in closely related professions. Early CPD policies based on the CPD cycle were developed by engineering and construction industry professionals. Separate from this, health professionals, and particularly doctors, had strong traditions of Continuing Professional Education. For example, it is only recently that CME has become infused with Continuing Medical Professional Development, or CMPD (du Boulay 2000; Peck *et al.* 2000). Articles about CPD often appear in the non-peer-reviewed house journals and magazines of professional bodies,[3] which are not only separated from academic peer review and critique, but also are rarely read by other professionals or even members of the same professions who are not members of those professional bodies. Even within the discipline of education, CPD rarely features. There are no general well-respected journals with CPD in the title, though there are ones on lifelong learning.[4]

Another difficulty in creating standard terms and practices is that the CPD field is both spreading and changing. It is spreading to new occupations. In occupations with CPD, the institutional wrapper is thickening: more are moving to outputs measures, more sophisticated supports are being put into place, such as via web-enabled systems that are electronically connected to general membership databases. These developments also make CPD doubly difficult for the general public to understand.

#### The strategic problem: CPD as an internal and somewhat hidden activity that may come to be regarded as a competitive strategic resource

Qualifications as issued by educational institutions are well understood by the general public and can be found in the public spaces of higher and further education institution brochures and websites. People know and recognize these qualifications, many of which are backed by licensure law as well as professional bodies. CPD is different. CPD is currently regarded by many professional associations as an internal policy towards its members. The general public are not invited to participate. Many keep information about CPD programmes in members-only sections of websites, unavailable to other professionals or CPD specialists or the general public.

Professional bodies may not recognize the value of linking their CPD programmes, and particularly their measurement schemes, to each other. Those who would use systems of CPD certification from professional bodies – suppliers of CPD activities or recruitment agencies for experienced professionals – find it difficult to translate systems across professions. Academics have not provided models that can be used to understand how programmes from different professions compare. This has been a problem for professional bodies entering the CPD field or wishing to develop their CPD programmes further.

> Instead of investigating systems that have already been designed, developed and put in place, many organizations have tended to start from the beginning. There is evidence though to suggest that this situation is changing and we are beginning to see more cooperation and more generic approaches to CPD.
>
> (Guest 2006: 275–6)

Webster-Wright (2009) recently noted that the substantial empirical research undertaken within the teaching profession, which was critical of traditional notions of professional development (essentially as formal courses), was virtually unknown among other professions.[5]

Professions have been characterized as primarily concerned with competition over jurisdictions by some academics, Abbott (1988) being the prime example. Certainly there have been many jurisdictional battles throughout the history of the professions. However, we regard this as a one-sided interpretation, much as interpreting the last 100 years of European politics as a history of territorial battles alone. Some professional bodies cover the same practitioners, and sometimes those covering different, but related, professions regard themselves as in competition on certain issues. It is possible that several professional bodies would come to regard their CPD programmes as terrain for competition and this may reduce communication among them and discourage a common language of CPD measurement and evaluation.

## 11.3.4 Lack of strategic links to universities

Universities may not realize a link between CPD and their need for new revenue streams, either because they regard the costs of serving this rapidly changing market as too high, or because they find it too difficult or disruptive to turn their staff towards what has been regarded by many as a distraction from the main business of research, or because other more lucrative opportunities are the focus of their efforts, particularly fees from foreign students.

Income streams from CPD teaching may not be compatible with university financing. High overheads require teaching of large numbers on courses, preferably long courses to justify prices charged to each student. The kinds of learning activities required for CPD are typically short. They are also potentially more varied and the kinds of information to be imparted change more quickly than traditional academic subjects. Unless only a few universities take up particular subjects the demand for what any one offers may be too low to justify the full costs of delivery.

Turning universities towards teaching more practical subjects and in more practice-oriented ways may be resisted by academics. Kudos attached to teaching based on subjects that are associated with strong research programmes and highly regarded peer-reviewed journals will lead few academics to risk their careers in what is currently a relatively barren area for research success. The legitimating of CPD research predicted in the previous chapter may not materialize sufficiently to support academics specializing in CPD to challenge for elite positions at universities.

### 11.3.5 Lack of links with employers

Some professional bodies have excellent links with the main employers of their members, but most do not. The Engineers Ireland scheme (Exhibit 10.2) is an exception. Links have weakened since the mid-twentieth century, when many employers would routinely allow their staff to work for professional bodies during working hours and regarded having staff members serving on professional body committees as valuable for their image. However, many large professional services firms continue to pay professional body subscription fees for employees. Nevertheless they regard professional body offerings and ways of measuring CPD as incompatible with how they assess staff development, and therefore simply ignore CPD.

In addition, organizations that are not primarily suppliers of particular professional services, but who hire a wide range of professionals to provide services internal to the organization, find differing CPD requirements and ways of demonstrating compliance too confusing and complex to link CPD to recruitment criteria or performance appraisal. Here a lack of linking of CPD among different professions constrains the ability for CPD to be more widely appreciated among stakeholders. This may point to the critical importance of making the links which allow a common language of CPD to become widespread.

## 11.3.6 General weakening of all links due to kaleidoscope of visions encouraging continuing Babel of terms

Among professional bodies views of CPD are shifting. Formalization of CPD has meant that Vision 1 of CPD (what professionals just did) has waned. In addition, what may in the past have been considered by those running professional bodies as satisfying the demand from practitioners for activities (Vision 2, a member service), is being transformed into a more conscious and strategic view of what activities would be needed to perform practitioner tasks competently (Vision 3, maintenance of professional standards) and to encourage and support professional development.

As these visions change, more space in the CPD field opens for other ways of viewing it. CPD is viewed as a key component of lifelong learning (Vision 5) by certain academics and policy makers; another label for training white-collar employees (Vision 6) by large organizations; and a label indicating a major market opportunity (Vision 7) for all kinds of private trainers and education institutions; so more definitions of CPD and more different ways of characterizing PDV will gain credence beyond the players and stakeholders from among whom these visions have emerged. It is likely that the term CPD itself will not be used by many of the stakeholders and may even fall into disuse among professional bodies. Already the term quality assurance is used by some regulatory bodies. It is possible that others will revert to terms that were often used just before the coming of CPD in the UK and which are commonly used in the United States; that is, to terms that distinguish the sector such as Continuing Medical Education, Continuing Legal Education or Continuing Engineering Education, but perhaps also Continuing Management Development and Continuing Human Resources Development. This may be expected to reduce the chances of the virtuous circle operating as techniques developed for improving CPD and studies of the effectiveness of CPD in one profession are not read across to others, because differences in terminology strengthen the traditional barriers to cross-professional benchmarking and understanding.

## 11.3.7 General weakening of all links due to backlash growing alongside success of the CPD field

Secondary effects on CPD (by which the flourishing of the CPD field affects players and stakeholders and this, in turn leads to negative 'rebound' effects on the field) must be considered. CPD may be come to be viewed in the following negative terms due to the very success of the field:

- A purely money-making exercise of professional bodies and a rip-off, because professionals must buy products which the professional bodies produce, or which they accredit for a fee as a condition of keeping up with professional body membership or registration: especially if these products

are regarded as more expensive or of lower quality than what is available elsewhere.
- A cause of increasing prices of professional services; prices reflecting the higher cost of maintaining a professional.

The first of these has been the view of CPD of a small number of professionals in the past. This may be expected to decline as new suppliers become accredited and as existing suppliers improve what they offer. However, this may not occur for two possible reasons.

First, if the fundamental link between CPD activities and PDV is in doubt because certain CPD activities are actually regarded as having negative effects on practice. Currently there are doubts about the value of training provided by suppliers, particularly suppliers of drugs and other products in the medical field (Campbell and Rosenthal 2009). Also some activities may be regarded as fashion or even misguided, such as certain types of training for race awareness (Anthony 2009). These are likely to remain limited cases but may harm the overall view of CPD and its effectiveness.

Second, if measurement and evaluation of CPD falls into disrepute, either because of widespread abuse or cheating, or because the measures are not perceived to be true measures of PDV. Will it be possible to recognize good PDV? Arguably, the first of these problems has occurred for inputs measures and a few examples for outputs measures were noted in Chapter 7. The problem is worse if the abuse is not merely opportunistic, but motivated by deeper misgivings about CPD. The second problem is nowhere near being solved at present. As noted in Sections 7.6 and 9.7, few studies have even attempted to show a clear link between CPD and positive outcomes for clients/patients. Most studies are limited to testing the opinions of professionals themselves as to the usefulness of CPD. These are important, but not likely to convince stakeholders. Until there are many serious research studies in many different professions, or preferably which show positive results across several professions, there will be doubters over the whole CPD enterprise.

These issues will contribute to Vision 4 – the professions as a sham – by holding up a set of aspirational policies of professional bodies that are subjected to research and found wanting. Stakeholders, having been alerted to the presence of the CPD field, come to see it as nothing more than other trappings of the unrealistic aspirations of the professions.

## 11.4 Alternative futures

A second set of reasons preventing realization of the picture of the CPD field described in the last chapter is that the field turns in a different direction. Professional development by practitioners continues and flourishes, with more and more professionals carrying out both formal and informal activities, but the circle of development is no longer centred on professional bodies and CPD specialists within them. Control over what are legitimate CPD activities, or what things are required to legitimate these activities, shifts elsewhere.

Three alternative centres are envisioned here, located among employers, education institutions (particularly universities), and government agencies or regulators in which professionals being regulated and their representative bodies have little or no influence. In the last of these scenarios the media, governments and the general public see thorough and regular inspection of professional practice by specialist agencies, which are not controlled or even influenced by the profession, coupled with strong disciplinary actions, as the only way to secure competent and ethical professionals. The three pillars of professional standards come to be dominated by the second pillar.

### 11.4.1 Employers as the centre of the field: the learning and development field

Arguably, Vision 6 – CPD as company training for higher level staff – which is part of a broad strategy to develop shared values and organizational learning, is most likely to encourage decentring CPD away from professional bodies. Many from a Business School perspective may regard this as having already occurred, at least for management and those professions that may be regarded as off-shoots of management, such as marketing management, and human resources management.

CPD, as legitimated by representative organizations from the professions themselves, would be regarded as a minor adjunct to company training for some employers and completely ignored by others. In addition, the terms of reference for post-qualification quality taken into account by company HR departments and specialist recruitment firms would ignore CPD and instead concentrate on company-specific recommendations and grades within company hierarchies or on purely formal extra qualifications provided by trainers and higher education institutions.

This seems to be the current situation for many large employers. Arguably this alternative vision of what is meant to be achieved, one interpretation of how CPD is defined, of PDV, has held the CPD field back. It is not merely that few organizations see CPD as a way of guaranteeing competence among their professional and managerial staff, but rather that this is not the way they interpret many of the activities that would be done under the label of CPD. Rather they see those things as something quite different. It is building organizational capacity, productivity, effectiveness and flexibility through training and development designed by or at least designed for, those particular companies. In addition, models of staff development for professionals may be developed that discourage connections to a profession and instead look to stimulate community-building for the organization as a whole or for their divisions defined geographically or by product produced rather than by professional group or department. This scenario is different from the mere lack of linkage with CPD as organized by professional bodies described in Section 11.3.5; it is not merely that CPD would be ignored, rather that it would be actively replaced by something else.

CPD would be submerged under organization controlled and approved training, much of which would be generated within organizations or by general human resources specialists or other new specialist management consultants. CPD would primarily entail learning about company specific knowledge and undergoing training required for job rotation between departments.

One way that this could occur would be for a revival of management and organizational theories spawned during the period of initial recognition and reaction to competition from Japan and the 'tiger' economies of the Far East in the late 1970s and 1980s, and in particular the management 'excellence' view of Peters and Waterman (Exhibit 8.2). These views were weakened in the late 1980s and 1990s when companies they used to demonstrate excellence faltered,[6] as did the Japanese economy, though they have remained in circulation.[7] Such management theories may be revived: that decry knowledge certified from both academic and professional bodies as potentially dangerous for shared organizational culture; that regard them as contributors to sclerosis of the company due to the solidity of management silos based on traditional professions.

One important aspect of CPD is that it is up to the professionals to decide what to do and how to do it. Arguably, that autonomy is needed to maintain professional integrity. The professional body institutional wrapper alters what professionals 'just do', but by and large it is, as we have emphasized, a thin wrapper. There is a danger that if employers, guided by certain theories, take on CPD, they will thicken the wrapper in such a way as to kill the goose that lays the golden egg. They may diminish that sense of calling that accompanies professionalism, that accompanies commitment to the knowledge base and serving clients, supposedly without complete subordination to (short-term) profitability.

Some employers are clearly committed to maintaining their knowledge base and to serving the long-term interests of their customers. However, it will often not be in an employer's interest to tie themselves to a particular knowledge base and there will be times when they may not be able to afford to sustain a training programme. They may lose interest when times are hard.

A related view of the future of the CPD field based on employer learning and development policies can be seen from the idea of the Learning Organization, associated with Peter Senge (see Exhibit 8.4). He describes Learning Organizations as places where collective aspiration is set free and people continually learn to see the whole of reality together, that is, the whole of the reality that the organization is part of. This involves sharing tools, methodologies and theories and creating common understandings of terms, concepts, categories and keywords that apply within the organization (see LOPN 2010).

Members of a Learning Organization recognize their own frames of reference and ways of thinking and recognize that these frames prevent them from seeing other's frames of reference. They can get in the way of the organization constantly redesigning itself. For professionals these frames will come from their professional backgrounds. The goal is to fill employees with as much intrinsic motivation and as deep a sense of organizational stewardship as any company executive. By applying these ideas to individual or group performance reviews, managers can create an incentive for employees to increase their commitment to continuous, non-routine learning and for implementing strategy (Cors 2003).

There is something of a contradiction here. Though redesign may appear to be an internal process, based on internally common concepts, language and frames of reference, Senge (1990) recognizes that framing requires perspective and perspective requires reflection. Together these achievements require thinking from outside the organization, exactly the sorts of things that CPD is intended to achieve.

Clearly, all or even most organizations will never become Learning Organizations as envisioned by Senge. However, if enough take this approach it is likely that CPD (or rather learning and development) will come to mean reflection on perspectives for organizations and on the organization-oriented learning and development that arises from such reflections and are deemed important for regular redesigning of these organizations: a different (though not always incompatible) approach from one based on reflection, on professional competence and professional ethics.

### 11.4.2 Universities as the centre of the CPD field: CPD as an extension of initial professional qualifications

Initial professional qualifications long ago migrated from professional schools to universities for many traditional professions. In addition, it is generally perceived that access to the professions, particularly those with a scientific knowledge base, is via an academic degree.[8] Thus, over time professional bodies have used universities to legitimate the standing of their initial professional qualifications. More recently, the UK government has been moving to higher education qualification requirements for certain professionals who are primarily employed in the public sector, such as social workers[9] and nurses.[10]

During this time students have little contact with a professional body, though in some cases professional bodies have made efforts to recruit students by offering very cheap or even free membership. Many university courses for which a profession is the common end destination include a period of work experience or of mixed university courses and work experience prior to qualification. For accountants and lawyers the student loses contact with their university after acquiring a degree and works towards passing exams set by the professional body, supervised largely by whoever is employing them. For others, universities continue to provide support either through courses designed to get these individuals through their professional exams, or by individual academics closely involved in the professional body helping to set the exams. Finally, after this transition period, the qualified professional severs ties with a university entirely (except as an alumnus and possibly a benefactor) and becomes a registrant and/ or member of a professional body, though many professions do not require a formal relation with a professional body to practice.

However, in future, universities could take on a role as important for CPD as they now do for initial professional qualifications. The period of initial practice experience before the qualifying professional exam could be used as a model for the rest of a professional's working life. The university would provide courses that would fulfil a programme of CPD. These 'courses' would have practice elements and require cooperation of employers. Courses would be very short and it would be possible to take them with minimal time off work during office hours via online delivery and exams, and even online supervisions. Say 50 of these courses or course equivalents from informal professional development would add up to a Diploma, 100 to a Master's Degree and 200 to a PhD. These would come to be appreciated by employers as marking certain experience milestones in a professional's working life. To bolster this, new degree categories would have to be created. Universities are moving in this direction already. Currently there are new degrees instead of PhDs such as the New Route DPhil degree at Sussex University[11] and the EdD degree at Bristol University.[12]

At first such a development might be welcomed by professional bodies, using universities to legitimate CPD requirements. Professional bodies may be involved in design of examinations set for the regular milestones. However, in time their role would diminish according to this scenario. Universities, through direct contact with employers and top practitioners, will design the relevant examinations as well as the courses and other activities required to get individual professionals past the milestones.

For such degrees to be clearly understood across the professions, allowing clients and employers to recognize a proper continually qualified professional, the way they are labelled is likely to change. The term CPD may be dropped in favour of something like revalidation at the tenth year after qualification. Eventually the term would be recognized as widely as the terms Bachelor's or Master's Degrees as BAs and MAs, called R10s, R20s and so on. If the revalidation label were used, the date it was achieved would be critical. If in 2011 a client notices the professional they are dealing with has a certificate labelled *R20 2000*, they would know that the professional is a year out-of-date in revalidation.

Another development needed for this scenario would be for knowledge used for CPD activities to be based more firmly on academic knowledge or at least academic research into practice. There is a plethora of house journals from professional bodies that could provide material for the content of CPD courses taught at universities. However, currently the journals most noticed by academic staff are largely generated by university staff, academically reviewed, and backed by Learned Societies centred at universities rather than representative or regulatory professional bodies. There is a clear academic hierarchy among these journals towards those that carry more abstract theory. There are a few respected journals on professional subjects designed to appeal to practitioners, such as the *Harvard Business Review* and the more recently launched *Academy of Management Executive* (renamed *Academy of Management Perspectives* in 2006).[13] However, many more of these journals will be required to support academic teaching of CPD because the knowledge base generally moves too quickly to be captured adequately in textbooks.

A third development required is the need to overcome the general reluctance of academics to become involved in this work. New incentives could be offered to them through incentivizing departments that devote more resources to CPD. Special budgetary arrangements could allow departments to retain some proportion of funds raised by CPD work and this could be used as incentives for individual academics to do this work. Availability of more journal outlets focusing on CPD would also go some way to solving the problem of academic reluctance. It would raise opportunities to make one's name as a researcher. This would also require practice-oriented materials to appear more often in traditional journals.

The chances of this future are likely to depend on many factors. Consider the following.

First, how quickly and easily can universities make the changes described above? This will depend on the importance they attribute to the CPD market and their ability to change what they do without prejudicing other universities' activities. At first there will only be a few that move down the path of CPD orientation. These are likely to be those that already provide practice support for training at employers, either sandwiched within a degree or between degree and formal professional qualification in a number of subjects. A danger for these pioneer universities is that they acquire a reputation within the academic community as 'mere' trainers as opposed to being 'serious' academics. If this leads to falling ratings among universities, the quality of entrants may fall and other funding sources based on academic reputation may decline. This trade-off may be acceptable for those with few other funding opportunities, but it will deter others. If pioneers are not followed and if those who do not follow them are regarded as the elite, or even as the only 'true' universities, the move towards CPD will falter.

A second problem may be regarded as the reverse of the first. Even in pioneer universities there is a tendency among academics to develop and impart principles and theories. Full-time academics, who by definition are separated from up-to-date personal experience of practice, are likely to academicize this activity; concentrating more on imparting ideas of why things are done, rather than techniques of what is done, how it is done and the practice environment that may support or hamper it being done. This may then lead to criticisms such as those aimed at universities in recent years by governments for not providing the 'skills' required for the labour force.[14] Employers may not recognize this CPD system if it becomes academicized. Of course, a solution to this problem will be for universities to maintain close relations with employers in designing programmes for these new types of qualifications. However, this would require universities to become much more open to influence from outsiders. Some academics are likely to regard too close a connection with large companies as a threat to academic autonomy and impartiality.

A third and perhaps the most critical factor will be the role of the UK government in pushing universities down a path of CPD provision. In 1980 the government did use financial incentives to push universities in this direction through the PICKUP scheme (Chivers 2006). Such incentives could be revived. However, the PICKUP scheme did not substantially orient universities towards practical or vocational or professional training for adults. It led to pockets of activity as described in Chapter 3, which were limited by both the size of the resources made available and the time the scheme operated. The scheme was launched in 1982 and there was some continuity through various versions of the policy, but the scheme virtually ended with the coming of the Labour Government of 1997. A much larger and more sustained financial incentive would be required to push the universities as a sector towards the possible CPD future discussed here. As noted above, some are likely to invest in this path, particularly those with lower traditional research ratings, but the whole university sector is unlikely to move in this direction on its own and in the near future it is unlikely that government will provide the push, given its continuing withdrawal of higher education funding in the wake of the banking crisis.

### 11.4.3 Government created regulatory bodies as the centre of the CPD field

Professional associations and regulatory bodies are likely to have different visions of CPD, particularly where the regulatory body has been set up by government, rather than emerging from an association. All regulatory bodies focus on public protection. Professional associations also have a public good mission, which is essential for maintaining the reputation of the profession, but it is one among other missions more directly linked to the benefit of members. The critical question is who should do what in relation to CPD. It seems fairly obvious that associations will concentrate more on providing content and supports for CPD activities and regulatory bodies will concentrate on disciplining practitioners who do not achieve specified CPD requirements where CPD is compulsory. However, between these two aspects of CPD management there is a wide 'grey area'.

Who will monitor and who will audit the CPD requirements? It could be either. The association can monitor and audit CPD in support of members' career ambitions, but pass over cases where the requirements are not fulfilled to the regulatory body. The regulatory body can do the monitoring and pass over issuance of certificates. Who will set the CPD standard required? Arguably, the association should; peers may be better placed to do it. Or it may be that the regulator will ask the association to co-operate with it in developing a standard or changing it. Who will promote CPD? Who will write the guidance materials? We would expect the association to do this, but some regulators have been regarding it as part of their public protection remit. Who will accredit third party providers? Again, one might expect it to be the association, but it could equally be the regulator. One division of labour could be for the accreditation standards to be developed by the association and the accreditation process to be carried out by the regulator.

Arguably, if the balance shifts too far towards regulatory bodies, CPD will become more like revalidation as suggested if universities become the centre of the CPD field. The comparative advantage of universities is to provide legitimate labels for the output of education and training. The comparative advantage of regulatory bodies is to provide disciplinary procedures for non-compliance with CPD requirements. The danger is that the institutional wrapping that CPD provides for internally directed professional development will no longer be 'light'; the wrapper will thicken. If professionals themselves are not sufficiently involved in the processes, CPD may become something they regard as separate from what they just did and adopt a compliance attitude towards it; finding ways to just do enough to pass the regulatory hurdles. This is likely to exacerbate the assessment dilemma discussed in Section 4.2 and Chapter 7.

In addition, there is the danger that CPD becomes subject to political fashion and the ping-pong-like alterations of policy that other aspects of education have been subjected to. It will depend on government budget considerations as well as the cycle of elections. Finally, and perhaps most importantly, removal of CPD from representative professional associations may remove some of the dynamism that is needed for CPD to be regularly refreshed.

On the other hand, it is likely that if this scenario comes to pass, CPD will become more standardized across the professions and therefore more widely recognized among all stakeholders. In particular, it may become firmly established in the minds of the general public as a means for securing competency and ethics of professionals, even if it has relatively little actual effect on client/patient, employer or public good outcomes.

## 11.5 Centring the CPD field within a wider vision of lifelong learning

European Union agencies have been developing common 'languages' towards education that cross-country boundaries. These are now being applied to lifelong learning and may come to apply to CPD. The European Credit Transfer System (ECTS) was introduced in 1989 to allow modules and courses of initial higher education degrees to be identified by a common set of terms, allowing them to be valued in a consistent manner. This facilitates student transfer of credits when moving between universities in the EU. This was extended towards lifelong learning by the Copenhagen Declaration of 2002 on vocational education and training (Copenhagen Declaration 2002).

The aim is to create a single framework for transparency of competencies and qualifications. The ECTS for Vocational Education and Training is being developed to promote both geographical and professional mobility by allowing the accreditation or validation of formal, non-formal and informal learning via the European Qualifications Framework. This would allow different national and higher education institution or even profession body level measures of value to be translatable. Rather than the individual countries or institutions developing local systems based on some view of best practice, the job is being carried out by committees at a supranational and supraoccupational level. It remains to be seen how successful this will be. Also, the extent to which the system that emerges takes into account the specifically professional aspects of CPD, that is, PDV, remains to be seen. In particular, will the distinction between skills or competencies and the broader notions of technical and ethical competence be taken into account? Are views of what is ethical professional behaviour compatible between European countries?[15]

If these initiatives succeed, they may encourage the future of the CPD field scenario discussed in the previous chapter. However, they are perhaps more likely to encourage governments to push for the regulatory body-centred or the university-centred scenarios discussed in this chapter.

## 11.6 Conclusions

We have been following a pattern of field development through a pair of very general concepts; the field/disposition distinction introduced in Chapter 2 whereby the field as a whole has 'shape' and structure, and individual players and stakeholders have dispositions towards and visions of CPD and the CPD field.[16]

On one hand, the field develops through the regularization of activities and development of administrative policies, structures and procedures that make up the practices of CPD. These are structured by a set of organizations, institutions and material conditions: types of professional bodies, education institutions, employers and governments; laws and technologies; conditions of competition and co-operation, both longstanding and recently emerging.

On the other hand, the field develops through understandings of what CPD is and is for and the extent to which this has become etched into actors' ways of thinking and being, or viewing CPD and professionalism, such that they become 'natural' dispositions. As we argued in Chapter 3, there has been no clear and consistent habitus in this field or vision of it. It is riddled with competing visions of the field and dispositions towards participating in it. It has been an emergent field, which has continued for at least 30 years in this rather early and ill-focused state, still in its adolescence.

Not only are there different norms in different professions because of different CPD policies and programmes and different relations established with suppliers of CPD activities, but also different groups of players and stakeholders appear to hold different visions of what CPD is. At the same time there are:

- Many professionals with a clear view of what CPD is and why they are doing it, who are guided by the policies and programmes of their professional bodies in accordance with the views of CPD specialists. These professionals accept the norms and are disposed to act in ways that are 'appropriate' to raising their PDV. For them CPD is not merely aspirational; it is part of what it is to be a professional.
- Some professionals who do not yet accept the line being pursued by their professional body. Some not taking up CPD opportunities offered under a voluntary or obligatory programme despite the exhortations of CPD specialists, and not taking these activities seriously enough. Some under compulsory schemes carry out CPD in a perfunctory manner: leaving annual requirements to the last weeks because they are 'too busy'; filling out planning and reflection forms without reflecting on them more than is necessary to satisfy whoever may audit them, or even less well if they believe the chances of audit are low.
- A continuing debate within many professional bodies as to whether to change policies and programmes. Should they make CPD compulsory? Should they move towards outputs measures and what level of investment should be put into this? Should they invest more in IT support for CPD and particularly in the use of new social networking technologies? To make these decisions, CPD specialists must engage with the CPD field beyond their own professional bodies. They must balance participation in the forward motion of the CPD field with risks of alienating the membership and raising costs. These are difficult decisions that must be sanctioned by people who are not CPD specialists: top management among paid staff and largely volunteer members of the governing bodies of professional bodies. This leads to a continuing plethora of different approaches to CPD in different professions. There continues to be no strong majority of professional bodies pursuing one of the three compliance policies discussed in Chapter 4; no strong majority favouring inputs or outputs measures; a range of models for relations between professional bodies and suppliers of CPD activities; competing awarding bodies, evaluation or accreditation schemes; and some taking a total laissez faire view as to what activities members are allowed to undertake.
- A possible overlap of CPD support and control between professional associations and regulatory bodies, as more regulatory bodies take on CPD as a third pillar of professional regulation, but realize that they need to support CPD participation rather than only punish those who neglect it.
- Relatively little understanding among professionals of what those in other professions do for their CPD and even less understanding among

employers and clients/patients or potential employers and potential clients/patients, attributable to the plethora of approaches described above and the lack of comprehensive research into the CPD field, which has meant that a common language to describe differences in approach to it has not yet emerged.

- A largely unrealized potential to supply CPD activities and materials needed for other phases of the CPD cycle on the part of higher education institutions. Primary suppliers of CPD currently being professional associations themselves and specialized private training organizations, as well as suppliers of material and techniques used by professionals.
- Lack of attention to CPD as worth policy initiatives from the UK government and lack of appreciation of CPD as different from training for skills.
- Lack of appreciation among commentators and policy makers concerned with lifelong learning that CPD is in fact the core of lifelong learning that is actually pursued; wrongly believing that most lifelong learning is remedial learning undertaken by those who missed out on education when young.

We argue that the combination of the complexity and divergence of CPD definitions and aims leading to different views of which activities represent Professional Development Value and how to measure or certify this value, has contributed to a continuing state of 'adolescence' of the CPD field. This has been framed and stimulated by what we have called the fundamental paradox of CPD – that we presume professionals to know what they should do to develop themselves and expect them to just do it, but at the same time we increasingly want reassurance that professionals have in fact done it (even if it is not clear to anyone other than the professionals themselves what it is). Not only does this make pre-specification of precisely what professionals need to do for their CPD complex, but it also makes it difficult to impose much structure on CPD from 'above'. For many, a critical aspect of CPD is encouraging professionals to plan their own development and to reflect for themselves on what they have learned and the implications of that learning for future behaviour and practice.

The first side of the CPD paradox suggests a light touch approach is best. However, the second side seems to be coming to dominate. The need for greater accountability through systems of measurement and credentializing are more compelling to whoever may come to be the core players in the field. Whether it is professional bodies or employers or higher education institutions, all are recognizing the need for evidence of CPD to be presented in ways that allow non-experts in CPD, or in the profession in question, to be reassured of the efforts professionals make. Both making this evidence easily translatable across professions and different situations within professions, and also allowing individual professionals leeway to take responsibility in a relatively autonomous manner for what they do for their CPD, will require standardization, or at the least easy translatability, which currently seems very far off.

While complexity and paradox will continue to restrain the progress of the CPD field, we believe the field will continue to flourish because of the underlying need for it: fed by a strong virtuous circle comprising the passion of professionals for self-development; their demands for value from their professional associations; in addition to other pressures on professional associations leading them to regard CPD as more and more important for their mission and sustainability (their 'killer application'); and the pressure of leaders in individual professions, government and the media on regulatory bodies to deal with CPD (the third pillar of professional standards); all these demands stimulating new and existing suppliers to raise the quality of what they offer. These mutually reinforcing pressures will propel professional bodies towards higher investments in CPD and particularly towards more robust and transparent accountability for the considerable CPD that their members and registrants do.

This self-reinforcing circle is likely to be pushed to spin more forcefully in the coming decades by highly public examples of individual misconduct and incompetence and by what seem to be whole sector failures (such as led to the banking crisis). Our prediction is that in time CPD will finally come to be recognized by the media, government and the general public for its importance as indicated in the Introduction. That is, the vision of CPD from professionals and professional bodies will come to be shared by the other stakeholders of the field.

As with any long-term view of the future, we must temper our prediction with consideration of what might confound it. One possibility is that restraining factors that have prolonged the adolescence of the field up to now will continue; that the babble of different systems will be added to as new techniques are slowly adopted and as new fashions and pressures are unevenly welcomed and reacted to among the professions. The slowly developing arenas for professional bodies to share experiences and to come to common understandings of why experiences and policies of some should be adopted more widely may be frustrated by lack of government and media understanding of the commonality of the situation of different professions. Agreements to commit to commonality may come up against ancient attitudes of hierarchy and snobbery among the professions and a concern to emphasize differences among them for purposes of reputation leadership as well as the more practical issue of jurisdictional disputes and also ideological visions of each profession as unique to itself and autonomous. These 'lesser governments' (Macdonald 1995) find it easier, just as national governments, to communicate regularly and make treaties bilaterally or with a limited number of neighbours or those recognized as having similar interests, rather than 'cede' power to an overriding national or even transnational authority.

We must also consider the possibility that what is now the CPD field could become decentred from professionals and professional bodies, to other stakeholders such as employers or HEIs.[17] There is also the possibility of a new set of stakeholders arising in future who 'take over' the CPD field. The Sector Skills Councils set up by the Labour Government have moved into the CPD field, stimulated by a view that there had been little to link higher education institutions to employers, or that the links were too limited to lead to these institutions producing graduates needed by employers. The Labour Government solution to this problem was to introduce a new set of institutions to achieve this linking. The vision focused on the ideal of 'skills' as a generic term to capture what was needed to raise labour productivity. Initially the focus was on 14- to 19-year-olds and on levels of skills below A levels. Since then Sector Skills Councils have been addressing higher level skills and some have 'discovered' there are professional bodies that have long provided the very link that was presumed to be absent. In addition, a Sector Skills Council was set up to focus on lifelong learning, Lifelong Learning UK (see http://www.lluk.org).

Finally we need to consider a future where there is even more confusion about CPD because multiple centres for the CPD field develop. In some economic sectors and in some parts of the world, employers may dominate what is understood as CPD. They come to use the label CPD to refer to their learning and development programmes for managers and other white-collar staff, feeding off the older use of the term legitimated by professional bodies. In addition, universities develop CPD offerings that are short and more digestible than most current offerings, but which can be added up to diplomas and degrees that are more appropriately labelled as indicating continuing competence. Also, new players such as the Sector Skills Councils enter the field to compete with professional associations and regulatory bodies.

Whichever scenario comes to describe the future CPD field, we are confident of one prediction. Increasingly, how the professions are regarded will depend critically on how the CPD field develops. The genie is out of the bottle! Initial professional qualifications are no longer regarded as a sufficient guarantee of professional competence, certainly not technical competence and increasingly not ethical competence. The dominant vision of CPD cannot remain as something that professionals just do. Professionals must be seen to carry out activities that support the maintenance and development of their competence as well as of other aspects of their personal and professional lives. They must be seen to be lifelong learners. Furthermore, the consequences of that learning must be visible. As long ago as 1992 Lord Benson declared in the English House of Commons, that, among other things, for a group to be considered a profession, training and education must not stop at qualification. They must continue throughout a professional's working life (Benson 1992). Though outputs measures of CPD have been slow in coming, we cannot see a future of CPD without greater emphasis on this aspect of it, particularly clarity in how CPD outcomes, particularly outcomes for clients/patients, are displayed and perceived by the various players and stakeholders of the CPD field, founded on serious research into the effectiveness of CPD.

# NOTES

## Introduction

1 The General Teaching Council for England (GTCE) was set up by the last Labour Government to encourage, some would say force, teachers to professionalize. However, at the time of writing the new Coalition Government elected in 2010 announced they were disbanding the GTCE.

2 We, in keeping with usage in the sector, use the term professional body to represent any organization that is concerned with representing, regulating, promoting or lobbying for an occupation as a profession. This involves having an educational or experience standard of entry, a code of ethics or conduct, and a commitment to CPD. There are many types of professional bodies (see Friedman and Mason 2007). Here, we particularly distinguish between professional associations and regulatory bodies. Professional associations are primarily concerned with representing the professional interests of their members and upholding the reputation of the profession. Regulatory bodies are primarily concerned with maintaining the standards of the profession, dealing with complaints and disciplining professionals in order to protect the public. In so doing they also uphold the reputation of the profession.

3 Continuing Professional Education or CPE is the more common term in Canada, though both terms are recognized. In Australia both are used and in most other Commonwealth Countries the term CPD is used. More recently other terms are being introduced, particularly continuing competency and quality assurance. The former of these reflects new competency frameworks that are being introduced in many professions to support monitoring and measurement of CPD or CPE activities. Quality assurance is a term that has been introduced into legislation in Canada for regulatory bodies to complement their work on complaints and discipline (see for example Ontario Regulated Health Professions Act of 1991). The term quality assurance has been borrowed from the 'quality movement', which long predates CPD (Gabor 1992; Deming 2000).

4 In 2009 it was estimated that 3.4 million professionals in the UK carried out CPD under a formal CPD policy of a professional body (Friedman and Afitska 2009).

5 In part this is because CPD is undertaken by individuals, at their own expense, or through employers, rather than through the public purse.

## 1 What is CPD? Complex and varied!

1 The very notion of professionalism may be viewed as bound up with considerations of validity. We consider what professional bodies primarily attempt to achieve is trustworthy, high quality services. Policies are developed to define acceptable qualifications for entry into the profession and standards of technical competence and ethical behaviour expected of practitioners. In defining and maintaining standards, professional bodies attempt to ensure that knowledge, competence and ethical behaviour of practitioners do not fall below levels considered acceptable or valid. While they may encourage excellent and innovative services, their primary aim is to ensure that services and behaviour do not fall below the standards. Standards define the profession. What is considered to be valid, up to standard, is crucial for the delivery, and the reputation for delivery, of reliable and therefore trustworthy services (see Friedman and Hanson 2010).

2 Structured and unstructured are terms that are often used in relation to CPD, but in different ways. Structured often means formal courses, but it can also mean using templates or forms to provide evidence of attendance or of learning achieved. As such it is close to another term used by some professional bodies: verifiable. The RIBA definition in Exhibit 1.1 defines CPD itself as structured rather than using the term structured to define a type of CPD: a subset of it.

3 For example the UK GDC (General Dental Council) allow up to 67 per cent of their required hours of CPD each year to be reading or self-directed study (GDC 2009).

4 What has been called 'embodied knowing' (Dall'Alba and Barnacle 2005) or 'authentic professional development derived from 'authentic lived practice' (Webster-Wright 2009).

5 This has been called *hot action* (Eraut 1994).

6 However, as we will show in the next chapter, while informal learning activities, and even learning from normal or 'authentic' practice, can be incorporated into CPD, it may not be for a particular profession. In addition, formalization can have negative consequences and be resented by professionals.

7 In an early influential publication on continuing professional learning in the USA, Houle (1980) regards its purpose to prepare professionals both to use the best ideas and techniques available and to be prepared for and willing to modify these ideas and techniques.

8 As will be elaborated in Section 1.5, some professional bodies only consider verifiable activities such as formal courses or events as counting towards CPD requirements. Some count informal activities, but give them a lower weight or impose a maximum allowance for them. However, some impose no limitation on what activities are undertaken, but rather allow individual professionals to self-assess their CPD according to the learning or practice changes that they believe have arisen from activities and/or practices.

9 Note in the CPD definition from IOSH (Exhibit 1.1) both career support and safeguarding professional status are mentioned. 'All Chartered Fellows, Chartered Members, Graduate and Technician Members have to carry out CPD to safeguard their professional membership status' (IOSH 2010).

10 The Royal College of Physicians implies this by defining CPD as 'postgraduate educational activities' (RCP 2008).

11 A major stimulus to adoption of the CPD cycle was the European Project for the Use of Standards of Competence in CPD for Construction Industry Practitioners (EUSCCCIP 1998). This led to adoption of the CPD cycle among all the project partners.

12 These distinctions are explored in relation to pharmacists by Black and Plowright (2010).

13 Of course what individuals regard as practice implications of their CPD activities, even after reflection, may not actually occur. In Chapter 7 we deal with the distinction between self-assessment of outputs of CPD and 'objective' measures.

14 This is not a simple matter as many scandals about improper reporting of profits such as those surrounding the ENRON scandal show (see Fusaro and Miller 2002; Fox 2003). However, there are generally accepted accounting procedures that are widely recognized and accounts are both independently audited and made public by law.

15 See for example, Postler-Slattery and Foley (2003) for effects of CPD on nurses; and Fleet *et al.* (2008) on what the objectives should be for health professionals.

16 For some this is a central tenet of professionalism: that professionals can be trusted to maintain standards and act in what is ultimately the best interests of those that rely on them. At least this was widely accepted in the past, though it no longer seems to be a universal given in the public mind or among those regulating professionals, as evidenced by the coming of formal CPD policies.

17 Several researchers have found that doctors are not very good at assessing their own learning needs (Tracey *et al.* 1997; Jennings 2007).

18 Interestingly, as evidence of complexity and confusion about CPD, the Association of Chartered Certified Accountants (ACCA 2003) reported that their members associated CPD with courses and did not recognize the range of CPD activities that were open to them (see also Rothwell and Herbert 2007).

19 We argue that a better way of distinguishing activities that should count towards CPD would be for the criteria to be based on an assessment of what each activity undertaken has actually contributed to that individual's professional development, to their PDV. This may only be measured after the activities are carried out. What the individual professional does for their CPD is not longer the focus, rather it is to what extent what they do contributes to the aims of CPD (see Chapter 7).

20 Again, the confusion between professions occurs because some use the term structured to mean the same thing as verifiable, but others, as noted above, use the term structured in a different way.

21 Webster-Wright (2009) implies it is impossible.

22 The questionnaires were mailed to a fixed sample of members of the four different professional bodies, 600 each to ACCA and CIMA members and 500 each to ICAEW and ICAS members. Of these 2,200 questionnaires 857 were returned. Of these 582 were from accountants in practice and only those were analysed by the authors. In 2000 membership was quite different for these bodies, with 103,478 ICAEW, 45,392 ACCA, 42,717 CIMA and 12,857 ICAS.

## 2 CPD: Who? Who from? For whom?

1 For example users of buildings and bridges designed and developed by professionals; members of the public who may be affected by infectious diseases from patients of medical and other health professionals; victims of crime committed by individuals who have been dealt with by social services or justice system professionals.

2 There is a tradition for distinguishing different types of stakeholders such as direct and indirect, core and peripheral, legitimate, urgent, powerful (Mitchell *et al.* 1997; Friedman and Miles 2006).

3 Groups we identify here are not homogeneous. The common way of dealing with aspects of the CPD field is to confine attention to a single profession, and sometimes to distinguish different situations within that profession. For example Paisey, Paisey and Tarbert (2007) distinguish accountants both by professional body membership and whether they are in practice or working in business (as employees) and also if they are working in audit or in insolvency. Here we concentrate on professions as a whole or on 'slicing' the category of professionals according to their approaches to CPD.

4 The Information Technology field has been regarded in this way in the first few post-war decades (Friedman 1994, 1999).

5 Personal communication from an individual at ACCA who described this situation as 'mad, as there is a huge crossover in business/management skills in particular' (Llewellyn 2009).

6 The general public may be considered stakeholders both as potential clients and as beneficiaries or those damaged by advice or actions of professionals to others.

7 Based on an estimate of 28 million labour force in 2007 according to the ONS.

8 For example the International Federation of Accountants (IFAC) now recommends all national accountancy bodies to adopt compulsory CPD (IFAC 2004).

9 For an idea of the range of professions that exist, as well as information about access to them, see www.totalprofessions.com.

10 There is considerable debate as to how much autonomy professionals have, particularly those who are not self employed (Adler *et al.* 2008). It clearly differs between occupations and employing organizations, and by their hierarchical position within those organizations. Nevertheless, compared with other employees, professionals can choose the kinds of work they do, the way they do this work, the ordering of their tasks, and the types of support they need to maintain their competence and professionalism.

11 Johnstone and Rivera 1965; Dao 1975; Cross 1981; Darkenwald and Merriam 1982; Scanlan and Darkenwald 1984; Darkenwald and Valentine 1985; Friedman and Phillips 2004; Henwood *et al.* 2004; Wessels 2007.

12 Certain professionals, particularly in professions with a high proportion of female practitioners, have been found to be particularly hampered by CPD competing with family responsibilities: nurses (Perry 1995), dieticians (Keim *et al.* 2001), occupational therapists (Townsend *et al.* 2006) and radiographers/sonographers (Henwood *et al.* 2004; Phillips 2010).

13 Notably situational deterrents concerning employer and family were not significantly related to perceived effectiveness of CPE courses. Paisey, Paisey and Tarbert (2007) found the most commonly cited barriers to CPD among accountants in practice in the UK were lack of time (67 per cent), cost of courses (51 per cent), location of courses being too far away (41 per cent), suitability of content (36 per cent). A long way below these was poor quality of courses (9 per cent).

14 Sadler-Smith and Badger (1998) found that people who had been members of the CIPD for a long time were less interested in CPD, but they found that age, gender and job level were not related to the value they attached to it. Bullock *et al.* (2003) found that dentists with the least experience had the highest participation in CPD. Hull *et al.* (2003) found that more female than male dentists undertook CPD and those that valued it most were females who had been registered for 11–20 years, with those valuing it least males registered for more than 30 years. However, Rothwell and Arnold (2005) found no significant correlation between perceived value of CPD and age or gender among CIPD members. Similarly, no significant relation between perceived effectiveness of CPE and years of experience in the profession or gender was found for accountants in the USA by Wessels (2007). She did find a significant negative relationship between those agreeing that CPE courses are less useful to them as they gain experience and perceived effectiveness of CPE courses.

15 Perry (1995) reported that nurse take-up of CPD was low because of lack of self-value, among other reasons, though mainly due to family responsibilities and lack of interest from managers.

16 This phenomenon was also found by Phillips (2010).

17 Varia (2006) distinguishes three categories of motivation for doing CPD: Values – 'emotionally charged beliefs acquired through interactions with others'. Attitudes – more specific than values, an attitude is described as a state of mind or a disposition. Drives – specific factors such as requirements of professional bodies or interests in particular topics or techniques, or changes in legislation that affect one's practice.

18 However, some have found that promotion rather than better patient care has been a prime motivation in certain professions (Spalding 2003; Evans *et al*. 2008).

19 This survey was administered by PARN rather than the particular professional bodies, though it was advertised to members by their respective professional bodies. Names were not asked for, so respondents were unlikely to concern themselves with what their professional body would think of their answers. Those public spirited enough to fill out this voluntary survey may bias the sample towards more worthily motivated individuals.

20 This result is consistent with Rothwell and Arnold's (2005) main finding, that the perceived value of CPD is mainly driven by professional commitment than by perceived enhancements to employability among CIPD members. Rothwell and Herbert (2007) found perceived value of CPD to be related to professional commitment and not significantly related to career orientation among accountants in England.

21 Not all professional bodies *require* members or registrants to do CPD, though all with a policy encourage it. In the UK 85 per cent of professional bodies reported having a CPD policy in 2006, compared with 71 per cent in Australia, 67 per cent in Ireland and 66 per cent in Canada (Friedman and Mason 2007).

22 Note the large number of items counting for CPD points by the Health Information Management Association of Australia under service to the HIMAA and service to other relevant associations/societies (Exhibit 1.6), and the number of items counting as CPD by the Health Professions Council under the heading professional activity, which recognize involvement in the workings of a professional body (Exhibit 1.5).

23 Among smaller associations early design work on CPD policies and programmes was carried out by committees of volunteers from among the membership of the profession. Even if a scheme was run by an administrator many were tightly overseen by a committee made up of volunteers (Friedman, Davis *et al*. 2000).

24 This survey covered 101 professional bodies in the UK with a CPD policy (out of 162 respondents to the survey that had been sent to 459 organizations that were on the PARN database at that time. It was discovered that several were not professional bodies and these were eliminated before the analysis. The survey period was during 1998/99 (Friedman, Davis *et al*. 2000).

25 PARN provides a network with opportunities to work on cross-professional projects and to attend cross-professional events on CPD (www.parnglobal.com). A professional body for CPD specialists has been established, based in the UK: CPD Institute (www.cpdinstitute.org), but it is not very active. In addition, the UK Inter Professional Group has an active section called Inter Professional CPD Forum (www.ukipg.org.uk).

26 As we will show in the next chapter, what is considered adult education or even lifelong learning is generally aimed at providing courses that are not work-related or encouraging learning among those who missed out on qualifications or even basic skills when they were young. The majority who carry out lifelong learning, that is professionals pursuing CPD, are largely ignored.

27 However, this view may not be so serious if employers view their staff as mobile anyway: 'They are likely to leave anyway if they are not able to get the training they want . . . We only rent them' stated a representative of HR from Asda at the Centre for Recording Achievement (CRA) conference 10 November 2009. They consider a certain amount of 'churn' to be beneficial or at least unavoidable (www.recordingachievement.org/news-and-events).

28 This is particularly associated with the great wave of enthusiasm for business process redesign or business process re-engineering of the past 20 years following Hammer (1990).

29 www.motorola.com

30 https://partner.microsoft.com

31 www.training.sap.com

32 www.premierit.com; www.skilsure.com; www.echelonit.com
33 This was announced at a Centre for Recording Achievement (CRA) conference 11 November 2009, though no data source was provided.
34 Some universities are also forming consortia to engage with communities and business on a regional level. Recently these units have come together into a national alliance and together they have developed a portal (www.thetraininggateway.com).
35 In the United States the term community college is used to describe this sector, rather than further education, however some FE colleges in the UK call themselves community colleges.
36 In the UK the plan in the 1960s was to develop further education through both colleges and polytechnics. However, during the 1970s polytechnics hired academic staff desirous of positions in traditional universities and the polytechnics were made over to look more and more like traditional universities. This was ratified by the government in 1992 when polytechnics were given university status. These post-1992 universities have been more ready and willing to provide CPD.
37 Lack of policy on supporting public sector institutions to provide CPD or for individual professionals to receive it can be linked to governments ignoring activities that might lead to new policies, that is, research into the value of CPD and policies that could improve PDV. One recent UK government initiative is worth noting: Gateways to the Professions (Langland 2005). Though its primary emphasis was on disadvantaged groups gaining entry to traditional professions, it did include a small project investigating links between HEIs and professional bodies in terms of collaborations over CPD (Friedman *et al.* 2008).
38 The position of any group of players/stakeholders will depend on both the range of positions of individuals in the group and the proportions of individuals at different ends of the range. Professional associations who have no CPD policy would clearly be far less dependent on CPD and have little or no influence on the CPD field as individual organizations. However, their members may expect CPD, if it appears that everyone else is doing it. As the proportion of professional associations with a policy grows, so we would shift the position of that category to the right. In addition, if those with a policy expend more resources on their CPD, this will also shift that category to the right.
39 Social capital is 'the aggregate of the actual or potential resources that are linked to possession of a durable network of more or less institutionalised relationships of mutual acquaintance and recognition' (Bourdieu 1986: 249). Economic capital is resources employed to produce goods and services (including labour), capital goods (tools and equipment) and sometimes includes land. However, the term can also apply to finance available to purchase these resources, that is, money above what is needed for personal consumption. Cultural capital is accumulated cultural knowledge that confers power and status.
40 The extent to which those in a profession are disposed to this sense of calling will largely depend on factors that are profession specific. The general public view of the worthiness of different occupations, the impact of decisions on client or employer interests and wellbeing, the role of the professional bodies and the traditions of the profession; all are likely to play a role.

## 3 Visions of CPD

1 There is much dispute about when this occurred, but traditional professions in the UK seem to have been well established in the seventeenth century. However, there are different opinions, for example: 'Sociologists regarded the professions as having distant medieval origins; more specifically, the three prototypical professions of learning, law, and medicine were seen as having 'differentiated' from a common medieval 'religious matrix.' The professions attained a nearly recognizable form in

the late eighteenth and nineteenth centuries and 'took off' at that time, eventually becoming, according to the sociological canon, one of the hallmarks of modernity in the West' (Goldstein 1984: 174).

2  These are the activities commonly thought of as CPE in the USA and Canada.

3  It is still unrecognized in most inputs-based systems of CPD (Chapter 7).

4  This had long been recognized by well known writers, though called different things, 'thinking processes' (Barnard 1938: 302); 'thinking what I am doing' (Ryle 1949: 32); 'tacit knowledge' or the 'tacit dimension' (Polanyi 1967); 'acting in the mind' (Harrison 1978).

5  It is notable that lawyers have been particularly resistant to formal CPD, particularly as 'time is money' in law firms that measure success by the number of billable hours (Watson and Harmel-Law 2010) and similar arguments have been applied to accountants (Hicks *et al.* 2005).

6  On the other hand, reframing is less likely to emerge in situations that are either totally routine, or where there is an emergency that needs to be dealt with very quickly.

7  In a later book, Schön (1987) makes recommendations for the type of professional education system he believes will enhance practitioners' abilities to reflect-in-practice.

8  This line of thinking has been more recently followed up by Koehn (1994).

9  Communities of practice have been defined as 'groups of people informally bound together by shared expertise and passion for joint enterprise' (Wenger and Snyder 2000: 139). They were originally thought of as bottom-up groupings of likeminded practitioners who through mutual engagement develop their community with 'an emergent structure, neither inherently stable nor randomly changeable' (Wenger 1999: 49). However, since his early work Wenger has concentrated on how agencies like corporations as well as professional associations, government and education institutions can cultivate such communities (Wenger *et al.* 2002). Others more proactively refer to the construction of communities of practice (Swan *et al.* 2002).

10  This term is used in the IT world to indicate an application that would be so compelling that it would sweep away any competition and represent a major leap in user value. It was applied to the development of spreadsheets beginning with VisiCalc for Apple II and Lotus 123 for the IBM PC (Downes and Mui 1998).

11  The most common reasons for instigating a CPD policy according to a sample of 20 UK professional bodies surveyed by Madden and Mitchell (1993) were 'improvements in professional standards' and the 'need to demonstrate professional standards'.

12  From this perspective, once established CPD can be viewed as a competitive device, a battalion on the potential battleground for jurisdictional control undertaken by different professions and professional bodies within a profession (Abbott 1988). There is competition particularly for what is thought of as generic CPD, that is, CPD subjects that cross professions, such as in management or team-working or IT skills. CPD may be a way of maintaining jurisdiction over a knowledge base as that base develops, particularly as new specialisms emerge.

13  Though interestingly it also echoes a guild-like view of expertise, based on 'secrets' of the occupational community into which novices are inculcated, rather than a more modern view, growing throughout the twentieth century, that expertise continually degrades without further training as technology develops.

14  Though there was a circularity in this traditional view; being of a certain class was assumed to make for a trustworthy professional, and being a professional made you a member of the professional class (Wilding 1982; Macdonald 1995).

15  It must be pointed out that Gold *et al.* cite no evidence or references for this claim.

16  Perhaps even Milton Friedman by reducing reliance on 'the ability to pass an examination twenty or thirty years earlier'.

17  The links implied in the following paragraphs are admittedly speculative, but provide at least a preliminary understanding of the emergence of CPD.

18 Criticisms of the health professions system and its institutions were epitomized by Ken Keasy's 1962 novel *One Flew Over the Cuckoo's Nest*, made into an academy award-winning film in 1975.

19 According to Houle (1996: 6) the first major delineation of adult education was published in 1919 by the Adult Education Committee of the British Ministry of Reconstruction by which it was described as 'general, humanitarian, nonutilitarian or humanistic'. This view has affected British and American adult education ever since according to Houle.

20 For example the University of Bristol's Department of Extra-mural Studies became the Department of Continuing Education in 1989.

21 Programmes can be traced back to the 1920s, with the first mandatory programme established in 1934 in the field of urology in the US (Sriharan *et al.* 2009).

22 An example of a stage in the transformation of CPE is the following definitions cited by Davis, Davis and Bloch (2008: 652):

> For the purposes of this work, continuing medical education is defined as any activity which serves to maintain, develop, or increase the knowledge, skills and professional performance and relationships that a physician uses to provide services for patients, the public, or the profession (American Medical Association 2007; Accreditation Council for CME 2007). The term continuing professional development (CPD) is broader than CPE and has become more popular in many areas of the world. As defined by Stanton and Grant, CPD includes educational methods beyond the didactic, embodies concepts of self-directed learning and personal development and considers organizational and systemic factors.
>
> (Stanton and Grant 1997)

It is not clear that 'any activity' positively affecting services a physician provides for patients and the public would exclude 'self-directed learning' or even 'personal development', 'organizational and systematic factors'. A more precise definition of CME which is cited as the common definition (Sriharan *et al.* 2009: 145) is 'education and training of doctors after completion of basic medical education and postgraduate training, thereafter extending throughout each doctor's professional working life' (Karle 2003). However, Peck *et al.* (2000: 432) state: 'There is no sharp division between continuing medical education and continuing professional development, as during the past decade continuing medical education has come to include managerial, social, and personal skills, topics beyond the traditional clinical medial subjects.' Finally, a very interesting comment about the relationship between the two was recently made by Bellande *et al.* (2010: 16):

> Traditional continuing medical education (CME) is necessary for keeping physicians current and competent, is insufficient in translating physician practice into better patient outcomes. CME, then, must be transformed from a system of episodic interventions to a more personalized, contextual, flexible and targeted process within a continuing professional development framework.

23 This is the experience of PARN which has been carrying out such surveys on a regular basis since 2000.

24 Of 101 professional bodies in the UK that responded to the 2000 survey on CPD, 86 per cent indicated that they had issued record cards (Friedman, Davis *et al.* 2000).

# 4 CPD governance: compliance policies

1 A spirited debate held at a conference in London on this issue seemed to have been 'won' by the side arguing CPD policies should be compulsory (UK Inter-Professional Group (UKIPG) CPD Forum, 28 January 2009).

2 See for example the professional credentializing scheme of the Health Information Management Association of Australia (Exhibit 1.4).

3 The estimate is based on a sample of 226 professional bodies who provided information on their membership figures and CPD policies and 26 professional bodies who provided estimates of the percentage of their membership that do CPD (Friedman and Afitska 2009).

4 www.gmc-uk.org/doctors/licensing.asp

5 www.rcgp.org.uk/_revalidation.aspx

6 Wessels (2007: 370) found a majority of accountants in the state of North Carolina in the US agreed that where CPE is required of them 'it makes it more likely that CPAs are competent (60 per cent agreed, though 16 per cent disagreed) though only 48 per cent agreed that compulsory CPE helps protect the public from incompetent professionals (and 28 per cent disagreed).'

7 Many professional bodies organize discounts for their members with companies providing professional indemnity insurance, see for example the relation between CIPD and Frank Glennon insurance (CIPD 2010b).

8 Though it is possible that the insurance companies are using CPD as a signal to indicate merely which individuals are more conscientious and therefore a better risk.

9 Wessels (2007: 370) found that 85 per cent of accountants (CPAs) in North Carolina agreed that compulsory CPE 'helps improve the image of the profession' and only 4 per cent disagreed.

10 The term ultrasonographer that was later shortened to sonographer identifies a person trained in performing ultrasound examinations in Australia from the early 1970s. In other countries this work is performed by radiographers or by physicians.

11 This argument was put at a PARN conference in 2007 in Australia in November 2007 where distances are considerable (see also the statement at the bottom of Exhibit 1.4).

12 This has occurred in Canada, not due to resistance to compulsory CPD, but rather resistance to assessment purely on an output measure basis. In 2007 the scheme of practice assessment among British Columbia pharmacists introduced in 2003 was altered in response to concerns voiced at annual general meetings of the regulatory body and the association in 2006 whereby a continuing education option was offered in addition to practice assessments (see British Columbia Pharmacy Association 2007).

13 Phillips (2010) cites many sonographers who complained of courses that were irrelevant, either because they were repetitions of previous courses or because they were aimed at too low a level to be of value to experienced practitioners. Such complaints are likely to have been conveyed more directly to course and workshop organizers if the evaluation was based on outputs and if there were alternative suppliers of courses and workshops.

14 I must have been asked that question more than 100 times in the past 11 years at various conferences and workshops run by PARN on aspects of CPD.

15 We call this regulation by exception (Friedman and Hanson 2010).

16 The Madden and Mitchell (1993) survey has not been used to show the diffusion path due to the very small sample size, which we believe has biased this estimate upwards by more than the other estimates. The proportion of larger professional bodies in their sample was higher than for the others.

17 The sample was still estimated to have a lower proportion of smaller professional bodies than the population at that time (Friedman, Davis et al. 2000).

18 According to the FEE survey of accounting professional bodies in Europe in 29 countries, only Greece and Portugal had failed to comply with mandatory CPD as at 31 December 2006. Not all accounting bodies in the world are IFAC members and some are associate rather than full members. As recently as spring 2009, ACCA supported the Society of Accountants in Malawi (SOCAM) to become compliant with IES 7 (personal communication from Sara Llewellyn of ACCA).

19 However, Canadians are proud of the self-regulatory aspects of their professions as distinguishing them from those in the United States. Both tend to have separated

professional associations from regulatory bodies, but in the United States those regulatory bodies are largely funded by and run as public sector agencies at state level. In Canada they are also constituted at the provincial level, but they tend to be funded largely by a levy on the professionals themselves and professionals either dominate or are strongly influential in the governance of these bodies.

20 There are also in several countries exemptions for non-practising members (Denmark, Spain) such as retired members (Ireland, Netherlands) or those on maternity leave or in temporary military service (Italy).

## 5 CPD governance: programme support

1 The Chartered Institute of Personnel Development has 132,000 members (CIPD 2010b).

2 Though in the past few years international bodies such as the International Federation of Accountants have been making recommendations and developing standards for CPD (IFAC Educational Committee 2004, 2010).

3 The situation is gradually changing in the UK with opportunities for cross professional fertilization occurring through several cross professional organizations focusing on CPD: UK IPG CPD Forum, PARN CPD events, CPD Institute.

4 These problems were identified in an earlier document published by the Institution when they were called the Institution of Electrical Engineers (IEE) *Mentoring: An IEE Guide to Best Practice* (Friedman, Davis *et al.* 2000).

## 6 CPD governance: regulatory procedures

1 Another way of viewing CPD may be as the last throw of the dice for lawyers and other professionals before their widely discussed end? (Broadbent 1997; Susskind 2008).

2 Except for the case of particular individuals who may have been considered for higher office, but this would have been carried out in an informal manner.

3 At best, or at least to benefit the active members, or those who contributed to the decision-making process, those who we have identified as super-members (Friedman and Williams 2006).

4 www.thecpa.co.uk

5 The FSA launched the Retail Distribution Review (RDR) in June 2006 to deal with 'insufficient consumer trust and confidence' in the products and services provided by the retail investment market in the UK. The FSA regard increasing the professional standards of investment advisers to be one of three broad ways of redressing this situation (the others being to improve the clarity with which services are described to consumers by firms and the potential for consumer outcomes to be distorted by systems of adviser remuneration). A new framework is due to come into effect at the end of 2012.

6 Examples of meta-regulators discussed in Friedman and Hanson include the Council for Healthcare Regulatory Excellence.

7 They were the General Medical Council and the RICS (for surveyors), but not ACCA (for Chartered Certified accountants), the Nursing and Midwifery Council or the Solicitors Regulation Authority (Friedman *et al.* 2009).

8 In Canada the term Continuing Professional Education (CPE) is commonly, but not exclusively, used instead of CPD. In the USA CPE is almost exclusively used.

9 That is, when there is a different distinct regulatory body for that profession.

10 In this the UK and other countries influenced by the Anglo Saxon model of relatively autonomous professions such as Australia and Canada, differ from American and Continental European models where licensing and re-licensing of professionals is a

state function, though professionals may be involved in the state organizations carrying out these functions. According to a representative of IOSH, which recently achieved Chartered Status, the Privy Council review of applications includes CPD requirements (Harvey 2010).

## 7 CPD measurement and the paradox of CPD

1 We define paradox as a regularly occurring unintended consequence that cannot be avoided in spite of being aware of it. Here we are using the term paradox to identify that CPD is two things at the same time and that those two things are not only different but they imply different interpretations of the reasons for doing CPD and the consequences of doing it. They give different impressions of what CPD is and what it is for, to those observing it and those who do it. Assessment of learning is a measure of what is learned and a stimulus to learning, but it also shapes behaviour towards achieving a high assessment and this can stimulate aspects of the intended knowledge to be ignored or learned in a manner that forgoes deeper understanding.

2 Arguably, it cannot be satisfactorily certified for two reasons. First, any examination would have to be specific to the circumstances in which that professional works. Second, the needed knowledge is always changing so that even if competence required could be certified, it would soon become out-of-date.

3 For example, for accountants in practice other than those in audit or insolvency the minimum requirements during the 1990s and early 2000s ranged from 30 hours (CIMA) and 35 hours (ACCA) to 55 hours (ICAS) and 150 points (ICAEW – with one hour of unstructured CPD counting as one point, but one hour of structured CPD counting for three hours) (Paisey *et al.* 2007). While ICAEW gave different weights through differential points for structured and unstructured hours, the other three had quota requirements for structured or unstructured CPD (21 hours structured and 15 unstructured for ACCA; 10 structured and 45 unstructured for ICAS; minimum 10 hours structured for CIMA). They also differed slightly in how they defined structured and unstructured CPD; generally defining structured as relevant to their field and training needs, but some more specifically such as for CIMA requiring structured hours to involve the stimulus of third-party contact. The field has come to be rationalized somewhat by the International Federation of Accountants (IFAC), to whom accounting bodies defer with respect to many policies. The accounting standard established by IFAC in 2004 for mandatory CPD was 120 hours over three years of which 60 must be verifiable (IFAC 2004).

4 These paragraphs are based on Friedman and Woodhead (2008: 12–13) but there the term results were used rather than outcomes.

5 For the distinction between competencies, technical competence and ethical competence see Friedman 2007.

6 This in part reflects a higher proportion of regulatory bodies in the Canadian sample, but may also be influenced by a North American view of concentrating on designing assessments that are simple and clear, a 'rules-based' rather than a 'principles-based' approach.

7 Friedman and Woodhead were influenced by the four levels for evaluation of training programmes proposed by Kirkpatrick (1994). These are: (1) Reactions – participant responses to training; (2) Learning – knowledge and skills acquired; (3) Behaviour – changes in behaviour or the application of knowledge and skills; (4) Results – or practice outcomes.

8 That is, the relation could be multiplicative.

9 Note that audit is different from assessment. Audit is to confirm the accuracy of reported assessment, not to make the assessment.

10 In May 2004 the 10,187 members of the North Carolina Association of Certified Public Accountants were invited to respond to a web based survey, 1,957 responded

(Wessels 2007). As noted in the Introduction (Note 3) the term Continuing Professional Education (CPE) is used instead of CPD in the USA. However, in this case CPE refers to formal courses only and is therefore rather limited compared with CPD in the UK, which usually includes some proportion of informal activities in the requirement even if the requirement is measured by inputs.

11 Some of these issues are best assessed long after the activities have occurred, such as enhancing employability.

12 'Any attempt to measure precisely the velocity of a subatomic particle, such as an electron, will knock it about in an unpredictable way, so that a simultaneous measurement of its position has no validity' [Britannica online; http://www.britannica.com/EBchecked/topic/486231/quantum-mechanics/77517/Heisenberg-uncertainty-principle (accessed 17 May 2011)].

13 See www.aqr.org.uk/glossary/?term=observereffect

# 8 Complexity, paradox and mystery

1 Summative assessment means summarizing the development up to a certain point. The purpose is to summarize what has been learned or achieved at the point of assessment. Formative assessment aims to promote further development (Crooks 2001). However, summative has come to be associated with the formal examination of a specified length of training.

2 Though this autonomy is not absolute and will vary by profession and by situation within the profession (particularly whether they are employed or self-employed).

3 All have not regarded CPD as a source of income, but rather promoted CPD as a member service, charging only enough to cover costs and also providing free learning opportunities. This has, for example, been the approach of ACCA (personal communication).

4 Phillips (2010: 116) states:

Professionalism can be seen as a major driver for CPD, and the push by sonographers for a recognised professional status was instrumental in the introduction of mandatory CPD for accreditation. It was evidenced by many comments that sonographers do perceive themselves as professional and in the main recognised that CPD is part of this. However, others felt that because they were professional there was no need to introduce a mandatory system. It has been recognised in the literature that professionals should be responsible for their own learning.

5 German federal states and the European Social Fund (ESF) offer a variety of on-the-job training programmes. Companies can be supported with subsidies covering up to 50 per cent of all training costs. European Union authorization is required if the amount awarded to a single company exceeds EUR 2M (German Trade and Investment, see www.gtai.com).

6 This view is certainly not shared by all players in the field of management. Note the Chartered Management Institute Manifesto of 2010 (CMI 2010).

7 Communication at presentation of the Training Gateway, at UKIPG CPD Forum 2008.

8 Nelson Croom, for example, provide online learning and development for professionals in the UK and support the CPD cycle (see www.nelsoncroom.co.uk).

9 However, Paisey and Paisey (2007) guest-edited an issue of *Accounting Education* with the theme of continuing professional development in December 2007.

# 9 Dynamics

1 PARN data show around 2/3 having a policy in Australia, Canada and Ireland (Friedman and Mason 2007), and it is likely that the proportion is at least as high in the USA.

2 Though this suffered a serious knock between late 2007 and early 2009 with the credit crunch, financial services have been growing again since then.

3 Though there is an argument that two opposing tendencies are operating. One to deprofessionalize traditional professions as they come to be characterized by more and tighter regulation and for some, with new technology leading to routinization of certain tasks. Second, more lower-level and new occupations are aspiring to the status and conditions that they perceive traditional professions have. In addition, some developments of new technology lead to the removal of certain tasks that had been taken on by lower level work within professional occupations (Adler *et al.* 2008).

4 Unfortunately the current picture of CPD has to be painted against the background of recession. First, it is leading employers to cut training budgets. Second, it gives additional impetus for individual professionals to take their CPD more seriously. The recession is therefore not likely to have a great effect on the overall spread of CPD as the two influences have opposing effects.

5 This assumes both more professionalized occupations as well as a higher proportion of professionals carrying out CPD, mainly because a higher proportion of professional bodies will have compulsory policies. Note this is based on a fairly wide definition of which occupations should count as professions (see Friedman and Afitska 2009).

6 Within a decade the Department for Education and Employment (DfEE) in the UK became the Department for Education and Skills (DfES) and then Department for Universities, Innovation and Skills (DIUS) and then became Department for Business, Innovation and Skills (BIS) in 2009.

7 The usual reason for this was that delivered systems could not cope with growth in numbers of records or features of records, which were obviously needed from professional bodies' point of view, but were not anticipated by suppliers, with neither party asking the right questions at the pre-specification stage. This may have occurred because suppliers presumed their experience with private sector companies could be easily transferred to membership organizations.

8 Professionals were sent a mailed questionnaire, 100 each from 14 professions via their professional bodies, with 376 responses received. The cited figures refer to uses of the internet for specialized professional learning.

9 2006 survey based on 110 responses from UK professional bodies representing a 33 per cent response rate, and 2009 based on 87 responses representing a 25 per cent response rate (Friedman and Afitska 2010).

10 Outputs measures of CPD are still not well understood, partly because many have only recently introduced them, and some do not even recognize that they are measuring CPD in output terms (they may not regard planning and reflection returns as outputs measures). Just as the definition of CPD varies among professional bodies, so what is considered an output measure varies. While this may hold back diffusion of outputs measures, we believe in future a more common view of these measures will develop, especially because they are being adopted by regulatory bodies.

11 Perhaps also time limited because the findings are not regarded as sufficiently robust to withstand the test of time.

12 See Chapter 3, Note 22 for a comparison of definitions of CME and CPD.

13 Meaning primarily that no control group was used in the studies reported, but also lack of quantitative data, randomization and descriptions of withdrawals or drop outs.

14 Education levels of pupils, in schools with different resources and of different sizes and sizes of classrooms, and schools with different remits and support from local authorities, all should be recognized as influencing factors.

## 10 CPD field beyond tomorrow

1 It is likely that some other label will emerge for this specific and partial aspect of lifelong learning.

2 Others have been less worried about this, either because of concerns that social capital may not be as cohesive as originally thought (strong communities mean high social capital for insiders, but raised barriers against outsiders), or because there are new forms of social capital (Ester and Vinken 2003). In the past more went to church, participated in the Boy Scouts, neighbourhood sports and recreational activities and charitable organizations. Now people are more likely to interact electronically, through email and on the internet through social networking sites such as Facebook or Twitter.

3 CPD – the new 'killer application' (see Section 3.3).

4 Friedman and Williams (2008) develop a model of degrees of closeness of the relations between professional bodies and higher education institutions, which specifies three degrees: recognition; approval and accreditation; partnership. Examples of partnership are given from a very large professional body – the CIMA programme of 'collaborative provision' such as its funding of a research Centre of Excellence at Bath University's Business School – and a very small one – the Institute of Translation and Interpreting (ITI) partnership with Leeds University.

5 In effect, the medium will become the message (McLuhan 1964).

6 Phillips (2010: 108) cites a sonographer on mandatory CPD. 'Initially mandatory CPD seemed like a burden. Once I had attended my first conference, I realised it was a necessary part of being a sonographer.'

7 This distinction was the justification for introducing preceptorships. A nurse may be fit for practice, able to do whatever is normally required of a nurse, however placed in a particular nursing environment, there are likely to be aspects of what is required specific to that environment, particular procedures that are hospital-specific or specific to a regional health authority. Mastering these things is required to be properly fit for purpose in that practice, rather than fit for practice in general or rather being capable of becoming fit for purpose with only light-touch supervision (Friedman *et al.* 2009).

8 Fordham (1973) noted the post-war change in universities away from what he perceived to be a liberal non-vocational framework towards more closed entry courses and more avowedly vocational orientation. He argued that this should lead to a change in situation for extramural or adult education staff to become less marginal to the process of university development. He called for a revival of university commitment to continuing education and for a debate on the separation of these departments from the rest of the university. Apart from a brief period of rising government commitment to these activities through the PICKUP scheme (Section 3.8.3), by the 1990s, universities were incorporating continuing education into mainstream subject departments. However, rather than leading to integration of such activity with traditional department work, the effect was to marginalize continuing education in individual departments and in some cases to quietly drop it from highly research-oriented departments (which were becoming even more focused on research in the 1990s, driven by national research assessment exercises). This was the experience at Bristol University for example.

9 This is due to more postgraduate students, and to undergraduates taking break years and moving between universities (with modularization and specific mobility programmes such as the EU Erasmus scheme).

10 University courses in the UK are examined by the Quality Assurance Agency for Higher Education (QAA). This is an independent body charged with ensuring standards of teaching across UK universities. It is funded by subscriptions from the

universities. The QAA publishes *The Framework for Higher Education Qualifications* (QAA 2005), which is an outcomes-based set of criteria for courses based on expected achievements of students on the course. Visits are carried out to ensure the specific standards are being met. Further to this the National Students Survey is used to measure the quality of courses, especially at degree level.

11 Sometimes the CPD unit is combined with these other units; sometimes they are loosely related through an umbrella organization; and sometimes they are completely stand alone and in some competition for university resources.

12 Though many universities in the middle ages dealt with medical as well as religious subjects, early medicine was closely associated with religion as through Christian traditions of healing and charity (Siraisi 1992).

13 Though there had been many other periods of radical fervour at universities over the centuries in many different countries, for example: German Student Associations (Burschenschaffen) from the early nineteenth century, late nineteenth-century post-Opium Wars Chinese nationalism, early twentieth-century Indonesian anti-colonialism, the 1956 Hungarian Revolution and of course the 1960s student movements in the USA, the UK, France and many other countries.

14 Conference run by UK IPG CPD Forum on 27 January 2009 in London.

# 11 Visions and fulfilment

1 The proposition that internal changes in CPD come soonest; and changes to CPD resulting from changes in stakeholders, wrought in part by CPD development, come only in the long run, is a logical speculation. Certainly some stakeholders change more quickly and their influence on the field may come at the same time as internal changes which themselves take time. We ignore this complication here.

2 Phillips (2010) observed a danger for linking CPD activities to outcomes, which was the criticism that activities on offer by professional bodies may reflect narrow opinions of committee members who set out programmes of workshops or lectures, rather than being based on the needs of the profession, which would require substantial effort. If new laws are passed or new techniques or materials become available, it will be important for professional bodies to develop CPD activities based on these developments or to encourage third parties to supply them.

3 Though the two above referenced articles did appear in a peer-reviewed journal.

4 There are the *International Journal of Lifelong Education* and the *LLI Review*. Note there was a failed online journal on CPD called *CPD Journal* that ran from 1998 for about five years. In addition, we found one profession-specific journal with CPD in the title – the *RCOG Quarterly CPD Journal*.

5 While published in 2009 the research was based on a search of literature in scholarly journals published during the period from April 2006 to March 2007 (Webster-Wright 2009).

6 At the end of 1984 an article appeared in *Business Week* ('Oops. Who's excellent now?') noting that of 43 'excellent' companies identified as such by Peters and Waterman, one-third were in financial difficulties after five years. Chapman (2003) wrote a successful book proposing that excellent companies in the high-tech industry were those who avoided 'stupid' mistakes with the title that parodied Peters and Waterman (*In Search of Stupidity*).

7 WorldCat (www.worldcat.org) identified *In Search of Excellence* as the most widely held library book in the United States from 1989 to 2006.

8 Though this is not strictly true in that even the traditional professions have minority routes of entry that do not require a university degree and most enter many of the newer and less well known professions without a degree (see www.totalprofessions.com).

9 Previously, a Certificate in Social Service and the Certificate of Qualification in Social Work were the qualifications undertaken. These, alongside the Diploma in Social Work, are still recognized qualifications for those returning to the workplace, but new social work students from 2009 have to take an academic degree with integrated work placements to qualify.

10 Currently a diploma or a degree are accepted for entry into nursing, but diploma courses will be phased out between September 2011 and early 2013 and new entrants to the nursing profession from September 2013 will have to have an academic degree.

11 This is still a research degree, but the programme information on the Sussex University website states: 'As well as extending your subject knowledge, the demands of your likely career path will be taken into account and professional skills development will be an integral part of your DPhil programme' (University of Sussex 2010). This site referred to professional skills development rather than continuing professional development, seeing this as a degree intended as an extension of education for the young rather than part of lifelong learning.

12 According to the Bristol University website the EdD programme:

> is tailor-made for ambitious, mid-career education and training professionals whose work requires them to have a high level of research capability. It is a structured programme with intensively taught units and coursework with a dissertation.
>
> (University of Bristol 2010)

13 The *AME* provided:

> practicing executives with relevant management tools and information based on advances in management theory and research. Articles enhance knowledge about the process of managing an organization, as well as techniques, trends, and issues growing out of management research of significance.
>
> (AOM 2010a)

However, 'AMP articles are aimed at the non-specialist academic reader, and should also be useful for teaching' (AOM 2010b).

14 The huge initiative of the UK government in recent years to establish the Sector Skills Councils and overarching agencies such as the Sector Skills Development Agency or the UK Commission on Education and Skills (http://www.ukces.org.uk/) was predicated on the idea that the publicly funded education system did not provide the skills required by employers.

15 See Common Values of the Liberal Professions in the European Union (http://www.ceplis.org/en/values.php).

16 This coincides with the fundamental duality in sociological thought between structure and agency or between social norms and individual ways of thinking and acting. According to Bourdieu this was his 'solution' to this duality; that is, to embrace what have been two very different approaches to sociological analysis (Bourdieu 1989).

17 This leads us to consider a second duality we have been dealing with throughout this book; between those at the core of the field (the players) and those on its periphery, or rather those operating more closely in other fields and therefore more affected by ways of thinking that are appropriate for those other fields (passive stakeholders). Professionals, professional bodies and direct suppliers of training aimed specifically at the 'CPD market' are at the core of the CPD field. Employers, academics, government policy makers and administrators, and journalists currently operate primarily in different fields and only on the periphery of the CPD field.

# BIBLIOGRAPHY

Abbott, A. (1988) *The System of Professions*, Chicago: University of Chicago Press.

ACCA (1993) *Continuing Professional Development – For Members Not in Public Practice* (Factsheet M25), London: ACCA.

—— (2003) *Global Consultation Report*, London: ACCA.

—— (2009) *The Coaching and Mentoring Revolution – Is It Working?* Online. Available at: http://www.accaglobal.com/allnews/global/2009/NEWSQ1/News/3176467 (accessed 13 September 2009).

Accreditation Council for CME (2007) in Davis, N., Davis, D. and Bloch, R. (2008) 'Continuing medical education: AMEE Education Guide No 35', *Medical Teacher*, 30(7): 652.

Acheson, H.W.K. (1974) 'Continuing education in general practice in England and Wales', *Journal of the Royal College of General Practitioners*, 24(146): 643–7.

Adler, P., Kwon, S. and Heckscher, C. (2008) 'Professional work: the emergence of collaborative community', *Organization Science* 19(2): 359–76.

American Medical Association 2007 in Davis, N., Davis, D. and Bloch, R. (2008) 'Continuing medical education: AMEE Education Guide No 35', *Medical Teacher*, 30(7): 652.

Anthony, A. (2009) 'Jane Elliott, the American schoolmarm who would rid us of our racism', *The Guardian*. Online. Available at: http://www.guardian.co.uk/culture/2009/oct/18/racism-psychology-jane-elliott-4 (accessed 27 October 2009).

AOM (Academy of Management) (2010a) *The Academy of Management Executive (AME)*. Online. Available at: http://www.aomonline.org/aom.asp?id=95 (accessed 23 December 2010).

—— (2010b) *Academy of Management Perspectives (AMP)*. Online. Available at: http://www.aomonline.org/aom.asp?id=263 (accessed 23 December 2010).

AoR (Association of Reflexologists) (2008) *AoR Approved Events*. Online. Available at: http://www.aor.org.uk/index.php?page=cpd-events-2008 (accessed 23 December 2008).

Apps, JW (1979) *Problems in Continuing Education*, Desoto, TX: McGraw-Hill.

ARB (Architects' Registration Board) (2010) *Maintenance of Professional Service and Competence: Guidance on Continuing Professional Development (CPD)*. Online. Available at: http://www.arb.org.uk/registration/returning_to_leaving_the_register/guidance_on_cdp.php (accessed 14 May 2010).

Argyris, C. and Schön D. (1978) *Organisational Learning: A Theory of Action Perspective*, Reading, MA: Addison Wesley.

Arthurs, H.W. (1971) 'The Ormrod Report: a Canadian reaction', *The Modern Law Review*, 34(6): 642–54.

ATA (Automotive Technicians Accreditation) (2008) Online. Available at: http://www.automotivetechnician.org.uk/ (accessed 12 March 2008).

Baranson, J. (1981) *The Japanese Challenge to US Industry*, Lexington, MA: Lexington Books.

Barnard, C. (1938) *The Functions of the Executive* (1968 edn), Cambridge, MA: Harvard University Press.

Bellande, B.J., Winicur, Z.M. and Cox, K.M. (2010) 'Urgently needed: a safe place for self-assessment on the path to maintaining competence and improving performance', *Academic Medicine*, 85(1): 16–18.

Benson, Lord (1992) 'Criteria for a group to be considered a profession' *Hansard (Lords)*, 8 July, 1206–7.

Black, P.E. and Plowright, D (2010) 'A multi-dimensional model of reflective learning for professional development', *Reflective Practice*, 11(2): 245–58.

du Boulay, C. (2000) 'From CME to CPD: getting better at getting better?' *British Medical Journal*; 320(7232): 393–4.

Bourdieu, P. (1986) 'The forms of capital', in Richardson J.G. (ed.) *Handbook for Theory and Research for the Sociology of Education*, Westport, CT: Greenwood Press, pp. 241–58.

— (1989) 'Social space and symbolic power', *Sociological Theory*, 7(1): 14–25.

Brien, A. (1998) 'Professional ethics and the culture of trust', *Journal of Business Ethics*, 17(4): 391–409.

British Columbia Pharmacy Association (2007) *Position Statement on the Professional Assessment and Development Program for B.C. Pharmacists*. Online. Available at: http://www.bcpharmacy.ca (accessed 28 September 2007).

Broadbent, J. (ed.) (1997) *The End of the Professions?: The Restructuring of Professional Work*, London: Routledge.

Brown, R., Bratton, S.L., Cabana, M.D., Kaciroti, N. and Clark, N.M. (2004) 'Physician asthma education program improves outcomes for children of low income families', *Chest*, 126(2): 369–74.

Bullock, A., Firmstone, V., Fielding, A., Frame, J., Thomas, D. and Belfield, C. (2003) 'Participation of UK dentists in continuing professional development', *British Dental Journal*, special edition on Continuing Professional Development: 136–44.

Burchell, G., Gordon, C.and Miller, P. (1991) *The Foucault Effect: Studies in Governmentality*, Hemel Hempstead: Harvester Wheatsheaf.

*Business Week* (1984) *Oops. Who's Excellent Now?*, November 5: 76–88.

Campbell, E.G. and Rosenthal, M. (2009) 'Commentary: reform of continuing medical education: investment in physician human capital', *Journal of the American Medical Association*, 302(16): 1807–8.

Canadian Constitutional Acts, 1867–1982. Online. Available at: http://laws-lois.justice.gc.ca/eng/Const/Const_index.html (accessed 13 August 2010).

Cannell, M. (2008) *Training: A Short History*. Online. Available at: www.cipd.co.uk/subjects/lrnanddev/general/thistory (accessed 25 November 2008).

Cantor, L.M. (1974) *Recurrent Education: Policy and Development in OECD Member Countries, United Kingdom*, Washington, DC: Organisation for Economic Co-operation and Development (OECD).

Chapman, M.R. (2003) *In Search of Stupidity*, New York: Springer-Verlag.

Cheetham, G. and Chivers, G. (2005) *Professions, Competence and Informal Learning*, Cheltenham: Edward Elgar.

Chivers, G. (2006) 'The work roles and development needs of vocational lifelong learning professionals in British higher education,' *Journal of European Industrial Training*, 30(3): 166–87.

CIM (Chartered Institute of Marketing) (2009) *Professional Development at the Chartered Institute of Marketing*. Online. Available at: http://www.cim.co.uk/cpd/careercentre.aspx (accessed 2 October 2009).

CIMA (Chartered Institute of Management Accountants) (2008) *Professional Development Cycle*. Online. Available at: http://www.cimaglobal.com/Members/CIMA-Professional-Development/Planning-your-CPD/CIMA-professional-development-cycle/ (accessed 4 December 2008).

—— (2010) *CIMA CPD Requirements*. Online. Available at: http://www.cpd-courses.org/CPD-points/CIMA-CPD.htm (accessed 23 November 2010).

CIPD (Chartered Institute for Personnel and Development) (2008) *What is CPD*. Online. Available at: http://www.cipd.co.uk/cpd/aboutcpd/whatiscpd.htm (accessed 12 July 2008).

—— (2010a) *Benefits of CPD*. Online. Available at: http://www.cipd.co.uk/cpd/benefitscpd.htm (accessed 14 July 2010).

—— (2010b) *Member Discounts*. Online. Available at: http://www.cipd.co.uk/Membership/benefits/discounts (accessed 14 July 2010).

CMI (Chartered Management Institute) (2010) *CMI Manifesto for a Better Managed Britain*. Online. Available at: http://www.managers.org.uk/research-analysis/research/influencing-public-policy/management-manifesto (accessed 06 September 2010).

Cohen, M. (1995) 'Technological disasters and natural resource damage assessment: an evaluation of the Exxon Valdez oil spill', *Land Economics*. 71(1): 65–82.

Coleman, J.S. (1988) 'Social capital in the creation of human capital', *American Journal of Sociology*, 94(S1), S95–120.

Committee on Higher Education (1963) *Higher Education: Report of the Committee Appointed by the Prime Minister under the Chairmanship of Lord Robbins 1961–63, Cmnd. 2154*, London: HMSO.

Construction Industry Council (CIC) (1986) in Memberwise (2009) *7 Habits of an Effective CPD Professional*. Online. Available at: http://memberwise.org/Documents/7%20Habits%20Presentation%20July%2009.pdf (accessed 14 June 2009).

Copenhagen Declaration (2002) *Declaration of the European Ministers of Vocational Education and Training and the European Commission*, Luxembourg: Office of Publications of the European Communities.

Cors, R. (2003) *What is a Learning Organization? Reflections on the Literature and Practitioner Perspectives*, University of Wisconsin-Madison. Online. Available at: http://www.engr.wisc.edu/services/elc/lor/files/Learning_Org_Lit_Review.pdf (accessed 20 December 2010).

Crompton, M. (2007) *Business Drivers: Michael Crompton Explains How the UK Bus Company Successfully Implemented a CPD Support Scheme for its Financial Professionals*, Financial Management (UK). Online. Available at: http://www.thefreelibrary.com/Financial+Management+%28UK%29/2007/October/1-p5756 (accessed 3 August 2008).

Crooks, T. (2001) *The Validity of Formative Assessments*. Paper presented at British Educational Research Annual Conference, University of Leeds 13–15 September. Online. Available at: http://www.leeds.ac.uk/educol/documents/00001862.htm (accessed 13 June 2010).

Cropley, A.J. (ed) (1979) *Lifelong Education: A Stocktaking*, Hamburg: UIE Monographs 8.

Cross, K.P. (1981) *Adults as Learners*, San Francisco: Jossey-Bass.

Dall'Alba, G. and Barnacle, R. (2005) 'Embodied knowing in online environments', *Educational Philosophy and Theory*, 37(5): 719–44.

Dao, M.N.S. (1975) *The Orientations Toward Nonparticipation in Adult Education*, Chicago: University of Chicago (doctoral dissertation).

Darkenwald, G.G. and Merriam, S.B. (1982) *Adult Education: Foundations of Practice*, New York: Harper & Row.

Darkenwald, G.G. and Valentine, T. (1985) 'Factor structure of deterrents to public participation in adult education', *Adult Education Quarterly*, 35(4): 177–93.

Davis, D.A., Mazmanian, P.E., Fordis, M.V., Harrison, R., Thorpe, K.E. and Perrier, L. (2006) 'Accuracy of physician self-assessment compared with observed measures of competence: a systematic review', *Journal of the American Medical Association*, 296(9): 1094–102.

Davis, N., Davis, D. and Bloch, R. (2008) 'Continuing medical education: AMEE Education Guide No 35', *Medical Teacher*, 30(7): 652–66.

Deming, W. E. (2000) *The New Economics for Industry, Government, Education* (2nd edn), Cambridge, MA: MIT Press.

Department for Education and Skills (2004) *The Future of Higher Education*, Norwich: Stationery Office. Online. Available at: http://www.bis.gov.uk/assets/biscore/corporate/migratedd/publications/f/future_of_he.pdf (accessed 14 June 2008).

Department of Education and Science (DES) (1972) *Teacher Education and Training (James Report)*, London: HMSO.

Dewey, J. (1916) *Democracy and Education: An Introduction to the Philosophy of Education*, New York: Macmillan.

Downes, L. and Mui, C. (1998) *Unleashing the Killer App*, Boston, MA: Harvard Business School Press.

Drucker, P. (1989) [1955] *The Practice of Management*, New York: HarperCollins.

—— (1993) [1946] *The Concept of the Corporation*, Rutgers, NJ: Transaction Publishers.

Durkhheim, E. (1957) *Professional Ethics and Civic Morals*, New York: The Free Press.

Ellis, S. and Williams, C. (2010) *Social Networking: Its Benefits and Challenges for Professional Bodies*, Bristol: PARN.

Elton, L. (2000) 'The UK research assessment exercise: unintended consequences', *Higher Education Quarterly*, 54(3): 274–83.

Engineers Ireland (2010) *The CPD Accredited Employer Standard*. Online. Available at: http://www.engineersireland.ie/cpd/cpd-employer/ (accessed 23 December 2010).

Eraut, M. (1994) *Developing Professional Knowledge and Competence*, London: Falmer.

—— (2000) 'Non-formal learning, implicit learning and tacit knowledge in professional work' in F. Coffield, *The Necessity of Informal Learning*, Bristol: Policy Press.

Ester, P. and Vinken, H. (2003) 'Debating civil society: on the fear of civic decline and hope for the internet alternative', *International Sociology*, 18(4): 659–80.

European Project for the Use of Standards of Competence in CPD for Construction Industry Practitioners (EUSCCCIP) (1998) *Framework for CPD Systems for Practitioners in the Construction Industry*, London: CISC.

Evans, K., Gallatin, A., Taylor, C. and Brodnick, M. (2008) 'Self-directed characteristics of participants in online CE programs', *Radiologic Technology*, 80(1): 11–19.

Faure, H., Kaddoura, A., Lopes, H., Petrovsky, A., Rahnema, M. and Champion Ward, F. (1972) *Learning To Be: The World of Education Today and Tomorrow,* Paris: UNESCO.

FEE (2007) *Continuous Professional Education in the European Accountancy Profession: A Survey of Current Practices,* Brussels: Fédération des Experts Comptables Européens.

Field, N. (2004) 'Mandatory continuing professional education: do we need it?' *The Radiographer,* 51(1): 5–9.

Fleet, L.J., Kirby, F., Cutler, S., Dunikowski, L., Nasmith, L. and Shaughnessy, R. (2008) 'Continuing professional development and social accountability: a review of the literature', *Journal of Interprofessional Care,* 22(S1): 15–29.

Fordham, P. (1973) 'University extra-mural departments and continuing education', *Higher Education,* 2(2): 180–1.

Foucault, M. (1963) *Birth of the Clinic,* translated by Sheridan, A.M. (1973), London: Tavistock.

Fournier, V. (1999) 'The appeal to "professionalism" as a disciplinary mechanism', *Social Review,* 47(2): 280–307.

Fox, L. (2003) *Enron: The Rise and Fall,* New York: John Wiley & Sons.

Freeman, R. (1984) *Strategic Management: A Stakeholder Approach,* Boston, MA: Pitman.

French, H.P. and Dowds, J. (2008) 'An overview of continuing professional development in physiotherapy', *Physiotherapy,* 94(3): 190–7.

Friedman, A. (1994) 'The Information Technology Field: Using Fields and Paradigms for Analyzing Technological Change', *Human Relations,* 47(4): 367–92.

—— (1999) 'Rhythm and the evolution of information technology', *Technology Analysis and Strategic Management,* 11(3): 375–90.

—— (ed.) (2005) *Critical Issues in CPD,* Bristol: PARN.

—— (2007) *Ethical Competence and Professional Associations,* Bristol: PARN.

Friedman, A. with Afitska, N. (2007) *Professionalism and Sustainability in the Professional Associations Sector: UK and Ireland,* Bristol: PARN.

Friedman, A. and Senior, C. (2001) *Professional Learning and the Internet,* unpublished report on projects to DfEE.

Friedman, A. and Mason, J. (2004) *Professional Associations in Ireland: A Comparative Study with the UK,* Bristol: PARN.

Friedman, A. and Phillips, M. (2004) 'CPD programmes of UK professional associations: developing a vision', *Journal of Education and Work,* 17(3): 361–76.

Friedman, A. and Miles, S.V. (2006) *Stakeholders: Theory and Practice,* Oxford: Oxford University Press.

Friedman, A. and Mason, J. (2007) *Distinguishing Australian Professional Bodies,* Bristol: PARN.

Friedman, A. and Williams, C. (2007) *Member Relations and Strategy: Supporting Member Involvement and Retention,* Bristol: PARN.

—— (2008) *Distinguishing Canadian Professional Bodies,* Bristol: PARN.

Friedman A. and Williams C. with Hopkins S. and Jackson L. (2008) *Linking Professional Associations with Higher Education Institutions (HEIs) in Relation to the Provision of Continuing Professional Development (CPD),* Report for Department of Innovation, Universities and Skills. Online. Available at: http://www.parnglobal.com (accessed 12 December 2010).

Friedman, A. and Woodhead, S. (2008) *Approaches to Continuing Professional Development (CPD) Measurement,* New York: International Federation of Accountants (IFAC).

Friedman, A. and Afitska, N (2009) *Estimating CPD: Lifelong Leaning of Millions,* Bristol: PARN.

—— (2010) *PARN International Benchmarking Survey 2009,* mimeo, Bristol: PARN.

Friedman, A. and Hanson, W. (2010) *Professional Standards Regulation*, Bristol: PARN.

Friedman, A., Durkin, C. and Hurran, N. (1999) *Building a CPD Network on the Internet*, Bristol: PARN.

Friedman, A., Davis, K., Durkin, C. and Phillips, M. (2000) *Continuing Professional Development in the UK: Policies and Programmes*, Bristol: PARN.

Friedman, A., Durkin, C. and Phillips, M. (2000) 'CPD: What are the true costs of Continuing Professional Development?', *CPD Journal*, 3: 78–87.

Friedman, A., Davis, K., Durkin, C. and Phillips, M. (2001) *Continuing Professional Development in the UK: Professionals' Reactions to Offerings from Professional Associations*, Bristol: PARN.

Friedman, A., Davis, K. and Phillips, M. (2001) *Continuing Professional Development in the UK: Attitudes & Experiences of Practitioners*, Bristol: PARN.

Friedman, A., Hanson, W. and Williams, C. (2009) *Professional Standards Bodies: Standards, Levels of Compliance and Measuring Success*, London: Financial Services Authority (FSA).

Friedman, M. (1962) *Capitalism and Freedom*, Chicago: University of Chicago Press.

FSA (Financial Services Authority) (2008) *Retail Distribution Review, November*, London: FSA.

—— (2010) *Delivering the RDR: Professionalism, including its Applicability to Pure Protection Advice with Feedback to CP09/18 and CP09/31, CP10/14*, London: FSA.

Fusaro, P.C. and Miller, R.M. (2002) *What Went Wrong at Enron: Everyone's Guide to the Largest Bankruptcy in U.S. History*, New York: John Wiley & Sons.

Gabor, A. (1992) *The Man Who Discovered Quality: How W. Edwards Deming Brought the Quality Revolution to America*, Harmondsworth: Penguin.

Gardner, R. (1978) *Policy on Continuing Education: A Report with Recommendations for Action*, York: University of York.

General Dental Council (GDC) (2002) *Lifelong Learning: Taking Dentistry Forward*, London: General Dental Council.

—— (2009) *What You Need to Know about Continuing Professional Development (CPD)* Online. Available at: http://www.gdc-uk.org/Current+registrant/CPD+requirements (accessed 29 July 2009).

—— (2010) *Continuing Professional Development (CPD) for Dentists*. Online. Available at: http://www.gdc-uk.org/NR/rdonlyres/095EBA4C-2EBC-4D87-8355-DEE3AAB 73554/0/CPDfordentists2010.pdf (accessed 4 May 2010).

Gilbert, C. (Department for Education and Skills) (2005) *2020 Vision: Report of the Teaching and Learning in 2020 Review Group*, DfES Publications. Online. Available at http://publications.education.gov.uk/eOrderingDownload/6856-DfES-Teaching%20 and%20Learning.pdf (accessed 13 December 2010).

Gold, J., Thorpe, R., Woodall, J. and Sadler-Smith, E. (2007) 'Continuing professional development in the legal profession: a practice-based learning perspective', *Management Learning*, 38(2): 235–50.

Goldstein, J. (1984) 'Foucault among the sociologists: the "disciplines" and the history of the professions', *History and Theory*, 23(2), 170–92.

Gould, M. (1979) 'When women create an organization: the ideological imperatives of feminism' in Dunkerley, D. and Salaman, G. (eds) *The International Yearbook of Women's Studies 1979*, London: Routledge & Kegan Paul.

Granovetter, M.S. (1973) 'The strength of weak ties', *American Journal of Sociology*, 78(6): 1360–80.

Grayston, Rupert (2007) 'CPD policy'. E-mail (6 November).

Guest, G. (2006) 'Lifelong learning for engineers: a global perspective', *European Journal of Engineering Education*, 31(3): 273–81.

Guskey, T.R. (2000) *Evaluating Professional Development*, London: Sage.

Hammer, M. (1990) 'Reengineering work: don't automate, obliterate', *Harvard Business Review*, July–August: 104–12.

Harris, M. (TNS Harris) (2000a) *Summary Report on the Lifelong Learning Survey undertaken by Harris Research*, London: TNS Harris Research/CIPD.

—— (2000b) *CPD 2000 Survey Graduate Members*, London: TNS Harris Research/CIPD.

Harrison, A. (1978) *Making and Thinking*, Indianapolis: Hackett.

Harvey, H. (2010) 'CPD book'. E-mail (15 April 2010).

HEFCE (Higher Education Funding Council for England) (2008) *Understanding Institutional Performance: Advice to the Secretary of State for Innovation, Universities and Skills.* Online. Available at: http://webarchive.nationalarchives.gov.uk/tna/+/http://www.dius.gov.uk/policy/understanding_Higher_Education.html/ (accessed 12 March 2008).

Henwood, S., Yielder, J. and Flinton, D. (2004) 'Radiographers attitudes to mandatory CPD: a comparative study in the United Kingdom and New Zealand', *Radiography*, 10: 251–8.

Hicks, E., Bagg, R., Doyle, W. and Young, J. (2007) 'Canadian accountants: examining workplace learning', *Journal of Workplace Learning*, 19(2): 61–77.

Hicks, S., Walling, A., Heap, D. and Livesey, D. (2005) *Public Sector Employment Trends 2005,* London: Office for National Statistics.

HIMAA (Health Information Management Association Australia) (2008) *Professional Credentialling Scheme.* Online. Available at: http://www.himaa.org.au/Credentialling/default.htm (accessed 4 December 2008).

HM Treasury (2002) SET for Success: *The Supply of People with Science, Technology, Engineering and Mathematics Skills (The Roberts Report)*, London: HMSO.

Holmes, L. (1995) 'Skills: a social perspective', in Assiter, A. (ed.) *Transferable Skills in Higher Education,* London: Kogan, pp. 20–8.

Houle, C.O. (1980) *Continuing Learning in the Professions*, San Francisco: Jossey-Bass.

—— (1996) *The Design of Education* (2nd edn), San Francisco: Jossey-Bass.

HPC (Health Professions Council) (2008) *Glossary of Terms.* Online. Available at: http://www.hpc-uk.org/registrants/cpd/glossary/ (accessed 16 November 2008).

—— (2009) *Continuing Professional Development.* Online. Available at: http://www.hpc-uk.org/education/cpd/ (accessed 22 July 2009).

Hull, H., Hunt, A. and Rutter, P. (2003) 'Community pharmacists' attitudes and approaches to the Royal Pharmaceutical Society of Great Britain continuing professional development initiatives', *International Journal of Pharmacy Practice*, 11: R50.

IET (Institution of Engineering and Technology) (2008) *We Work Better Together.* Online. Available at: http://www.theiet.org/careers/mentoring/resources/ (accessed 17 May 2011).

Illich, I. (1971) *Deschooling Society*, New York: Harper & Row.

—— (1977) *The Right to Useful Unemployment and its Professional Enemies*, London: Marian Boyars.

Illich, I., Zola I. I. and McKnight, J. (1977a) *Disabling Professions*, London: Marion Boyars.

—— (1977b) *The Right to Useful Unemployment and its Professional Enemies*, London: Marian Boyars.

International Federation of Accountants (IFAC) Educational Committee (2004) *Continuing Professional Development: A Program of Lifelong Learning and Continuing Development of Professional Competence, International Education standard for Professional Accountants*, IES 7, New York: IFAC.

—— (2010) *Proposed Redrafted International Education Standard,* New York: IFAC.

IOSH (Institution of Occupational Safety and Health) (2010) *About CPD.* Online. Available at: http://www.iosh.co.uk/membership/about_membership/about_cpd.aspx (accessed 22 November 2010).

Ipsos MORI (2007) *Trust in the Professions.* Online. Available at: http://www.ipsos-mori.com/researchpublications/researcharchive/poll.aspx?oItemId=232 (accessed 13 November 2010).

Jamal, K. and Bowie, N. E. (1995) 'Theoretical considerations for a meaningful code of professional ethics', *Journal of Business Ethics,* 14: 703–14.

Jarausch, K. H. (2004) 'Graduation and Careers' in Rüegg, W. (ed.) *A History of the University in Europe (Vol. III) Universities in the Nineteenth and Early Twentieth Centuries,* Cambridge: Cambridge University Press.

Jarvis, P. (1995) *Adult and Continuing Education* (2nd edn), London: Routledge.

Jennings, S. (2007) 'Personal development plans and self-directed learning for healthcare professionals: are they evidence based?' *Postgraduate Medical Journal,* 83: 518–24.

Johnstone, J.W.C. and Rivera, R.J. (1965) *Volunteers for Learning,* Chicago: Aldine.

Jones, N. and Fear, N. (1994) 'Continuing professional development, perspectives from human resource professionals', *Personnel Review,* 23(8): 67–79.

Kallen, D. (1979) 'Recurrent education and lifelong learning: definitions and distinctions' in Schuller, T. and Megarry, J. (eds) *Recurrent Education and Lifelong Learning in World Yearbook of Education,* New York: Kogan Page.

Kamm, O. (2009) 'Blame incompetent bankers, not the rules', *The Times.* Online. Available at: http://www.timesonline.co.uk/tol/comment/columnists/guest_contributors/article6523843.ece (accessed 16 December 2009).

Karle, H. (2003) *Global Standards for Continuing Professional Development: Who Should Be Responsible for Providing CME?,* The World Federation of Medical Education. Online. Available at: http://www.game-cme.org/meeting/archive/2003_Program.pdf (accessed 2 March 2010).

Keim, K., Gates, G. and Johnson, C. (2001) 'Dietetics professionals have a positive perception of professional development', *Journal of American Dietetic Association,* 101(7): 820–4.

Khurana, R. and Nohria, N. (2008) 'It's time to make management a true profession,' *Harvard Business Review,* October: 70–7.

Kirkpatrick, D. L. (1994) *Evaluating Training Programs: The Four Levels,* San Francisco: Berrett-Koehler.

Knapper, C. and Cropley, A. (2000) *Lifelong Learning in Higher Education,* London: Kogan Page.

Koehn, D. (1994) *The Ground of Professional Ethics,* London: Routledge.

KPMG (2010) *Learning and Development.* Online. Available at: http://www.kpmg.com/MY/en/JoinUs/WhyKPMG/Pages/LearningDevelopment.aspx (accessed 22 October 2010).

Kultgen, J. (1982) 'The ideological use of professional codes,' *Business and Professional Ethics Journal,* 1(3): 53–69.

Lambert, R. (2003) *Lambert Review of Business–University Collaboration,* London: HMSO.

Langland, Sir A. (2005) *Gateways to the Professions Report,* Nottingham: Department for Education and Skills (DfES) Publications.

Lengrand, P. (1976) *An Introduction to Lifelong Education,* London: Groom Helm.

Llewellyn, S. (2009) 'CPD book'. Email (22 April).

LOPN (Learning Organization Practitioners' Network) (2010) *The Sixty Tools of Learning Organization.* Online. Available at: http://www.lopn.net/60_Tools.html (accessed 26 November 2010).

Lynn, K. (1963) 'Introduction to the issue: "the professions"', *Daedalus: Journal of the American Academy of Arts and Science*, Fall: 649–54.

Macdonald, K. M. (1995) *The Sociology of the Professions*, London: SAGE.

MacDonald Ross, G. (2005) 'Plagiarism: the Leeds approach', *Learning & Teaching Bulletin*, 8, February, internal publication at the University of Leeds. Online. Available at: http://www.ldu.leeds.ac.uk/l&tbulletin/issue8/ross.htm (accessed 5 June 2010).

McIntosh, N.E. (1979) 'To make continuing education a reality', *Oxford Review of Education*, 5(2): 169–82.

McLuhan, M. (1964) *Understanding Media: The Extensions of Man*, London: Routledge.

Madden, C. A. and Mitchell, V. A. (1993) *Professions, Standards and Competence: A Survey of Continuing Education for the Professions,* Bristol: Department for Continuing Education, University of Bristol.

Marinopoulos, S.S., Dorman, T., Ratanawongsa, N., Wilson, L.M, Ashar, B.H., Magazine, J.L., Miller, R.G., Thomas, P.A., Prokopowicz, G.P., Qayyum, R. and Bass, E.B. (2007) *Effectiveness of Continuing Medical Education*, AHRQ Publication No. 07-E006, Rockville, MD: Agency for Healthcare Research and Quality.

Marshall, T.H. (1939) 'The recent history of professionalism in relation to social structure and social policy', *Canadian Journal of Economics and Political Science*, 5(3): 325–40.

Megginson, D. and Whitaker, V. (2007) *Continuing Professional Development*, London: CIPD.

Middlesex University (2009) *Understanding APEL: Making Your Experience Count.* Online. Available at: www.mdx.ac.uk/aboutus/Schools/iwbl/wbl_explained/apel (accessed 3 March 2009).

Mitchell, R.K., Agle, B.R. and Wood, D.J. (1997) 'Toward a theory of stakeholder identification and salience: defining the principle of how and what really counts', *Academy of Management Review* 22(4): 853–86.

Murray, T. and Campbell, L. (1997) 'Finance, not learning needs, makes general practitioners attend courses: a database survey', *British Medical Journal*, 315(7104): 353.

O'Connor, J. (1973) *The Fiscal Crisis of the State*, New Brunswick, NJ: Transaction Publishers.

O'Neill, O. (2005) 'Accountability, trust and professional practice: the end of professionalism' in N. Ray (ed.) *Architecture and its Ethical Dilemmas.* New York: Taylor & Francis, pp. 75–88.

OECD (Organisation for Economic Co-operation and Development) (2004) *Thematic Review on Adult Learning: United Kingdom (England) Background Report.* Online. Available at: http://www.oecd.org/dataoecd/49/49/2471965.pdf (accessed 26 May 2010).

Office of Fair Trading (2001) *Competition in Professions*, London: HMSO.

*Official Consolidation of the Regulated Health Professions Act* (1991) Statutes of Ontario, 1991, Chapter 18, 15 December 2009 to current. Online. Available at: http://www.canlii.org/en/on/laws/stat/so-1991-c-18/latest/so-1991-c-18.html (accessed 14 April 2010).

Ouchi, W. (1981) *Theory Z: How American Management Can Meet the Japanese Challenge*, New York: Addison-Wesley.

Owen, T. and Powell, J. (2006) '"Trust", professional power and social theory', *International Journal of Sociology and Social Policy.* 26(3): 110–20.

Padfield C. and Schaufelberger, W. (1998) *Lifelong Learning in Engineering Education: A Call to Action*, SEFI Document no 20, Brussels: European Society for Engineering Education.

Paisey C. and Paisey, N.J. (2004) 'An analysis of accounting education in *Accounting Education: an international journal*: 1992–2001', *Accounting Education*, 13(1): 69–99.

—— (2007) 'Guest editorial: continuing professional development', *Accounting Education*, 16(4): 315–8.

Paisey C., Paisey, N.J. and Tarbert, H. (2007) 'Continuing professional development activities of UK accountants in public practice', *Accounting Education*, 16(4): 379–403.

Parboosingh, J. (1998) 'Revalidation for doctors', *British Medical Journal*, 317(7166): 1094–5.

PARN (2008a) *Analysis of Survey of Professional Body Members on Continuing Professional Development (CPD), Higher Education Institutions (HEIs) as Providers of CPD, and Online Delivery*, Report for the Open University, Bristol: PARN. Online. Available at: http://www.parnglobal.com (accessed 14 June 2010).

—— (2008b) *How Can Professional Associations Embed Awareness and Support for Diversity in their Organisations?* Report for Department of Innovation, Universities and Skills, Bristol: PARN. Online. Available at: http://www.parnglobal.com (accessed 24 September 2010).

Parsloe, E. and Leedham, M. (2009) *Coaching and Mentoring* (2nd edn), London: Kogan Page.

Parsons, T. (1954) 'Professions and the social structure', in Parsons, T., *Essays in Sociological Theory*, Glencoe, IL: The Free Press.

Pascale, R.T. and Athos, A.G. (1981) *The Art of Japanese Management*, New York: Warner Books.

Paxton, P. (1999) 'Is social capital declining in the United States? A multiple indicator assessment', *American Journal of Sociology*, 105(1): 88–127.

Peck, C., McCall, M., McLaren, B. and Rotem, T. (2000) 'Continuing medical education and continuing professional development: international comparisons', *British Medical Journal*, 320(7232): 432–5.

Penuel, W.R., Fishman, B.J., Yamaguchi, R. and Gallagher, L. (2007) 'What makes professional development effective? Strategies that foster curriculum implementation', *American Educational Research Journal*, 44(4): 921–58.

Perry, L. (1995) 'Continuing professional education: luxury or necessity?', *Journal of Advanced Nursing*, 21(4): 766–71.

Peters, T. and Waterman, R.H. (1982) *In Search of Excellence: Lessons from America's Best-run Companies*, New York: Harper & Row.

Phillips, M. (2010) *The Role of Self-Direction in Australian Sonographers' Professional Development*, unpublished PhD, Melbourne, Deakin University.

Phillips, M., Cruickshank, I. and Friedman, A. (2002) *Continuing Professional Development: Evaluation of Good Practice*, Bristol: PARN.

Piatt, J., Lensink, C., Butler, W., Kendziorek, M. and Nysewander, D. (1990) 'Immediate impact of the Exxon Valdez Oil Spill on Marine Birds', *The Auk*, 107: 387–97.

Pidd, Helen (2008) 'Burger bar A-level for staff at McDonald's', *The Guardian*, 28 January. Online. Available at: http://www.guardian.co.uk/uk/2008/jan/28/schools.furthereducation (accessed 14 December 2010).

Polanyi, M. (1967) *The Tacit Dimension*, New York: Doubleday.

Postler-Slattery, D. and Foley, K. (2003) 'The fruits of lifelong learning', *Nursing Management*, 34(2): 35–7.

Putnam, R.D. (1995) 'Tuning in, tuning out: the strange disappearance of social capital in America', *Political Science and Politics*, 28(4): 664–83.

—— (2000) *Bowling Alone: The Collapse and Revival of American Community*, New York: Simon & Schuster.

QAA (Quality Assurance Agency for Higher Education) (2005) *The Framework for Higher Education Qualifications*, London: QAA.

Rapkins, C. (1996) 'Best practice for continuing professional development: professional bodies facing the challenge' in Woodward, I. (ed.) *Continuing Professional Development: Issues in Design and Delivery*, London: Cassell.

Revel, T. and Yussuf, H. (2003) 'Taking primary care Continuing Professional Education to rural areas: lessons from United Arab Emirates', *Australian Journal of Rural Health*, 11(4): 271–6.

RICS (Royal Institution of Chartered Surveyors) (2008) *Assessment of Professional Competence: RICS Education and Qualification Standards*. Online. Available at: http://www.rics.org/site/download_feed.aspx?fileID=1067&fileExtension=PDF (accessed 12 October 2010).

Rockhill, K. (1983) 'Mandatory continuing education for professionals: trends and issues', *Adult Education Quarterly*, 33(2): 106–16.

Rogers, G.A. (1982) *General Practitioners and Continuing Education: Aspects of Patient Management*, Dundee: University of Dundee (MPhil thesis).

Rothwell, A. and Arnold, J. (2005) 'How HR professionals rate continuing professional development', *Human Resource Management Journal*, 15(3): 18–32.

Rothwell, A. and Herbert, I. (2007) 'Accounting professionals and CPD: attitudes and engagement – some survey evidence', *Research in Post-Compulsory Education*, 12(1): 121–38.

Royal College of Physicians (RCP) (2008) *CPD*. Online. Available at: http://www.rcplondon.ac.uk/education/cpd/Pages/cpd.aspx (accessed 13 July 2008).

Royal College of Psychiatrists (RCPsych) (2009) *Policy for CPD*. Online. Available at: http://www.rcpsych.ac.uk/training/cpdandrevalidation/cpdpolicy.aspx (accessed 26 July 2009).

Royal College of Veterinary Surgeons (RCVS) (2006) *Continuing Professional Development Policy 2006*. Online. Available at: http://www.rcvs.org.uk/Templates/Internal.asp?NodeID=94975&int2ndParentNodeID=94971&int1stParentNodeID=94964 (accessed 15 August 2009).

Royal Institute of British Architects (RIBA) (2008) *CPD at the RIBA*. Online. Available at: http://www.architecture.com/ (accessed 12 July 2008).

—— (2009) *CPD at the RIBA*. Online. Available at: http://www.architecture.com/EducationAndCareers/CPD/CPDAtTheRIBA.aspx (accessed 8 August 2009).

Royal Institution of Chartered Surveyors (RICS) (2009) *Education and Qualification Standards: Requirements and Competencies*. Online. Available at: http://www.rics.org/site/download_feed.aspx?fileID=3729&fileExtension=PDF (accessed: 28 May 2010).

Royal Pharmaceutical Society of Great Britain (RPSGB) (2008) *CPD FAQs*. Online. Available at: http://www.uptodate.org.uk/faqs/General.shtml (accessed 13 July 2008).

—— (2009) *Continuing Professional Development: A Guide to Getting Started: 2. A Journey Round the CPD Cycle*. Online. Available at: http://www.uptodate.org.uk/PlanandRecord/getting_started_guide/getting_started_2.pdf (accessed 16 August 2009).

Ryle, G. (1949) *The Concept of Mind*, London: Hutcheson.

Sadler-Smith, E. and Badger, B. (1998) 'The HR practitioner's perspective on continuing professional development', *Human Resource Development Quarterly*, 6(2): 215–26.

Sadler-Smith, E., Allinson, C.W. and Hayes, J. (2000) 'Learning preferences and cognitive style: some implications for continuing professional development', *Management Learning*, 31(2): 239–56.

Sankar, R. (2003) 'Big Brother is watching (your CPD)', *British Medical Journal*, 327(7419): 855.

Sargeant, J. (2008) 'Toward a common understanding of self-assessment', *Journal of Continuing Education in Health Professions*, 28(1): 1–4.

Scanlan, C.L. and Darkenwald, G.G. (1984) 'Identifying deterrents to participate in continuing education', *Adult Education Quarterly*, 34(3): 155–66.

Schön, D.A. (1973) *Beyond the Stable State. Public and Private Learning in a Changing Society*, Harmondsworth: Penguin.

—— (1983 first published, 1991 this edition) *The Reflective Practitioner: How Professionals Think in Action*, New York: Basic Books.

—— (1984) 'The crisis of professional knowledge and the pursuit of an epistemology of practice' in Raven, J. and Stephenson, J. (eds) (2001) *Competence in the Learning Society*, New York: Peter Lang, pp. 185–207.

—— (1987) *Educating the Reflective Practitioner*, San Francisco: Jossey-Bass.

SCOPME (Standing Committee on Postgraduate Medical and Dental Education) (1999) *Equity and Interchange: Multiprofessional Working and Learning*, London: SCOPME.

Senge, P. (1990) *The Fifth Discipline*, New York: Doubleday.

Shaw, G.B. (1911 first published, 1987 this edition) *The Doctor's Dilemma*, London: Penguin.

Shepard, L. (2000) 'The role of assessment in a learning culture', *Educational Researcher*, 29(7): 4–14.

Siraisi, N. (1992) 'The faculty of medicine' in W. Rüegg and H. De Ridder-Symoens (eds.) *A History of the University in Europe: Volume 1: Universities in the Middle Ages*, Cambridge: Cambridge University Press.

Smiles, S. (1860) *Self-Help: With Illustrations of Character and Conduct*, New York: Harper & Brothers.

Smith, I. (2004) 'Continuing professional development and workplace learning 8: human resource development – the return on investment', *Library Management*, 25(4/5): 232–4.

Smith, J. (2004) *Fifth Report Safeguarding Patients: Lessons from the Past – Proposals for the Future*, Command Paper Cm 6394. Online. Available at: http://www.the-Shipman-inquiry.org.uk/reports.asp (accessed 2 November 2010).

Snadden, D. (1999) 'Portfolios – attempting to measure the unmeasurable?', *Medical Education*, 33(7): 478–9.

Sockett, H. (1981) 'Researching educational futures', *Educational Review*, 33(2): 97–103.

Spalding, M. (2003) 'Towards continuing education and professional development: drivers for change in therapy radiography', *Journal of Radiotherapy in Practice*, 3(3): 131–8.

Sriharan, A., Murray, R., Pardell, H. and Silva, H. (2009) 'An overview of CME/CPD credit systems around the world', *Journal of Medical Marketing*, 9(2): 145–50.

Stanton, F. and Grant, J. (1997) in Davis, N., Davis, D. and Bloch, R. (2008) 'Continuing medical education: AMEE Education Guide No 35', *Medical Teacher*, 30(7): 652.

Strategic Forum for Construction, chaired by Egan, Sir E. (2002) *Accelerating Change*. Online. Available at: http://www.strategicforum.org.uk/pdf/report_sept02.pdf (accessed 14 June 2009).

Susskind, R. (2008) *The End of Lawyers?*, Oxford: Oxford University Press.

Swan, J., Scarborough, H. and Robertson, M. (2002) 'The construction of communities of practice in the management of innovation' *Management Learning*, 33(4): 477–96.

Tawney, R.H. (1921) *The Acquisitive Society*, New York: Harcourt, Brace & Howe.

Thompson, S. and Thompson, N. (2008) *The Critically Reflective Practitioner*, Basingstoke: Palgrave Macmillan.

Todd, F. (1987) *Planning Continuing Professional Development*, London: Croom Helm.

Tovey, P. (1994) *Quality Assurance in Continuing Professional Education: An Analysis*, London: Routledge.

Townsend, E., Sheffield, S., Stadnyk, R. and Beagan, B. (2006) 'Effects of workplace policy on continuing professional development: the case of occupational therapy in Nova Scotia, Canada', *Canadian Journal of Occupational Therapy*, 73(2): 98–108.

Tracey, J., Arroll, B., Barham, P. and Richmond, D. (1997) 'The validity of general practitioners' self-assessment of knowledge: cross sectional study', *British Medical Journal*, 315(7120): 1426–28.

The Training Gateway (2010) Online. Available at: http://www.thetraininggateway.com (accessed 23 December 2010).

—— (2011) 'Permission for publication'. Email (17 January 2011).

Tredwin, C.J., Eder, A., Moles, D.R. and Faigenblum, M.J. (2005) *'British Dental Journal* based continuing professional development: a survey of participating dentists and their views', *British Dental Journal*, 199(10): 665–9.

*UK Public Spending* (2009) Online. Available at: http://www.ukpublicspending.co.uk/ (accessed 13 September 2009).

Unger, S. (1994) *Controlling Technology: Ethics and the Responsible Engineer* (2nd edn), New York: Wiley.

United Nations Scientific Committee on the Effects of Atomic Radiation (UNSCEAR) (1988) *United Nations Scientific Committee on the Effects of Atomic Radiation: Sources, Effects and Risks of Ionizing Radiation*, New York: United Nations.

University of Bristol (2010) *Doctoral Programmes*. Online. Available at: http://www.bristol.ac.uk/education/students/doctoral/ (accessed 12 December 2010).

University of Kent (2009) 'Training and professional development'. Email (16 February 2009).

University of Sussex (2010) *New Route – DPhil*. Online. Available at: www.sussex.ac.uk/Units/publications/newrouteDPhil/ (accessed 12 December 2010).

*US Government Spending* (2009) Online. Available at: http://www.usgovernmentspending.com/ (accessed 13 September 2009).

Varia, S. (2006) 'Motivation theories to engage people in CPD', handout to accompany presentation at the NHS London Pharmacy Education & Training CPD Facilitators' Network Meeting, 4 April. Online. Available at: http://www.londonpharmacy.nhs.uk/educationandtraining/cpd/meetings/download/003%20April%202006%20%20Motivation%20theories%20to%20engage%20people%20in%20CPD%20handout.pdf (accessed 1 November 2010).

Vaughan, P. (1991) *Maintaining Professional Competence: A Survey of the Role of Professional Bodies in the Development of Credit-bearing CPD Courses*, Hull: University of Hull.

Venables, P. (Committee on Continuing Education, Open University) (1976) *Report of the Committee on Continuing Education*, Milton Keynes: Open University Press.

Vickers, J. (2001) *Report on Competition in the Professions*, London: Office of Fair Trading.

Watkins, J., Drury, L. and Bray, S. (1996) *The Future of the UK Professional Association*, Cheltenham: Cheltenham Strategic Publications.

Watson, S. and Harmel-Law, A. (2010) 'Exploring the contribution of workplace learning to an HRD strategy in the Scottish legal profession', *Journal of European Industrial Training*, 34(1): 7–22.

Webster-Wright, A. (2009) 'Reframing professional development through understanding authentic professional learning', *Review of Educational Research*, 79(2): 702–39.

Weisaeth, L. (1994) 'Psychological and psychiatric aspects of technological disasters' in Ursano, R.J, McCaughey, B.G. and Fullerton, C.S. (eds), *The structure of human chaos*, Cambridge: Cambridge University Press.

Welsh, L. and Woodward, P. (1989) *Continuing Professional Development: Towards a National Strategy*, Glasgow: Planning Exchange.

Wenger, E. (1999) *Communities of Practice: Learning, Meaning and Identity*, Cambridge: Cambridge University Press.

Wenger, E. and Snyder, W. (2000) 'Communities of practice: the organisational frontier', *Harvard Business Review*, Jan/Feb: 136–45.

Wenger, E., McDermott, R. and Snyder, W. (2002) *Cultivating Communities of Practice: A Guide to Managing Knowledge*, Cambridge, MA: Harvard Business School Press.

Wessels, S.B. (2007) 'Accountants' perceptions of the effectiveness of mandatory Continuing Professional Education', *Accounting Education*, 16(4): 365–78.

Whitmore, Sir J. (1992) *Coaching for Performance: Growing People, Performance and Purpose*, London: Nicholas Brealey Publishing.

Wilding, P. (1982) *Professional Power and Social Welfare*, London: Routledge.

Wilensky, H.L. (1964) 'The professionalization of everyone?' *American Journal of Sociology*, 70(2): 137–58.

Williams, C. and Friedman, A. (2008) *Online Support for CPD: Lessons from Practice*, Bristol: PARN.

# AUTHOR INDEX

Abbott, A. 70, 215, 237
Afitska, N. 34, 85, 92–4, 169, 179, 180, 194, 231, 239, 243
Argyris, C. 172
Arnold, J. 39, 64, 176, 234–5
Arthurs, H.W. 75

Benson, Lord. 230
du Boulay, C. 63, 214
Bourdieu, P. 32, 54–5, 236, 246
Bowie, N. E. 115
Brien, A. 115, 124
Brown, R. 186
Burchell, G. 129

Cannell, M. 77
Cantor, L.M. 74
Cheetham, G. xvii, 28
Chivers, G. 28, 33, 41, 76, 224
Crompton, M. 44
Cohen, M. 70
Colman, J.S. 194
Cropley, A.J. 72

Davies, K. 10, 14, 35–6, 58, 73, 84, 85, 90–3, 104–7, 109–10, 115–20, 141, 176–7, 182, 235, 238–40
Dewey, J. 71–2, 202
Dowds, J. 58
Drucker, P. 171
Durkheim, E. 65
Durkin, C. 10, 73, 84, 90–4, 104–5

Elton, L. 49
Eraut, M. 164, 232

Faure, H. 72
Fear, N. 83
Field, N. 88
Foley, K. 88
Foucault, M. 70, 129
Fournier, V. 129
French, H.P. 58
Friedman, A. 10, 14–15, 17–20, 26, 35–6, 38, 41, 47, 52, 58, 63, 73, 84–5, 90–4, 104–7, 109–11, 113–20, 126–7, 133, 135–8, 141, 146–9, 151–5, 169, 176–7, 179–80, 182–3, 187, 194, 196, 231–44
Friedman, M. 65–6, 167

Gardner, R. 75–6
Gilbert, C. 65
Gold, J. 60, 67, 141, 237
Gould, M. 73
Granovetter, M.S. 189
Guest, G. 73, 215

Hanson, W. 52, 114, 120, 126, 182, 187, 232, 239–40
Harris, M. 36
Herbert, I. 26, 176–233, 235
Holmes, L. 71
Houle, C.O. 63, 232, 238

Illich, I. 70, 74

Jarvis, P. 73–4
Jones, N. 83

Kallen, D. 73
Kamm, O. 124
Khurana, R. 124
Kultgen, J. 115

Lengrand, P. 72
Lynn, K. 69

MacDonald, K.M. 229, 237
MacDonald, R.G. 89
McIntosh, N.E, 74
Madden, C.A. 78, 92–3, 237, 239
Mason, J. 92–4, 118, 135–6, 231, 235, 242
Megginson, D. 11, 36–7, 112
Mitchell R.K. 233
Mitchell, V.A. 78, 92, 237, 239

Nohria, N. 124

O'Connor, J. 70
O'Neill, O. 65, 124
Owen, T. 65

Paisey, C. 27–8, 96–7, 176, 233–4, 241–2
Paisey, N.J. 27–8, 96–7, 176, 233–4, 241–2
Parsons, T. 65
Paxton, P. 194
Peck, C. 214, 238
Penuel, W.R. 187
Perry, L. 88, 234
Peters, T. 172, 220, 245
Phillips, M. 10, 73, 84–5, 87, 90–4,104–5, 107, 116–18, 120, 182
Pidd, H. 46
Putnam, R.D. 70, 166, 194
Postler-Slattery, D. 88, 233

Rapkins, C. 77–8, 137, 153
Rockhill, K. 87
Rogers, G.A. 77
Rothwell, A. 26, 39, 64, 176, 233–5

Sankar, R. 36
Sargeant, J. 141
Schön, D.A. 12, 59–61, 64, 68–9, 115, 164, 172, 174, 203, 237
Senge, P. 173–5, 220–1
Shepard, L. 130
Snadden, D. 130, 132, 158
Sockett, H. 74

Tarbert, H. 27–8, 233–4
Tawney, R.H. 65
Thompson, N. 61
Thompson, S. 61
Todd, F. 76
Tovey, P. 90

Unger, S. 70

Vaughan, P. 92–3
Venables, B. 74
Vickers, J. 115

Webster-Wright, A. 26, 215, 232–3, 245
Welsh, L. 77, 91–3
Weisaeth, L. 70
Wessels, S.B. 35, 88, 96, 156–7, 176, 234, 239, 242
Wilensky, H.L. 2
Williams, C. 20, 63, 94, 103, 113, 117, 126, 133, 177, 183–4, 196, 240, 244
Woodhead, S. 15, 17–18, 26, 111, 137–8, 141, 146–9, 151–5, 241
Woodward, P. 77, 91–3

# ORGANIZATION INDEX

Architects Registration Board (ARB) 123, 125

Association of Chartered Certified Accountants (ACCA) 26, 94, 97, 110, 136, 233∂–4, 239–42

Association of Reflexologists (AoR) 41–2

Centre for Recording Achievement (CRA) 235, 236

Chartered Institute of Management Accountants (CIMA) 15–16, 26, 44, 97, 111, 153–4, 233, 241, 244

Chartered Institute of Marketing (CIM) 93, 105, 111

Chartered Institute of Personnel and Development (CIPD) 11, 36–7, 39, 63, 101–2, 112, 234–5, 239–40

Chartered Institute of Public Finance and Accountancy (CIPFA) 136

Construction Industry Council (CIC) 9–10, 14–15, 146

Department for Education and Employment (DfEE) 82

Department for Education and Skills (DfES) 243

Department of Education and Science (DES) 77

Department for Universities, Innovation and Skills (DIUS) 243

General Dental Council (GDC) 122, 232

General Teaching Council for England (GTCE) 231

Health Information Management Association of Australia (HIMAA) 23–5

Health Professions Council (HPC) 11, 20–2, 122–3, 235

Higher Education Funding Council for England (HEFCE) 50, 202

Institute for Archeologists (IfA) 126

Institute of Chartered Accountants in England and Wales (ICAEW) 26, 97, 233, 241

Institute of Chartered Accountants of Scotland (ICAS) 27, 97, 136, 233, 241

Institute of the Motor Industry (IMI) 3, 86

Institute of Physics (IoP) 56

Institute of Translating and Interpreting (ITI) 244

Institution of Electrical Engineers (IEE) 240

Institution of Engineering and Technology (IET) 108–9

Institution of Occupational Safety and Health (IOSH) 11

International Federation of Accountants (IFAC) 95, 97, 189

Institution of Occupational Safety and Health (IOSH) 11, 232, 241

Marketing and Sales Standards Setting Body (MSSSB) 111

Office of Fair Trading (OFT) 115

Office for National Statistics (ONS) 234

Open University (OU) 33

Organisation for Economic Co-operation and Development (OECD) 50, 73

Professional Associations Research Network (PARN) 28, 38, 56, 78, 83, 93–5, 98–9, 118, 133, 135, 179–80, 182–4, 194, 235, 238–40, 243

Quality Assurance Agency for Higher Education (QAA) 244–5

Royal College of Physicians (RCP) 10, 232
Royal College of Psychiatrists (RCPsych) 138–40
Royal College of Veterinary Surgeons (RCVS) 10
Royal Institute of British Architects (RIBA) 10–11, 123–5, 232

Royal Institution of Chartered Surveyors (RICS) 110, 164, 240
Royal Pharmaceutical Society of Great Britain (RPSGB) 10, 14–16

Standing Committee on Postgraduate Medical and Dental Education (SCOPME) 77

The Society of Accountants in Malawi (SOCAM) 239

UK Department for Business, Innovation and Skills (BIS) 243
UK Inter-Professional Group (UKIPG) 235, 238, 242
United Nations Scientific Committee on the Effects of Atomic Radiation (UNSCEAR) 70

# WORD AND CONCEPT INDEX

Page numbers in **bold** denote subject definitions

accountants 15–16, 26–7, 34–5, 40, 44, 89, 95–7, 153, 155–7, 196, 221, 223–5, 237, 239–41

Accreditation of Prior Experiential Learning (APEL) 211

acquisitive society 65

adult education 34, 42, 46, 49–50, 68, 71–8, 169, 193, 199, 206, 235, 238, 244

Anglo Saxon model (of professions) 240

appraisal 38–9, 43, 102, 135, 139, 151, 166, 170, 175, 196, 204, 210, 216

apprentice 66, 164, 170

archaeologists 34, 126

architects 10, 13, 62, 123–5, 242

assessment: summative 164; formative 164, 242

Assessment of Professional Competence (APC) 110

audit(s) 20–1, 40, 87, 97, 99, 117–18, 129, 141–2, 146, 150–6, 189, 205, 224, 227, 233, 241

Automotive Technician Accreditation (ATA) 86–7

Australia 2, 23, 28, 38, 69, 79, 87, 94, 98–9, 135–6, 231, 235, 239–40, 243

bankers 124

barristers 60, 115

benefits model 77–8, 137

blogs 51, 168, 183, 184

boardroom (board) 124, 155

branch 12, 20–1, 24–5, 30, 55, 58, 62–4, 70, 103, 105 , 116, 166, 184, 194

Bristol University 222, 238, 244, 246

broadcast media 51, 183

bureaucracy 13, 36, 87

calling (noun) 55, 70, 167, 174, 220, 236

Canada 2, 28, 38, 69, 75, 79, 94, 98–9, 123, 126, 128, 135–6, 231, 235, 237, 239–40, 243

charter/chartered 11, 15, 26, 35, 38, 40, 44, 85, 91, 93–4, 96, 102, 105, 107, 110–11, 118, 126, 136, 153, 166, 196, 232–3, 240–2

cheat/cheating 88, 90, 111, 152, 218

coaching 21, 45, **107**, 110, 113

code of ethics 37, 59, 90–2, 96, 111, 115, 125, 192, 195, 231

communities of practice 62, 166, 194, 237

community college 236

competence 4, 10, 17, 19–22, 26, 35–6, 33, 39–40, 65–71, 77–8, 84–6, 92, 95, 97, **110**, 115–6, 120–7, 130, 134, 141, 143, 145–7, 154, 158–9, 163–6, 168, 173, 177, 181, 189, 193, 195, 197, 210, 219, 221, 226, 230, 232, 234, 241

competencies 3, 14–15, 26, 86, 103, 110–11, 126, 131, 134, 141, 144, 147, 150–3, 158, 170, 203, 226, 241

competency framework 26, 104, **110–11**, 141, 150–2, 164, 183, 189, 205, 211, 231

compliance mentality **88**, 130, 141, 152

compliance policies: compulsory 45, **81–9**, 107–11, 117–132, 165, 180–3, 192–3, 224, 227, 234, 238–9, 243; experimental **92–3**; mixed; 83, **91–9**, 117–19, 135; obligatory **77–8**,

81, 83, 90–111, 116–17, 181, 227;
voluntary 33–4, 45, 77, **81–5**, 91–6,
98–9, 101, 107, 110, 116–19, 129, 181,
227
Continental Europe 240
continuing education 10, 41, 73, **74**, 75–7,
123, 128, 169, 232, 238–9, 244
Continuing Medical Education (CME)
75, 77, 186, **214**, 238, 243
Continuing Medical Professional
Development (CMPD) 214
Continuing Professional Development
(CPD) **9, 14, 18, 124, 228**;
accreditation 11, 41, 44, 86–7,
**106–7**, 194, 199, 202, 204–5, 210,
225, 227, 242, 244; benefits to an
organization 102; compulsory 81, 188;
cost 43, 100; credits/points 38, 82, 133;
cycle 103, 210–12; early years 77–8;
field **29–34**, 41–3, 45, 51–4, 169;
history 57–8, 64–71, 91–6; individual
centred 107; individual's attitudes 36–9,
58, 67, 78; inputs 78, 132–3, 142–5,
151–6, 231, 241; internationally 98–9;
measurement 146; mystery 69; for
non-compliance 30, 39–40, 78, 84, 91,
116, 118–20, 126, 129, 157, 181, 210,
225; not welcomed by organization 35,
44; outcomes **127–8**, 133–58, 184–9,
202–3, 211–13, 218, 225, 230;
outputs 132–58, 178, 184, 188–9, 230;
selling 82; sham 78, 114–15, 168–9,
218; specialists 32–3, 40–3, 52–4, 76,
87, 90, 104, 113, 115, 141, 178, 188–9,
192–3, 195, 197–8, 207, 215, 227, 235;
structured and unstructured 5, 10–11,
22, 133, 178 , **232**, 233, 242, 246;
professionalization 188
Continuing Professional Education
(CPE) 5, 34–5, **75–7**, 126, 156–7, 186,
190, 231, 234, 237–40, 242
Continuing Vocational Education (CVE)
76
convergence **193**, 199

deprofessionalization 190
discipline: (a process) 40, 90, 116, 120–2,
181, 231; a subject or field 24, 30, 35,
173–5, 200, 214
disposition(s)/dispositional 31, 34–5,
54–6, 60, 78, 82, 89, 131, 165, 191–2,
226, 234
divergence/divergent **193**, 228
doctors 1–4, 13, 34, 36, 60, 62–3, 77, 84,
116, 124, 170, 186–7, 214, 233, 238–9

duality 246
duty 38, 55, 70, 90, 111, 131

effectiveness 35, 60, 105, 137–8, 142,
146, 156–7, 186–92, 198, 204, 210–13,
217–19, 230, 234
emergent/emergence 7, 60, 64–5, 67–8,
75, 170, 191, 196, 209, 226, 237
engineers 34, 73, 77, 86, 204–5, 213, 216,
240
England 26, 50, 75, 202, 231, 235
epistemology 203
ethics 23, 37, 64–5, 90, 147, 221, 225, 231
European Credit Transfer System (ECTS)
225
European Project for the use of
Standards of Competence in CPD for
Construction Industry Practitioners
(EUSCCCIP) 17, 77
excellence 71, 172, 199, 220, 240, 240–5
expert witness 21,
Extra-Mural Studies, Department of 46,
238

fairness 88, 90
Fédération des Experts Comptables
Européens (FEE) 96, 99, 137, 239
fit for practice 244
fit for purpose 197, 244
formal 5, **9–13**, 17, 22–3, 26, 29, 33–5,
38–40, 57–8, 62–3, 67, 71–77, 82–3, 87,
89, 95, 106–7, 131, 133, 135, 137, 147,
153, 166, 168, 171, 179, 181, 183, 185,
201, 205, 210–11, 215, 218–19, 222–3,
226, 231–3, 237, 242
formalization **12–13**, 26, 63, 81, 165, 217,
232
free ride 170
further education colleges (FECs) 49,
52–3, 207

general (medical) practitioners (GPs) 75
German 154–5, 170, 242, 245
government 5, 14, 29, 33–4, 47–8, **49–54**,
62, 67–70, 76, 87, 101, 111, 116, 120,
129, 131, 145, 161, 163, 167, 169–70,
179–81, 206–8, 221–5, 229–31, 236–7,
244, 246
grey literature 5, **186**, 213

habitus 54–6, 165, 226
Heisenberg Uncertainty Principle 158, 242
higher educations institutes (HEIs)/
universities 5, 11, 28, 31, 33, 41, 45–53,
64, 69, 71, 74–7, 89, 142, 166, 169,

175, 184, 192, 196, 199–203, 207, 211, 215–16, 219, 221–6, 229–30, 236, 238, 243–6

human resources (HR) 42–3, 46, 60, 102, 175, 204, 217, 219, 220

human resources development (HRD) 43

informal 5, **12–13**, 23, 26, 28, 62, 65, 76–7, 83, 107, 133, 164–6, 179, 183, 185–6, 190, 200, 218, 222, 226, 232, 240, 242

information technology 41, 45, 111, 182, 234

in-service 21, 77

International Benchmarking Survey (IBS) 83, 95, 118, 133, 184

International Education Standards (IES) 95, 239

internet 1, 3, 20, 22, 30, 41, 50, 89, 168, 178, 182–6, 199, 204, 243–4

Ireland 28, 38, 79, 86, 94–5, 98–9, 135–6, 204–5, 216, 235, 240, 243

job rotation 21, 220

killer application **64**, 166, 229, 244

kitemark 86–7, 196–7

knowing-in-action 59

knowing-in-practice 60

laity 65, 168

language 18, 58, 164, 190, 196, 204, 212, 214–16, 221, 225, 228

law 2, 35, 47, 84, 89, 122, 170, 215, 226. 233, 236–7, 245

lawyers 2, 3, 34, 62, 75, 89, 221, 237, 240

learned society/societies **30**, 32, 63, 72, 197–8, 222

learning organization 170–5, 220–1

lesser governments 229

liberal professions 246

lifelong learning 5, 41–2, 46, 50, **71–8**, 88, 169, 173, 193–9, 202, 206, 210–11, 214–17, 225–30, 235, 243, 246

management 5, 15, 21, 30, 36, 43–4, 58, 76, 104, 109, 116, 125, 153, 170–3, 175, 179, 182–3, 199, 203, 205, 217, 219–20, 223–4, 227, 134–5, 237–8, 242, 246

media 4, 5, 34, 49, 51–4, 67, 131, 161, 167, 176, 184, 186, 192–3, 198, 207–8, 214, 219, 229

medical 1, 38, 63, 70, 75–7, 84, 120, 127, 139, 168, 179, 185–7, 193, 199, 214, 217–8, 233, 238, 240, 245

mentee/mentor/mentoring 12, 21, 44–5, 100–1, 103, 107–10, 164, 185–6, 197, 205, 240

monitor 20, 22, 30, 36, 40, 78–9, 82, 84, 97, 90, 100, 103, 114–18, 120, 121–3, 129, 134–5, 139, 142–3, 154–5, 158, 165, 167, 173, 175, 177–8, 181, 194, 214, 224, 231

moral suasion 90, 119

motivation 19–20, 35–9, 44, 56, 112, 156, 221, 234–5

nurses/nursing 34, 62, 124, 221, 233–4, 244

observer effect 158

organizational skin 172

paradox 67, 90, 130–59, **163–5**, 166–7, 176–7, 228–9, 241–2; fundamental paradox of CPD **130–1**, 229

paraprofessionals 2, 34

participation 11, 78, 84, 107, 116–19, 133–6, 140–3, 147, 150, 153, 158, 166, 184, 194, 227, 234

peer review 21, 24, 134, 138–9, 147, 155, 213–14, 216, 245

peers 20, 62, 138, 152, 157, 167, 189, 224

performance review 140, 155, 221

personal development 13, 39, 102, 131, 134, 163, 170, 193, 238

physiotherapists 2–3, 34

planning 13, 15–16, 22, 30, 44, 62, 76, 100–4, 1112, 134–7, 148–51, 163, 170, 175, 178, 180, 182, 188–9, 210–11, 227, 243

players **7**, 29 – 34, 38, 43, 46, 51–3, 55, 57, 67, 71, 78, 89, 161, 165, 169, 173, 176, 178, 191–3, 207–9, 211, 217, 226–8, 230, 236, 242, 246

post-nominals **91**, 168

power 51–6

preceptorship 197, 244

principles-based 241

Privy Council 241

professional autonomy 67, 81–2, 87, 167, 197

Professional Conduct Committee (PCC) 125

professional development **33–4**, 56, 116, 134

Professional Development Value (PDV) 9, 17–19, 23, 26, 88, 90, 100, 111, 126, 130–2, 135, 145–58, 184, 186, 188, 190, 192–3, 195–8, 204, 206, 210–11,

213, 217–19, 226–8, 233, 236; PDV
measurement level 142–3, 146–53
professional indemnity insurance **85**, 118,
166, 239
Professional, Industrial and Commercial
Updating Programme (PICKUP) 76,
224, 244
professional services firms 42–3, 85, 170,
175, 206, 216
professionalization 2–3, 167, 171, 178–80,
188
profit(s) 18, 220, 233

qualifications 3–5, 24, 41, 45, 52, 57, 62,
73, 84, 105, 111, 114–16, 127, 145,
166–8, 181–2, 189, 196–7, 204, 206,
214, 221–6, 232, 235, 244–5
quality assurance 49–50, 115, 120, 123,
126–8, 217, 231, 244

radiographers 23
Recognised Professional Body (RPB) 97
record card 77, 104, 106, 117, 238
recurrent education **73–4**, 169
reflecting-in-action 59
reflection 4, 11, 13, 15–17, 30, 32, 59–62,
76, 88, 100–4, 112, 134–7, 141–2, 144,
147–51, 153–5, 163, 174–5, 178, 180,
182, 188–9, 193, 210–11, 221, 227, 233,
243
reflection-in-practice **12**, 59, 60–1
reflection-on-practice **12**, 60–1
reflective practice **12**, 16, 21, 59
reflexologists 41–2
regalia 168
Registered Supervisory Body (RSB) 97
reliability 3, 149, 185, 210
Retail Distribution Review (RDR) 124,
240
revalidation 84, 127, 168, 222, 225, 239
rules-based 241

sanctions 77–8, 84, 87, 90–1, 103, 114,
116–20, 122, 126, 129, 137, 142, 157,
173, 181, 188, 194, 210
sanctions model **77–8**, 137

Scandinavia 74
self-assessment 21, 87, 107, 111–12,
137–8, 141, 148, 150, 152–3, 156, 164,
233
situational 35
social networking 168, 182–4, 188, 199,
227, 244
solicitors 60, 115, 240
sonographer 87, 234, 242, 244
specific, measurable, achievable, realistic
and time-bound (SMART) 102
stakeholders 7, **29–30**, 31–4, 43, 46, 51–3,
55, 57, 59, 78, 81, 116, 143, 145, 154,
156, 161, 165, 168–9, 173, 176, 185,
191–3, 207, 209–11, 216–18, 225–7,
229–30, 233–4, 236, 245–6
super-members 240
strengths, weaknesses, opportunities and
threats (SWOT) 104
systems thinking 175

tacit knowledge **237**
teachers 1–4, 13, 62, 77, 130, 175, 187, 231
technology 41, 71, 98, 108, 121, 143, 146,
184–5, 192, 234, 237, 243
template(s) 88, 101, 103–4, 112, 137, 150,
178, 181, 183, 189, 232
three pillars of professional
standards **120–5**, 187, 219,
tick box 82, 120, 126
totalprofessions.com 234
TV 20, 22
twitter 51, 244

USA 2, 68–9, 72, 75, 84, 94, 200, 203, 232,
234, 237–40, 242–3, 245

validity 134, 138, 184–5, 232, 242
verifiable 25, 232–3, 241
Vietnam War 69
Vocational Lifelong Learning (VLL) 41, 76
volunteer/volunteering 46, 58, 104, 146,
194, 227, 235

Web 2.0 178, 183–4, 188, 192
welfare state 179

9 780415 679251